New NF /NF
MAR 11 2008
658.562
W37q
WITHDRAWN
W9-DDL-904

Quality Control For Dummies®

Cheat Sheet

Obtaining ISO Certification

Quality standards provide a common language for companies to trade across the globe. The most recognized quality standards are those developed by the International Organization for Standardization (ISO), whose members are the national standards organizations of 150 countries. Meeting ISO quality standards by following these steps gives your customers confidence that you'll provide them with a quality product. (See Chapter 2 for more details on ISO and quality standards in general.)

1. Get commitment from top management to ensure success.
2. Train all employees on the basics of quality.
3. Prepare your quality policy manual.
4. Document operating procedures.
5. Perform an internal audit.
6. Select an ISO certification agency to use.
7. Have the certification agency perform the audit.
8. If you pass the audit, congratulations!
9. If you don't pass the audit, take necessary corrective action and repeat the audit.

Conquering Obstacles to Change

Organizations, much like people, are reluctant to change. Many in the organization will see the introduction of a quality control process as an unwelcome change. The following steps can help you rally the support of the willing, ease the fears of the reluctant, and overcome the obstacles put up by the unwilling. (Chapter 5 has the full scoop on overcoming obstacles to change in your organization.)

- Identify the risks to your project.
- Calculate the costs for each risk so you know which ones to worry about the most.
- Plan for the prevention of the risks.
- Monitor and manage the risks as your project progresses.
- Believe in your goal, and focus on the benefits that quality will bring to your organization.
- Don't go it alone; find support from the quality sponsor or other experts in your organization.
- Remain rational when you face challenges.
- Keep everything in perspective.
- Break down an obstacle into manageable pieces.

Introducing Quality Control to Your Organization

You must carefully plan and precisely execute the introduction of a quality control program into your organization. Like any other major new program that you introduce, thorough planning and careful attention to detail will greatly increase the odds of success. Just follow these steps, and see Chapter 5 for more information about introducing quality to your company.

1. Create a roadmap to guide your organization to its quality goals.
2. Obtain a sponsor to be the organization's champion of quality.
3. Select a quality control manager.
4. Create an effective communications program.
5. Provide employees training on quality control.
6. Select a pilot project.
7. Perform the pilot, prove its value, and apply the lessons learned.

For Dummies: Bestselling Book Series for Beginners

FOR DUMMIES™

BESTSELLING
BOOK SERIES

Quality Control For Dummies®

Cheat Sheet

Gathering and Evaluating Customer Feedback

We must never forget the reason why our organization exists — to provide for the needs of our customer. Don't assume that you know what the customer wants or wait for them to tell you. Actively seeking the voice of the customer with the following steps ensures that you know exactly what the customer wants, which is the only way to keep your organization in business. (Chapter 6 has the full scoop on listening to the voice of the customer.)

1. Define your objectives; know what you hope to accomplish before you begin.
2. Think about how you'll analyze the data you gather; consider your objectives as well as time and budget restraints.
3. Use good questions that fit within your objectives and data-analysis method.
4. Keep the data-collection process simple to minimize errors.
5. Use an unrelated party to collect data to prevent bias.
6. Train your data collectors to ensure consistency and accuracy.
7. Perform a trial run to work out any bugs in the collection process.
8. Make any modifications necessary and gather more information from a larger customer population.

Getting Your Quality Project Back on Track

Even the best-laid plans sometimes run into problems. While we don't plan to fail, things rarely go as smoothly as planned. Be ready for trouble and use the following steps to get your quality project back on track. (Check out Chapter 5 for more details on steering a project back on track.)

✔ Review your goals and focus on what's really important.

✔ Evaluate where your project stands — look at what you've achieved and where the project truly has problems.

✔ Get professional help from an outside expert.

✔ Learn from your mistakes to prevent them in the future.

✔ Determine your minimum acceptable goals; you may have to scale back the project.

Measuring Your Current Quality Process

You can't manage what you can't measure. Careful measurement is key to managing your quality processes. Use the following steps to ensure that you measure the right things in the right way. (Head to Chapters 7 and 8 for details on measuring a quality process.)

1. Determine what to measure (the items or processes you decide to measure are called *metrics*).
2. Determine your measurement process by selecting the best process for your needs.
3. Define exactly how you'll use the selected measurement process.
4. Train your employees on the proper measurement process.
5. Perform a gauge R&R to determine measurement variation.
6. Perform the measurements and compare to customer specifications.
7. Confirm the quality of your data with compare-and-review checks.
8. Make sense of your data with coding and different data charts.

Wiley, the Wiley Publishing logo, For Dummies, the Dummies Man logo, the For Dummies Bestselling Book Series logo and all related trade dress are trademarks or registered trademarks of John Wiley & Sons, Inc. and/or its affiliates. All other trademarks are property of their respective owners.

Copyright © 2007 Wiley Publishing, Inc. All rights reserved. Item 6909-0. For more information about Wiley Publishing, call 1-800-762-2974.

For Dummies: Bestselling Book Series for Beginners

Quality Control FOR DUMMIES®

by Larry Webber and Michael Wallace

ELISHA D. SMITH PUBLIC LIBRARY
MENASHA, WISCONSIN

BICENTENNIAL
1807
WILEY
2007
BICENTENNIAL

Wiley Publishing, Inc.

Quality Control For Dummies®

Published by
Wiley Publishing, Inc.
111 River St.
Hoboken, NJ 07030-5774
www.wiley.com

Copyright © 2007 by Wiley Publishing, Inc., Indianapolis, Indiana

Published simultaneously in Canada

No part of this publication may be reproduced, stored in a retrieval system, or transmitted in any form or by any means, electronic, mechanical, photocopying, recording, scanning, or otherwise, except as permitted under Sections 107 or 108 of the 1976 United States Copyright Act, without either the prior written permission of the Publisher, or authorization through payment of the appropriate per-copy fee to the Copyright Clearance Center, 222 Rosewood Drive, Danvers, MA 01923, 978-750-8400, fax 978-646-8600. Requests to the Publisher for permission should be addressed to the Legal Department, Wiley Publishing, Inc., 10475 Crosspoint Blvd., Indianapolis, IN 46256, 317-572-3447, fax 317-572-4355, or online at http://www.wiley.com/go/permissions.

Trademarks: Wiley, the Wiley Publishing logo, For Dummies, the Dummies Man logo, A Reference for the Rest of Us!, The Dummies Way, Dummies Daily, The Fun and Easy Way, Dummies.com and related trade dress are trademarks or registered trademarks of John Wiley & Sons, Inc. and/or its affiliates in the United States and other countries, and may not be used without written permission. All other trademarks are the property of their respective owners. Wiley Publishing, Inc., is not associated with any product or vendor mentioned in this book.

LIMIT OF LIABILITY/DISCLAIMER OF WARRANTY: THE PUBLISHER AND THE AUTHOR MAKE NO REPRESENTATIONS OR WARRANTIES WITH RESPECT TO THE ACCURACY OR COMPLETENESS OF THE CONTENTS OF THIS WORK AND SPECIFICALLY DISCLAIM ALL WARRANTIES, INCLUDING WITHOUT LIMITATION WARRANTIES OF FITNESS FOR A PARTICULAR PURPOSE. NO WARRANTY MAY BE CREATED OR EXTENDED BY SALES OR PROMOTIONAL MATERIALS. THE ADVICE AND STRATEGIES CONTAINED HEREIN MAY NOT BE SUITABLE FOR EVERY SITUATION. THIS WORK IS SOLD WITH THE UNDERSTANDING THAT THE PUBLISHER IS NOT ENGAGED IN RENDERING LEGAL, ACCOUNTING, OR OTHER PROFESSIONAL SERVICES. IF PROFESSIONAL ASSISTANCE IS REQUIRED, THE SERVICES OF A COMPETENT PROFESSIONAL PERSON SHOULD BE SOUGHT. NEITHER THE PUBLISHER NOR THE AUTHOR SHALL BE LIABLE FOR DAMAGES ARISING HEREFROM. THE FACT THAT AN ORGANIZATION OR WEBSITE IS REFERRED TO IN THIS WORK AS A CITATION AND/OR A POTENTIAL SOURCE OF FURTHER INFORMATION DOES NOT MEAN THAT THE AUTHOR OR THE PUBLISHER ENDORSES THE INFORMATION THE ORGANIZATION OR WEBSITE MAY PROVIDE OR RECOMMENDATIONS IT MAY MAKE. FURTHER, READERS SHOULD BE AWARE THAT INTERNET WEBSITES LISTED IN THIS WORK MAY HAVE CHANGED OR DISAPPEARED BETWEEN WHEN THIS WORK WAS WRITTEN AND WHEN IT IS READ.

For general information on our other products and services, please contact our Customer Care Department within the U.S. at 800-762-2974, outside the U.S. at 317-572-3993, or fax 317-572-4002.

For technical support, please visit www.wiley.com/techsupport.

Wiley also publishes its books in a variety of electronic formats. Some content that appears in print may not be available in electronic books.

Library of Congress Control Number: 2006936764

ISBN-13: 978-0-470-06909-7

ISBN-10: 0-470-06909-0

Manufactured in the United States of America

10 9 8 7 6 5 4 3 2 1

1B/RT/RS/QW/IN

WILEY

About the Authors

Larry Webber is a certified Six Sigma Black Belt and holds a Masters of Project Management degree from West Carolina University. He has supported quality initiatives at multiple major manufacturers and in software development companies. He's currently a Project Manager and Six Sigma Black Belt working for Computer Science Corporation. Larry is also retired from the Army Reserve as an infantry First Sergeant, is a certified Master Business Continuity Planner and a certified Project Manager, and holds an MBA and BSBA from Rockhurst College. He can be reached at ljwljw88@hotmail.com.

Michael Wallace has more than 25 years of experience in the information systems field. He graduated magna cum laude from Wright State University with a bachelor of science degree in Management Science. Michael has worked as an application developer, a systems analyst, and a technical and business consultant and has assisted the state of Ohio in developing statewide IT policies. He's active in the local technical community, is President of the Columbus International Association of Microsoft Certified Partners (IAMCP), is a Competent Toastmaster with Toastmasters International, and graduated from the Executive MBA program at the Fisher College of Business at The Ohio State University. Michael is now the Vice President of Application Engineering at Result Data, which provides its clients with guidance on IT strategy, application development, business intelligence, disaster-recovery planning, and policies and procedures. He's also an adjunct faculty member at The Ohio State University and at DeVry University's Keller Graduate School of Management, and he has published several articles and books on business and technology topics. He can be reached at michaelw@columbus.rr.com.

Larry and Michael have co-authored several books, including *The Disaster Recovery Handbook* (American Management Association, 2004). Here are their annually updated works:

IT Policies and Procedures, 2003–2007 editions (Aspen Publishing)

IS Project Management Handbook, 2004–2006 editions (Aspen Publishing)

Larry recently co-authored a book with his son, Fred, called *IT Project Management Essentials* (Aspen Publishing, 2007).

Dedication

Larry dedicates this book to his wife, Nancy, in honor of their upcoming 25th anniversary, and Michael dedicates the book to his wife, Tami, and his children, Phillip and Sarah, for their patience and support while this book was being created.

Authors' Acknowledgments

We would like to acknowledge the contributions of several people who made this book possible. First, Dennis Dreyer (www.DreyerSolutions.com) for his contribution of the chapter on Lean techniques, based on his many years of experience implementing supply-chain-management and logistics solutions at General Motors and at many other organizations. Thanks also to Larry's son, Fred Webber, for his assistance in researching several of the chapters, and to his daughter, Katrina Webber, for cleaning up his poor grammar and oversized words. We would also like to thank literary agent extraordinaire Marilyn Allen for all her help in getting this book off the ground, acquisitions editor Mike Lewis for sharpening the book's focus, and editors Georgette Beatty and Josh Dials for guiding us to a safe landing. Finally, we would like to thank Rob Bryant for his many fine-tuning points, which we borrowed heavily from in our chapters.

Publisher's Acknowledgments

We're proud of this book; please send us your comments through our Dummies online registration form located at www.dummies.com/register/.

Some of the people who helped bring this book to market include the following:

Acquisitions, Editorial, and Media Development

Project Editor: Georgette Beatty

Acquisitions Editor: Michael Lewis

Copy Editor: Josh Dials

Technical Editor: Rob Bryant

Editorial Manager: Michelle Hacker

Editorial Assistants: Erin Calligan, David Lutton

Cartoons: Rich Tennant (www.the5thwave.com)

Composition Services

Project Coordinator: Patrick Redmond

Layout and Graphics: Carl Byers, Lavonne Cook, Laura Pence

Anniversary Logo Design: Richard Pacifico

Proofreaders: Laura Albert, Jessica Kramer, Techbooks

Indexer: Techbooks

Special Help Danielle Voirol

Publishing and Editorial for Consumer Dummies

Diane Graves Steele, Vice President and Publisher, Consumer Dummies

Joyce Pepple, Acquisitions Director, Consumer Dummies

Kristin A. Cocks, Product Development Director, Consumer Dummies

Michael Spring, Vice President and Publisher, Travel

Kelly Regan, Editorial Director, Travel

Publishing for Technology Dummies

Andy Cummings, Vice President and Publisher, Dummies Technology/General User

Composition Services

Gerry Fahey, Vice President of Production Services

Debbie Stailey, Director of Composition Services

Contents at a Glance

Table of Contents

Introduction

* *

*W*elcome to *Quality Control For Dummies,* the book that helps anyone unfamiliar with quality control find their way around a quality program. Quality improvement techniques have been around for a very long time. They apply to every type of endeavor — business (most likely why you're here), educational (the reason you may have taken those test-taking courses or joined study groups), and even personal (self-help books, anyone?). We all want to do things faster and for less cost while getting more desirable results. A company's quality system strives for the same goals: better, faster, and cheaper. With this book, you'll be able to understand the various and ever-changing quality initiatives underway or under discussion at your company.

About This Book

Most quality control books have a single theme: They push their own theory as the "one right way" to solve all of a company's problems. But this book isn't like that. It addresses every major quality improvement program and describes how to choose the applicable parts for a company.

The design of this book allows you to pick it up and begin reading at any point — much like a reference book — so we suggest you start with a topic that interests you. You can use the table of contents to identify general areas of interest or broad topics. You'll come to find, however, that the index is your best friend for identifying detailed concepts, related topics, or particular quality issues. After you find what you need, you can toss the book on a shelf on your way out the door and tackle whatever tasks you set for yourself with confidence — and without wading through unrelated details.

Conventions Used in This Book

To guide you through this book, we include the following conventions:

- *Italics* point out defined terms and emphasize certain words.
- **Boldface** text indicates key words in bulleted lists and actions to take in numbered lists.
- `Monofont` highlights Web addresses.

During printing of this book, some Web addresses may have broken across two lines of text. If you come across a Web address spread over two lines, rest assured that we haven't put in any extra characters (such as hyphens) to indicate the break. Just type in exactly what you see, pretending as though the line break doesn't exist.

What You're Not to Read

You can safely skip any text that we mark with the Technical Stuff icon; the information is interesting, to be sure, but it's not essential to your understanding of quality issues. You can also skip sidebars (those shaded gray boxes within the chapters); we like the stories in them, but we won't be offended if you don't read them.

Foolish Assumptions

We don't think that anything in this book is foolish, but we *have* made the following assumptions about our readers:

- You're a business owner or CEO who needs to know more about quality and the right quality methods for your organization.
- You're a staff member or mid-level manager who's in charge of introducing quality methods to your organization.
- You're a team leader looking for ideas on improving how a team works to reduce costs and improve service.
- You're an average worker trying to figure out what all the funny names for the different quality techniques really mean.

How This Book Is Organized

This book is organized into the following five parts, each of which has several chapters. Each chapter discusses a major topic related to quality control, and we divide the chapters into sections, which discuss particular issues related to those topics. The book is organized to support both a linear and modular read, but how you read it is up to you. Choose a part, a chapter, or a related topic — whatever floats your boat — and start reading!

Part 1: Understanding the Basics of Quality Control

Part I reviews the basic concept of "quality" and how it fits into an organization's products, services, and strategies. We provide an overview of what quality really means, why it's important in the modern business world, and the standards used to govern it. We also cover quality assurance, which examines the tools used to create a product or service, and inspection, which examines the results of a process to determine the degree to which it conforms to what it's supposed to be.

Part II: Putting Fundamental Quality Control Methods to Use

In Part II, we explore some fundamental processes for improving quality. For example, we explain how the customer defines quality with what's called the *voice of the customer*. We also explore ways to measure and evaluate quality characteristics, such as Statistical Process Control (not as scary as it sounds).

Part III: Whipping Quality Control into Shape with Lean Processes

Part III provides you with an explanation of the various Lean techniques in order to show how they build on one another. A *Lean organization* has examined all its processes and has squeezed out all the waste by cleaning up the workplace. Identifying waste and squeezing it out of your processes provides many savings, because a big money sink in many companies is an excess-materials inventory. Eliminating this bloat saves money and improves quality all around. Let us show you how!

Part IV: Surveying Other Quality Control Techniques

Part IV looks at some of the better-known quality methodologies that have been in fashion recently. Interestingly enough, the methods we outline here seem to use varying amounts of the Lean tools we identify in Part III — they just add their own spins on how to use them. And as you're probably aware, all "expert" consultants have their own spins on things because that's how they justify their fat salaries.

Part V: The Part of Tens

Part V follows in the grand tradition of *For Dummies* books providing Parts of Tens. Here you find ten steps for incorporating quality into a new process and ten Web sites that give you some quality control tips and present some quality techniques. This supplemental information is designed to be both helpful and informative.

Icons Used in This Book

The icons used in this book point you to important (and not so important) topics in the text:

Keep these facts in mind when making decisions about different aspects of the quality control process.

This icon signals that helpful advice is at hand. We use it to offer insights that we hope make quality control interesting or easier.

This icon means what it says and says what it means — you'd better be careful with the information that comes after. It warns you to avoid situations that can have nasty consequences for your organization.

This icon tips you off to interesting but nonessential information. Read it or skip it — the choice is yours.

Where to Go from Here

Each chapter in this book can stand on its own and will provide you with unique, useful information. So, find a subject that interests you or that you need to bone up on, turn to the page, and be ready to learn! Feel free to mark up the book, fill in the blanks, copy any tables, dog-ear the pages, or do anything else that would make a librarian blush. The important thing is that you make good use of the book and enjoy yourself in the process.

If you're new to quality systems, we suggest that you read Parts I and II in their entirety. You'll find that many quality improvement techniques are built on previous models, and they all point back to the basics of quality control.

One last thing: Check out the Web page at www.dummies.com. Feel free to take the opportunity to register your purchase online or to send the authors e-mail with feedback about your reading experience.

Part I
Understanding the Basics of Quality Control

The 5th Wave   By Rich Tennant

"Okay, I'm getting confused. Can we define 'quality junk' again?"

In this part . . .

*Q*uality control is a term often used to cover the entire concept of product quality. Every businessperson has a unique idea of what a "quality" product should be. In this part, we explore the basics of what makes up quality along with examples of how you can apply it.

We cover quality standards, which are like "the rules of the road." If every employee understands and follows them, every employee knows what to expect. We also discuss quality assurance, which examines the materials you use to create a product or service. "Good cakes require good ingredients," and so do good business products.

To wrap up the first part, we explain how quality control examines the results of a process to determine the degree to which it conforms to expectations. In many companies, this process is the "final inspection" to ensure that they pass on only good results to customers. However, catching poor quality means that you've already wasted the money making a product that isn't ready for sale. The ideal situation is to prevent an error from ever occurring.

Chapter 1

Defining and Explaining Quality Control

*W*elcome! Because you're reading this book, you've probably

✔ Been asked to lead a quality control initiative.

✔ Been assigned to a quality team.

✔ Heard your company CEO say quality is job #1.

✔ Heard rumors about new quality programs at your company.

Of course, you may simply be curious about the topic of quality control, and you want to discover more about how quality control affects your company and your job. We commend your dedication and initiative!

Quality control is a critical concept in every industry and profession. As globalization continues and the world becomes smaller, making it possible for consumers to pick and choose from the best products worldwide, the survival of your job and of your company depends on your ability to produce a quality product or service. In this chapter, we define the term "quality," and we introduce some important quality control concepts and methods.

Looking at Different Definitions of "Quality"

Everyone says that they want quality products or services, or a high level of quality, but what do they really mean? Is it possible to have too much quality? Without a clear definition of quality, you can't even begin to measure and evaluate it. In the following sections, we define quality in customer-oriented and statistical terms.

A customer-based definition of quality

What does the word quality mean to you? For most people, quality is associated with the idea of a product or service that's well done, looks good, and does its job well. We think of a quality product as one that lasts, holds up well under use, and doesn't require constant repair. A quality product or service should meet a high standard in many areas, such as form, features, fit and finish, reliability, and usability.

Most people use the word *quality* to mean "having a high degree of excellence," but like beauty, quality is in the eye of the beholder. If a consumer's desire is to have basic transportation at a low price, he would buy a Toyota rather than a Lexus. The Toyota may be a lesser grade of car, but is it of lower quality than the Lexus? That's up to the consumer to decide.

To complicate matters, the definition of quality changes over time. The Ford Model T was once thought of as a quality product, but if a dealership sold it today, it would be in the same quality class as the Yugo. Consumers' quality standards for cars have changed over time, just like they have for other products. As products and services evolve, consumer expectations tend to increase so that yesterday's quality product becomes tomorrow's junk.

What do these facts mean to your business? Quality, in the eyes of a business, revolves around meeting customer expectations — expectations that may be stated or implied. One action that sums up quality from a business perspective is when the customer returns after the sale and the product doesn't. Repeat business is probably the most basic measure of quality, because customers vote on the quality of your product or service with their pocketbooks. But unlike political elections, your customers vote daily, and new opposing candidates appear just as often to try to win your customers' votes.

The statistical definition of quality

As you may expect, the statistical definition of quality is a little more precise than other definitions, such as the customer-based concept, and is based on mathematics. When you measure quality statistically, you look for variation in a measurement between what the customer asks for and what you produce. The less variation you have, the higher the quality of your product or service.

All processes have some natural variation; you use statistics to detect abnormal variation that could cause you to produce a bad product or service. You can also use statistics to avoid testing every item that you produce. By testing a sample of what you make or deliver, you can use statistics to measure its quality and find out whether it meets customer requirements.

Setting Quality Standards

After you as an organization decide on a definition of quality (see the previous section), you need standards against which to measure your quality. Why? Many standards are driven by the desire to safeguard the health and well-being of the people who use the products or services companies provide. Quality standards also are critical in support of international trade.

Almost every industry has an association or trade group that sets quality standards against which companies can measure the quality of their products or services. Industries also have their own government- or business-supported standards bodies for products important to them. The International Organization for Standardization (ISO) is an international body made up of the national standards organizations for almost every country. We cover standards in detail in Chapter 2.

Preventing Errors with Quality Assurance

Quality assurance focuses on the ability of a process to produce or deliver a quality product or service. This method differs from quality control in that it looks at the entire process, not just the final product. Quality control is designed to detect problems with a product or service (see the next section); quality assurance attempts to head off problems at the pass by tweaking a production process until it can produce a quality product.

Don't get us wrong; we're not saying that quality assurance and quality control are unrelated. By continually improving your process, you improve the quality of your product or service. Probably the most well-known technique for improving a process is called the *Plan-Do-Check-Act,* or the *PDCA Cycle.* This simple but powerful tool requires you to

✔ Plan improvements to your process by looking for problems that affect the quality of your product or service.

✔ Make improvements by implementing small changes to minimize disruption to your process.

✔ Check production results to see if you've actually made an improvement.

✔ Act on what you discover and roll it out to the entire process.

Check out Chapter 3 for more information about quality assurance concepts.

Controlling Quality with Inspection

The most basic quality control technique is to inspect the results of your production or service-delivery process to make sure it conforms to customer requirements. In quality control terms, *conforming* means that an item meets customer specifications, and *nonconforming* means it doesn't. You inspect your product or service by measuring one or more of its properties and comparing the measurements to customer specifications.

Although inspection can ensure that 100 percent of the products or services you deliver to your customers are good, it can be a very expensive process, especially for high-volume, low-value items (such as common nails or shirt buttons). Also, inspection is impossible for items where testing can damage the product (such as testing a bullet).

Head to Chapter 4 for details about the role of inspection in quality control. We explain the challenges of inspection, how to overcome the challenges, and how to choose the best inspection method for your organization.

Applying Fundamental Quality Control Concepts

Your organization can implement several fundamental quality control processes to ensure that you produce or deliver a high-quality product or service. The following sections present the information you need to determine how you can integrate quality control processes into your organization.

Introducing quality control to your business

The introduction of a quality control process into an organization can be a major shock to its system. The following components are crucial if you want to lessen the shock and gain acceptance within your organization:

- ✔ Advertise acceptance of the program from important stakeholders within your organization.

- ✔ Give communication power to a sponsor who can articulate the need for change and who has the political power to gain compliance when required.

- ✔ Communicate the reasons for the change and the benefits it will bring to everyone in the organization.

- ✔ Train employees in the new ways of the organization. You want workers doing the right things consistently because success helps to gain support.

Like most other changes, quality control is best introduced in small bits. One way to do this is to create a pilot project that allows you to make a small change to a small part of your process to see the change's effect. If the results are good, you can implement the change on a wider basis; if the change is bad, you've limited the damage done. See Chapter 5 for the scoop on successfully introducing quality methods to your company.

Listening to your customers

An important concept in quality control is listening to the customer; we call this listening to the *voice of the customer* (the VOC). Although this task seems pretty simple (can't you just ask?!), you may find that your customers don't know exactly what they need, or they can't articulate their needs. The customer typically has three desires:

- ✔ They want it good.
- ✔ They want it fast.
- ✔ They want it cheap.

Of course, in the real world, consumers seldom get all three, so you need to identify what's most important in your customers' buying decisions, and you need to make sure you satisfy those needs.

You have several ways to hear the VOC:

- ✔ You can ask by handing out questionnaires, conducting interviews, reviewing complaints, holding focus groups, reviewing purchasing patterns, and interviewing field personnel.

- ✔ You can borrow good ideas from your competitors. Don't be afraid to use good ideas, no matter where you find them.

- ✔ You can use a good customer relationship management (CRM) system, which is a handy tool for gathering and analyzing data about customers.

Chapter 6 has details on listening to the VOC to improve the quality of your product or service.

Measuring your quality

The old management saying "You can't manage what you can't measure" rings especially true in quality control. A good measurement system helps you to know where you've been and where you're going. Customers typically require that you measure certain attributes of your product or service against their specifications. Your job is to determine what to measure, how to measure it, and when to measure it.

Employee training is critical to ensure that everyone involved in your process measures the same specifications in the same way. You also need to collect data in a usable format so that you can analyze it to determine the effectiveness of your quality process. The effectiveness of your quality process is directly related to the quality of your data collection and analysis process. If you don't have good data, you can't make good decisions.

Check out Chapters 7 and 8 for the nitty-gritty on measuring your current quality process.

Evaluating your quality

The most common way to analyze the data you collect is to use statistics. Statistics serve many purposes within quality control:

- ✔ Statistics allow you to determine which processes or parts of processes are causing your company the most problems (by using the *80/20 rule* — 80 percent of your problems are caused by 20 percent of what you do).

- ✔ You can use statistics for sampling so that you don't have to test 100 percent of the items you make.

- ✔ Statistics can help you spot relationships between the values you measure — even if the relationships aren't obvious. They also allow you to identify small variations in your process that can lead to big problems if you don't correct them.

Although statistics can seem daunting, you can use many simple tools to greatly improve your quality — tools that don't require an advanced degree in statistics! Chapter 9 has all the information you need to evaluate your quality process with simple statistical tools.

Although much of statistics allows you to look back only at what has happened in the past, Statistical Process Control (SPC) allows you to identify problems before they can negatively impact the quality of your product or service. The basic idea behind SPC is that if you can spot a change in a process before it gets to the point of making bad products, you can fix the process before bad products hit the shelves. We cover SPC in Chapter 10.

Trimming Down with Lean Processes

Lean processes are the latest diet craze in the world of quality control! *Lean* is a quality control technique you can use to identify and eliminate the flab in your company's processes. The "flab" is all the dead weight carried by a process without adding any value. The customer doesn't want to pay for dead weight, so why should you?

Most company processes are wasteful in terms of time and materials, which often results in poorer quality to the customer — a concern for all businesses. Lean focuses on customer satisfaction and cost reduction. Proponents of the technique believe that every step in a process is an opportunity to make a mistake — to create a quality problem, in other words. The fewer steps you have in a process, the fewer chances for error you create and the better the quality in your final product or service.

You can apply the Lean techniques in the following sections to all types of processes and in environments ranging from offices, to hospitals, to factories. In most cases, applying Lean concepts doesn't require an increase in capital costs — it simply reassigns people to more productive purposes. And, oh yes, Lean processes are much cheaper to operate. For a greater overview of Lean processes, check out Chapter 11.

Value Stream Mapping

People think in images, not in words, so giving them a picture of how something is done is often better than telling them about a process. After all, the quote is "Show me the money!" not "Tell me about the money!"

Value Stream Mapping (see Chapter 12) visually describes a production process in order to help workers locate waste within it. *Waste* is any activity that doesn't add value for the customer. Typically, eliminating waste involves reducing the amount of inventory sitting around and shortening the time it takes to deliver a product or service to the customer upon its order.

The 5S method

Work areas evolve along with the processes they support. As your organization implements new actions and tools, you must find a place for them "somewhere." Over time, clutter can slowly build as piles of excess materials or tools grow and gradually gum up the smooth flow of work.

The 5S method is an essential tool for any quality initiative that seeks to clear up the flow of work. Five Ss describe five Japanese attributes required for a clean workplace:

✔ Seiri (organization)

✔ Seiton (neatness)

✔ Seiso (cleaning)

✔ Seiketsu (standardization)

✔ Shitsuke (discipline)

Removing all the clutter from a process eliminates hidden inventories, frees floor space for productive use, improves the flow of materials through the workplace, reduces walk time, and shakes out unnecessary items for reuse elsewhere or landfill designation. Head to Chapter 13 for details about 5S.

Rapid Improvement Events

No one knows a process like the workers who touch it every day. They know how the work should flow, they can identify obstacles that slow everyone down, and they deal with problems that never seem to go away. So, why not tap this source of institutional knowledge and turn it loose to fix the problems that vex workers day in and day out?

A Rapid Improvement Event (RIE), which we discuss in Chapter 14, is an intensive process-improvement activity, where over a few days a company's workers bone up on Lean techniques and rebuild their processes to incorporate its principles. The workers take apart their work areas, rearrange items, and reassemble the spaces for more efficient work. The improvements are immediate, and the workers have ownership of the process and feel motivated to further refine it.

Lean Materials and Kanban

A company's materials are essential for the organization to work well, but they also tie up a large part of a company's capital. And while the company does its business year in and year out, its materials are stolen, damaged, rotting, corroding, and losing value in many other ways.

A key part of the Lean approach is to minimize the amount of materials (both incoming and finished goods) you have sitting around in your facility. (What do you know? This minimization is called Lean Materials.) Excess materials hide problems with purchasing, work scheduling, scrap rates, and so on. Eliminating these excess materials provides an immediate financial benefit to your company — if you eliminate correctly.

You don't want to eliminate so thoroughly that you cause shortages. One method you can use to fix the problem of excess materials without causing shortages is Kanban. Kanban is a materials system controlled by the customer. When a consumer buys an item, action cascades back up the production line to make one more of that item.

Turn to Chapter 15 for more information about Lean Materials and Kanban.

Checking Out Additional Quality Control Techniques

Okay, so Lean is interesting (see the previous section), but what other quality control techniques are available? Other quality methodologies have recently come into fashion, and we cover a few big ones in the following sections. They borrow from previous quality schools but provide their own twists that make it easier to accommodate different environments.

Total Quality Management

Total Quality Management (TQM), which we cover in Chapter 16, combines the work of important quality leaders, such as W. Edwards Deming, Joseph Juran, and Phillip Crosby, into a single quality improvement approach. You use TQM to improve the performance of processes by controlling variation — especially if your organization's products don't change frequently. TQM is very flexible and suitable to all types of organizations. It promotes a "quality culture," where a company trains everyone to focus on continuously improving the quality of everything the organization does. The concept includes the publication of a "quality strategy," whose application workers discuss at every meeting. It also requires the creation and use of quality measurement and monitoring tools.

Six Sigma

Six Sigma (see Chapter 17) is a great tool for driving difficult process problems back to their root causes. It uses process-analysis techniques and a broad application of statistics to determine the process inputs that cause the undesired outputs. Minimizing the variation of inputs produces a more consistent product or service.

Six Sigma is designed to provide "breakthrough" results, whereas the results from Lean improvements are bit by bit. Six Sigma is the best tool for fixing stubborn, it's-always-been-this-way problems. However, it isn't the right tool for every difficult situation. Six Sigma techniques take time to work their magic. You should apply it only after other quality techniques, such as Lean, have removed the waste and clutter from your process.

Quality Function Deployment

Quality, as we note in the earlier section "A customer-based definition of quality," is how well a product's or service's characteristics fulfill customer needs and wants. Quality Function Deployment (QFD), which we cover in Chapter 18, is a disciplined approach to identifying customer needs and wants and translating them into product or service characteristics. Its technique is easy to understand but time consuming to implement.

Many businesses like the structured way that QFD breaks down customer requirements into various components. When complete, QFD assembles the information into a busy matrix called the *House of Quality*.

QFD's power is in improving cross-functional communication and decision-making within an organization. It focuses all workers on the true requirements of the customer and minimizes misinterpretation of customer needs.

The Theory of Constraints

Every company has goals it wants to achieve, usually tied directly to revenue. Company goals are the result of a chain of activities or processes. However, each chain has a weak link that limits how much it can produce — a limitation known as its *constraint*. The pace at which a chain produces is its *drum* (or *drumbeat*). In order to achieve company goals, you need to increase your drumbeat in order to increase overall process throughput.

The Theory of Constraints (see Chapter 19 for details) is a comprehensive technique for identifying and managing an organization's constraints for obtaining maximum throughput. In short, with this concept, you find the constraint, focus it on maximum throughout by eliminating its distractions, and only then, if required, expand it by hiring more workers or putting in more machinery. In many cases, a company's own policies and metrics are its worst enemies (even though they're so cheap to fix).

Chapter 2

Understanding the Importance of Quality Standards

In This Chapter

▶ Securing the right level of "quality"

▶ Discovering how quality standards work

▶ Checking out the roles of quality standards in commerce

▶ Proving to the world that you run a quality organization

*I*magine trying to build a house with pieces of lumber that measure at different sizes, depending on where you buy them, or working on a car made with bolts that vary by manufacturer. Without quality standards, these tasks are much harder than they need to be. Quality standards ensure that the wood you purchase is the same no matter what lumberyard you buy it from. Standards also make it possible to buy one set of wrenches to work on all your cars. In a general sense, quality standards make it possible for companies across the globe to trade with each other. You should have confidence that the products you buy will mesh with the products you build.

In this chapter, you discover how quality standards make the modern world of global trade possible. You find out what level of quality is right for your company. You set the quality standards that will govern your production. You examine the role of quality in the global marketplace. Finally, you find out how ISO certification enters the quality picture.

Getting the Quality Just Right

As a child, you probably heard the story of *Goldilocks and the Three Bears*. Just as Goldilocks wants the soup, the chair, and the bed to be "just right," your customers want something that fits their needs.

You measure quality by how well a product or service conforms to the customer's desired specifications. (Chapter 6 has details on detecting the voice of the customer in quality issues.) Quality isn't a statement of the value of a product. Although one bear's soup is too hot for Goldilocks, and one bear's soup is too cold, the food is all high-quality soup for the intended diners. Goldilocks finds the teeny, tiny bear's soup to be "just right" because she happens to share the same taste in soup as that bear, not because that bear's soup is any "better" than the others.

In the following sections, we explain the costs of not meeting your customers' expectations (and why exceeding them can sometimes be bad).

Falling short: The cost of offering too little

The idea that insufficient value is bad is easy for everyone to understand. If I ask for a ladder that holds 300 pounds (I'm a big guy!), and the ladder you sell me holds only 250 pounds, I'm going to have a problem with the quality of your ladder. I will incur a cost (a medical cost!) that you created because you sold me, in my opinion, a ladder of poor quality.

The impact of providing too little quality is such an important concept in the field of quality control that it has a formal name: *cost of poor quality,* or *COPQ.* COPQ consists of all the costs that result from producing a poor-quality product or service. This expense consists of the costs of

- ✔ Improving the actual product or service to fill the gap between what the customer wants and what you currently offer
- ✔ Materials you added to the product or work you put into the service before the customer rejected it
- ✔ Lost labor and resources you need to fix the poor-quality product
- ✔ Potential lost market share (you may lose orders to competitors that offer better quality)
- ✔ Getting rid of the poor-quality product rejected by a customer (because you can't resell it)

COPQ doesn't include any costs associated with attempting to detect or prevent the lack of quality.

Calculating COPQ for your organization helps you determine the potential savings you can gain by putting quality process improvements into practice (see Chapter 3 for more on assuring quality). How do you calculate COPQ? Just follow these steps:

1. **Identify all activities that are necessary only because of poor quality.**

   Conduct a brainstorming session with people familiar with the process to identify all tasks that workers perform solely to fix quality problems. This could include processes such as inspection, rework, repair, and returns.

2. **Determine where in the production process these activities occur.**

   In other words, you look at which production steps cause the quality problems.

3. **To calculate the total cost of poor quality, identify the percentage of effort that each corrective activity consumes in its part of the production process; multiply by the total costs in that area.**

   For example, if workers perform 10 percent of the effort in a production area solely to fix quality problems, 10 percent of the entire cost of that production step is the cost of poor quality for that area.

4. **Sum the cost of poor quality for each area to get the total for your organization.**

   Sadly, the COPQ for most companies ranges from 15 to 25 percent. Reducing this value can increase the quality you provide to your customers.

Overshooting: Providing too much

Can exceeding the customer's requirements in some attribute of a product ever be bad? For example, if a customer wants a ladder that supports 250 pounds, and you sell him one that holds 300 pounds, have you done any harm?

If all a customer cares about is how much the ladder can hold, the fact that it holds more probably doesn't matter. But the material and engineering that went into adding 50 pounds to the holding capacity of the ladder likely added cost to the product. So, at the very least, the customer can find a ladder from another company that meets his needs and costs less. The customer also may have unspoken requirements, such as the weight of the ladder; a more heavy-duty ladder probably weighs more than the ladder the customer really wants.

Exceeding the customer's requirements for other types of items may also cause problems later in the production chain for products that use your parts. The production process is configured to work with the product exactly as specified; what you think are "improvements" may simply get in the way when your product becomes part of the final result that you deliver to the customer.

Doing more than the customer asks for is rarely a good thing, and it almost always adds unnecessary cost to the product. The key to maintaining quality is to make sure you know exactly what the customer wants and deliver it — nothing more, nothing less. Conduct market research often to ensure that you include features that are considered industry standards in your products or services.

Setting Quality Standards as the Rules of the Road

Quality standards are to producing a product or service what traffic laws are to driving. Imagine driving across a country where every state or town has its own traffic laws. Stop signs could be red in one town and yellow in another. Some country folk may drive on the right, and some city folk may drive on the left. Without a commonly understood set of rules, driving would be difficult, if not impossible.

You can say the same about the products you make or the services you provide; what you produce needs to conform to standards and interact with other products to function properly. Standards are critical for most products and services in use today.

Following quality standards is to everyone's benefit. Quality standards promote customer confidence in your products or services and can encourage the growth of the entire market. Because almost all products people can buy today contain parts or materials purchased from outside suppliers, a customer can get stuck with a poor-quality product if one supplier fails to follow quality standards.

In the following sections, we define quality standards, show you how to create them, and give you a sampling of different organizations that oversee them.

Defining quality standards

Quality standards provide a common language and measurement system for describing the quality attributes of the products or services you sell. The term *standards* describes things such as specifications, metrics, or statements about a process. Quality standards are designed to help you document what you're making or doing (specifications) so you can prove you followed and made exactly what you said you would.

For our discussion about quality standards, we focus on quality management standards. *Quality management standards* deal with the training, quality assessment, and quality management needs of the organization. These standards are designed to ensure that your process is capable of creating a quality product or service.

One example of a quality standard is ISO 9000, which describes the requirements for quality assurance and quality management. (Quality assurance involves examining *how* you do things so you can prevent flaws in your products and services; see Chapter 3 for details.) ISO 9000 is an international standard that helps organizations effectively document the processes they need to maintain complete quality systems. The standards aren't industry specific; they're designed to fit any process that creates a product or service. Check out "Securing ISO Certification," later in this chapter, for more about ISO 9000.

Creating quality standards

Quality standards, for the most part, are voluntary standards set by organizations that represent a particular industry. (See the following section for a sampling of quality governing bodies.) Although the quality standards may technically be voluntary, your customers may require that your business prove that it follows the quality standards before they buy from you. Most countries have a national standards body that sets the rules by which standards are created and maintained.

Most standards result from the collaborative effort of all the stakeholders in a production process. As a standard develops, the people who outline the standard consider the customer and the needs of the market. This collaboration increases the chances that consumers will accept products conforming to the standard, but it still allows room for innovators to differentiate their products or services.

Most formal standards start out as informal ones, created when an organization develops a new product, service, or process to which no existing standard applies. The market leader establishes a *de facto* standard — one that the market recognizes as a standard but that isn't officially spelled out. As the new product, service, or process becomes more popular, the need for a new or amended formal standard becomes evident. The creation of a formal standard usually follows these steps:

1. **Someone submits a proposal for a new standard (after you conduct research to find the appropriate standards body).**

2. **The standards body accepts the proposal.**

3. **The body drafts a proposed standard.**

4. **The body publishes the draft and solicits public comment.**

5. **The final standard is published.**

6. **The standards body reviews the standard on a periodic basis.**

Most organizations refer to this process as an *open standards process* because it gives anyone who has a stake in the outcome of the standard creation an opportunity to make comments and suggestions.

Surveying quality governing bodies

A number of organizations develop quality standards; we list some examples in the following sections. These and numerous other organizations work in almost any industry or profession you can think of to develop and implement quality standards that make sense for the producer and the consumer.

Check with industry trade groups that serve the business you're in to find out which quality organization(s) apply to you. A search engine on the Internet is also a good source of information on quality standards organizations.

The International Organization for Standardization

If you've heard or read anything about quality certification, you've seen the TLA *(three-letter acronym)* ISO (the study of quality is full of TLAs). The International Organization for Standardization (ISO) is made up of the standards organizations of approximately 150 countries. They work together to develop standards to facilitate international trade. The ISO is the 800-pound gorilla in the field of quality standards.

ISO's quality standards fall under the heading *ISO 9000.* These standards are, by far, the most widely recognized and followed. Although the majority of the standards that ISO produces are very specific to particular industries, products, processes, or materials, the ISO 9000 group of standards is known as *generic management system standards.*

In this case, *generic* means that the standards can apply to any

- Product or service
- Size of organization
- Type of industry
- Type of organization (corporate, government, or nonprofit)

Management system means that the standards focus on the processes companies use to create the products or services (quality assurance — see Chapter 3), as well as on how these processes satisfy the customers' requirements (quality control).

These quality standards are grouped under the designation ISO 9000:2000. The 2000 refers to the year of the standards' last update.

The ISO 9000 standards have become the most widely known and implemented quality standards ever developed, used by over 750,000 organizations. We discuss the requirements that make up ISO 9000 later in the chapter. You also can check out www.iso.org for more information.

The American National Standards Institute

The American National Standards Institute (ANSI) is a private, nonprofit organization that governs and oversees the voluntary standardization and conformity-assessment system that covers industries of all types in the United States. ANSI originally began as the American Engineering Standards Committee (AESC) in 1918, and its goal was to serve as the national coordinator in the standards development process; as an impartial party, the organization intended to approve national consensus standards and to stop user confusion on acceptability. Today, ANSI is also a founder and the sole U.S. representative of ISO (see the preceding section), and it plays a major role in the workings of that organization for setting international standards. Visit www.ansi.org for more information.

The Joint Commission on Accreditation of Healthcare Organizations

The Joint Commission on Accreditation of Healthcare Organizations (JCAHO), pronounced *JAY-co,* evaluates and provides accreditation for hospitals and other healthcare organizations in the United States. As an independent, non-profit organization, JCAHO focuses on improving the quality and safety of the care that healthcare organizations provide. Its accreditation process evaluates compliance with JCAHO standards. Visit www.jointcommission.org for more information.

Recognizing the Roles of Quality Standards in Commerce

Quality standards play a critical role in commerce. In the following sections, we explain how quality standards indicate customer needs, trim costs, and ensure safety.

Standardizing ISO's name

According to ISO's Web site at www.iso.org, the full name of ISO is *International Organization for Standardization,* which should be the acronym IOS in English. Because the organization has members from many countries, the abbreviation for the name is different in different languages (IOS in English, OIN in French for *Organisation internationale de normalisation*). To avoid confusion, members of ISO decided to use a name derived from the Greek *isos,* which means "equal." Using ISO as the standard short form of the organization's name makes the acronym the same in any language or country.

Communicating customers' requirements

Quality standards communicate to the seller of a product exactly what the buyer requires. They document what's important to the customer and clearly define what the producer needs to deliver to the customers. Standards provide a common language to reduce problems and misunderstandings as a product moves from raw materials to the consumer.

Well-defined quality specifications tell the producer how "well" to build something. Although a Toyota buyer may appreciate the extra human effort that goes into a Rolls-Royce, she definitely doesn't want to pay for that extra effort. (See the nearby sidebar for more about Rolls-Royce and Toyota.)

Cutting costs

Quality standards allow companies to focus on their roles in the production process instead of spending valuable time and resources inspecting incoming materials and parts. Imagine the cost involved in inspecting every part or material that a vendor sends you. Multiply that over the entire production process, and you can see how individual inspections don't give companies an efficient way to ensure quality. (For information on how to make sure your suppliers are up to standard, see Chapter 3; for details on the role of inspection in quality control, see Chapter 4.)

Ensuring safety

Quality standards play an important role in safety. In fact, most standards have their roots in providing safe products to consumers and providing safe working conditions for employees.

For example, quality standards for food and beverages help prevent illness. The Occupational Safety and Health Administration (OSHA) facilitates communication between the public and private sectors on creating standards that affect safety in the workplace. OSHA also works with the Consumer Product Safety Commission (CPSC) to develop quality standards related to consumer products.

Want another example? A main driver for the creation of standards in healthcare is the concern for patient safety. Each year, JCAHO (see the earlier section "The Joint Commission on Accreditation of Healthcare Organizations") adds new standards called "Patient Safety Goals," which focus on different areas of patient safety. For 2006, the new standards focus on areas such as assisted living, behavioral healthcare, critical access hospitals, and laboratories.

Man versus machine: Choosing alternative production methods

Rolls-Royce and Toyota are both known for the high quality of their cars, yet the processes they use to produce their products couldn't be more different. Although both companies use machines to produce the parts that go into their cars, Rolls-Royce does much of the assembly by hand, relying on human touch to make sure everything fits just right. Toyota relies on automation to meet its goal of consistent quality from car to car.

Following quality standards doesn't mean that you have to do everything the same way as everyone else; it simply means that your customers get what they expect when they buy your product or service.

Securing ISO Certification

How can you tell that you know what you need to know about quality? How do your suppliers know that you know about quality? And most importantly, how do your customers know that you know about quality? Like anything else you've had to learn in your life, passing "the test" shows others and yourself that you know what you need to know about a subject. Quality is no different. You can prove to the world that your organization knows quality by passing "the test" — in this case, becoming certified as an organization that knows and follows the practices that lead to quality.

Just as passing the bar exam doesn't guarantee that you're an expert lawyer, becoming quality certified from the International Organization for Standardization (ISO) doesn't guarantee that you'll always produce a quality product or service. What it does mean is that your organization has made an effort to become knowledgeable in the ways of quality and has processes in place to make the best quality product or service possible. The following sections show you the steps of the quality certification process and how the process can help your organization reach its quality goals. For general information about ISO, see "The International Organization for Standardization," earlier in this chapter, and be sure to visit www.iso.org for additional information about the certification process.

Looking at the basics of ISO certification

ISO certification is becoming the "standard" for certifying the ability of an organization to produce a quality product or service. Certification shows that your organization has proven its ability to consistently provide a product or service that meets the needs of your customers. It also means that you meet any regulatory requirements that apply in your industry and that your processes are designed to enhance customer satisfaction.

ISO's standards, grouped under the name *ISO 9000,* are a family of standards primarily concerned with quality management. Quality management involves an organization's ability to

- Meet its customers' quality expectations
- Enhance its customers' satisfaction in the product
- Follow applicable regulatory requirements
- Continually improve the product

Going through the ISO 9000 certification process can really improve how your organization functions. The basic aim of the process is to help your organization

- Set quality goals and objectives
- Ensure that customer requirements are understood and met
- Train employees on producing a quality product
- Control production processes
- Purchase from quality suppliers
- Correct any problems found and adjust the process to prevent the problems in the future

Both the improvements in your processes and the quality seal of approval can really pay off. Benefits of ISO certification to your organization include

- Increased productivity
- International recognition of the quality of your company
- Improved employee satisfaction
- Ability to compete with larger businesses
- Increased customer satisfaction
- Increased profits
- Opportunities to sell your products to new markets

For these reasons, many companies are finding that being ISO 9000 certified isn't simply good for business, it's becoming a *requirement* for doing business.

Checking out ISO standards

As we mention in the preceding section, ISO 9000 is really a set of standards. The main parts of the ISO 9000 standard are as follows:

- ✔ **ISO 9000:2000:** This standard covers the basics of the attributes of a quality management system. It also defines the core language of the ISO 9000 standard series.

- ✔ **ISO 9001:2000:** This standard defines the requirements for an organization to meet customer expectations through consistent products and services (see the next section). It's designed for use by any organization that designs, manufactures, installs, and/or services any type of product or provides any type of service.

  This standard is the one to which you can be certified by outside auditors; this is what we mean when we say an organization is ISO 9000 *compliant.*

- ✔ **ISO 9004:2000:** This standard is for organizations that have already achieved ISO 9001 certification, and it covers standards for continuous improvement.

The 2000 in the standard designation is the year the standard was revised. The previous versions from 1994 also included ISO 9002 and ISO 9003, but these were incorporated into ISO 9001 and are no longer in use. To make matters more confusing, some ISO standards that are referenced in the ISO 9000 standards aren't in the 9000 series of numbers. For example, some of the standards in the 10,000 series also discuss quality issues. People use the term ISO 9000 to refer to the three ISO quality standards: ISO 9000:2000, 9001:2000, and 9004:2000.

Examining the requirements for ISO 9000

Although the ISO 9000 standards may seem overwhelming at first, they're really nothing more than good business practices. Five groups of requirements make up the standard:

- ✔ **Quality management system:** These requirements are broad statements that apply to all aspects of your quality process. They outline the requirements for your quality manual and how to control your documentation and records.

- ✔ **Management responsibility:** These requirements describe the role of upper management in determining the customers' needs, planning, identifying responsibilities, setting objectives, and reviewing the performance of a process.

- ✔ **Resource management:** This group covers the requirements for managing the resources of the organization through activities such as training employees and providing the proper tools and equipment.

- ✔ **Product realization:** This group is the meat of the standard; it includes all the requirements for how you make your product or deliver your service. Topics include communicating with your customers, the design of your product or service, and how you deliver to your customers.

- ✔ **Measurement analysis and improvement:** These requirements are what you do to check your performance; they involve issues of how you measure performance, fix problems, and make improvements to a process.

As you can see, the standards really just prove that you know what your customers want; that you have a plan to give it to them; that your people are well-trained; and that you have a well-thought-out and documented process for delivering to your customers. You also need a way to determine whether your customers are satisfied and to demonstrate that you can identify and fix problems. These areas are all things that any successful business must do. ISO 9000 certification is simply a way to prove to your customers that you know how to run your business.

Preparing for ISO 9001 certification

Preparing for ISO 9001 certification is complex and time consuming, and it requires a lot of documentation. It also involves almost everyone in your organization. The following list presents the steps to follow when preparing your organization for ISO 9001 certification:

1. **Get the commitment of top management.**

   As with any other program within the organization, support from upper management is critical for success. The quality control process requires extra time and resources from almost everyone, so management needs to be prepared to see it through.

   Form a quality committee to evaluate the process and its impact on your organization. The committee should make sure that management understands the total cost and schedule of the process. (See Chapter 5 for more on forming quality teams.)

2. **Train all employees.**

   Make sure that everyone in the organization receives basic quality training (this book can help), and select and train your internal auditors.

3. **Prepare your quality policy manual.**

   Determine how the ISO 9001 requirements apply to your organization. Develop vision and mission statements to reflect these requirements. Write a basic quality policy manual outline for review by management, and then complete the first draft of the manual. If customers request ISO 9001 compliance, send them copies to review.

4. **Document operating procedures.**

   Define responsibilities in each part of your process, using the quality manual you develop as a guide. Have each person document procedures for his or her part of the process.

5. **Perform an internal audit to determine your compliance with ISO 9001 standards.**

   The audit is basically a gap analysis between what the ISO standards are and the current state of your production process. (This internal audit should resemble the actual audit; see "Moving through the steps of the audit," later in this chapter, for details.) Develop a list of corrective action items from the audit.

After you correct any problem items you find in the internal audit, you're ready to take the plunge and have a real audit performed.

Industry associations and trade groups that serve your industry are good sources of information on ISO certification. The ISO Web site at `www.iso.org` can get you started.

Sweating through an ISO audit

If you've prepared and practiced (see the preceding sections for the right steps to take), you're ready for your ISO 9001 audit. In the following sections, we show you how to select a certification agency, and we walk you through the steps of the audit.

Choosing a certification agency

The ISO doesn't directly certify organizations; you have to engage an outside organization that specializes in assessing compliance with the standard. Most countries have formed accreditation agencies to authorize certification organizations (also called *registrars*), which then audit organizations applying for ISO compliance certification. Both the accreditation agencies and the certification organizations charge fees for their services. The accreditation agencies in different countries have mutual agreements with each other to ensure that certifications issued by any of the certification organizations are accepted worldwide.

With approximately 100 registrars in the United States, how do you select the best one? As with most decisions, you have to consider a number of factors when making your selection. All countries have a body responsible for controlling the activities of registrars and for ensuring that they have their own ISO equivalent quality systems. The countries maintain lists of approved registrars and check to make sure the registrars continue to meet the standards. In the United States, you can check out the ANSI-ASQ National Accreditation Board Web site at www.anab.org to find approved registrars.

Some registrars work only within a specific industry, which may be an advantage because the one that works in your industry will be more familiar with the processes commonly used in your industry. Review a registrar's process and check references to try to determine the quality of service.

When comparing costs, make sure you compare apples to apples, as fees vary widely. Costs may include application fees, administrative fees, and document-assessment fees before the auditor even shows up. You also have to pay fees for an annual or semiannual review of your quality process. Ask how registrars calculate expenses. Some registrars with local offices fly in auditors from other locations and expect payment for expenses. If applicable, also ask whether an auditor has a special fee structure for small companies.

Moving through the steps of the audit

After selecting the registrar, you're ready to go through the audit process. Review the audit process with the registrar to make sure you're ready. Hold a pre-assessment audit as a final check to correct any last-minute issues (see "Preparing for ISO 9001 certification," earlier in this chapter, for information).

After the audit is complete, take any corrective action needed and re-audit if necessary.

After you pass the audit, your registrar can certify that you follow the ISO 9001 standards. Your auditor will provide your organization with a letter and a certificate suitable for framing to let the world know that you're officially a "quality" organization!

Chapter 3

Using Quality Assurance for the Best Results

*I*n the 1980s, companies around the world discovered that if they wanted to compete in the marketplace, they had to dramatically improve quality while reducing costs. Companies who survived accomplished this by shifting how they managed their quality processes. Instead of relying on inspection alone to identify and correct problems (see Chapter 4 for more about inspection), they moved toward a focus on preventing problems before they occurred. Quality control programs evolved into a more comprehensive quality assurance process. Quality control changed from being a post-manufacturing step performed at the end of each process to being part of the process itself.

In this chapter, we explain the general concept of quality assurance and provide a few methods you can use to improve quality in your product or service from start to finish.

Understanding the Concept of Quality Assurance

The International Organization for Standardization (ISO; see Chapter 2 for more on the ISO) defines *quality assurance* as "providing confidence that requirements will be met." To meet the goal of the quality assurance process, a company has to look not only at the product or service that's the output of its production process, but also at activities such as design, development, production, installation, service after the sale, and documentation.

In other words, quality assurance is more than just checking to see that the product or service meets the customers' expectations; you also have to look at the process involved in creating the product or service to see if you're capable of producing a quality product or service each and every time. Part of this is

- ✔ Verifying that the materials or parts you receive are correct before they go into whatever product or service you make or provide.
- ✔ Ensuring that the specifications for your product or service are crystal clear.

Quality assurance is more effective the earlier it occurs in the process. In fact, quality assurance should begin before the product is assembled or the service is designed. How is this possible, you ask? It all starts with the suppliers!

This chapter covers these important issues and more. But before we dive into the details of incorporating quality assurance into your workplace, we want to discuss a few basics. In the following sections, we clarify the differences between quality assurance and quality control and explain the overall importance of catching errors before they occur.

Recognizing how quality assurance differs from quality control

Here's a good description of the difference between quality control and quality assurance: Whereas quality control includes all the tactical activities necessary to produce a quality product or service, quality assurance looks at quality from a strategic prospective. Quality control focuses on identifying problems after they occur; quality assurance is a process for preventing problems from occurring in the first place. Quality assurance looks at the entire system used to create the final product or service for the customer, not just at individual parts of the process.

Measuring quality while you create the product or carry out the service can prevent bad output from reaching the customer. This has been a standard practice in most industries for a long time, but a number of successful organizations have adopted a dramatically different approach. Driven by competitive pressures, they've significantly improved quality in their products and services while reducing oversight and inspection costs.

The striking difference between the way companies have traditionally managed quality and the manner in which world-class companies practice quality assurance is that the latter defines quality assurance much more broadly, making it an integral part of the entire process — from development to production to sales. Several crucial techniques are common to the quality assurance approach:

✔ Focusing on creating complete, accurate, and producible designs before production begins by requiring communication between key players.

✔ Making use of process controls to design products and control the production process as it occurs. (See Chapter 10 for details on controlling your production process.)

✔ Developing programs with key suppliers to ensure the quality of incoming products and materials. (See the section "Developing Trusted Suppliers" later in this chapter for more details.)

Catching errors before they occur

Because bad processes can transform good products into bad products, and because bad parts lead to bad products or services, a key goal in quality assurance is to catch errors before they occur. This practice allows companies to avoid making bad parts in the first place or putting bad parts into otherwise good products. It's always cheaper and easier to do things right the first time instead of doing something over to correct a mistake (this thought process leads to the saying "quality is free").

Bad parts result in bad products

You just can't make a good product with bad parts. Most finished products contain a tremendous number of parts, and each part must work correctly; if not, partial or total product failure occurs. If your suppliers can't provide you with quality parts, you can't make a quality product.

An example most people can relate to is the modern automobile. You don't think about the thousands of processes that the manufacturer performed in bringing your car into existence until something goes wrong. It boggles the mind thinking about the art and science that goes into building millions of cars and trucks every year. Given the huge amount of companies, parts, materials, people, and processes required, mistakes will be made and problems will occur. How the participants in the supply chain deal with problems once they happen determines whether quality is improved.

For want of a nail

Leave it to a nursery rhyme to sum up the quality assurance process:

For want of a nail, the shoe was lost. For want of the shoe, the horse was lost. For want of the horse, the rider was lost. For want of the rider, the battle was lost. For want of the battle, the kingdom was lost. And all for the want of a nail.

As this old English nursery rhyme shows, it takes only one bad part to turn a good product into a bad one!

See the section "Developing Trusted Suppliers" later in this chapter to find out how to ensure quality materials from your suppliers.

Bad processes turn good products or services into bad ones

If the process of putting together a product or providing a service is bad, the final product or service will be bad — no matter the quality of the parts involved. For example, an automaker can buy the highest-quality parts, but if the car is poorly designed, the result will be a shoddy car.

One effective technique for improving a process is to educate workers about not only their pieces of the process, but also about how their work fits into the entire production system (with formal or on-the-job training, for example). With this knowledge, workers can see how what they do affects others further down the production process. You can also give them the opportunity to make suggestions for improving the processes that lead up to theirs. Initiatives such as these help everyone in the goal of making a better product. (For additional information on improving an overall process, see "Focusing on the Process with Plan-Do-Check-Act" later in this chapter.)

A good example of how looking at an entire system can improve quality is in how hospitals provide drugs to patients. The number one cause of non-illness-related complications suffered by hospital patients is problems with the process of prescribing and administering drugs. The traditional process is for a doctor to see a patient, determine what drug is appropriate for treatment, and then send the prescription to a pharmacy to be filled. Errors can occur at the last stage, because the pharmacist simply fills the prescription without knowing much about the patient. An error at this stage is not only costly, but also can be hazardous to the patient's health.

By examining the treatment process and gathering information from doctors and pharmacists, hospitals have found that including pharmacists on hospital rounds is a low-cost way to catch drug errors before they occur. Doctors spend about 5 percent of their time thinking about drugs, whereas pharmacists spend all their time thinking about drugs. By including input from the pharmacist earlier in the process, hospitals can prevent many potential errors.

Developing Trusted Suppliers

Every company today has suppliers in one form or another. The days of totally vertically integrated manufacturing plants, where nothing but raw materials come in and finished products go out, are mostly gone. Almost all manufacturers of goods sold to consumers use numerous suppliers to provide the parts that make up the finished products. Your relationship with your suppliers is critical to producing a quality product or service.

Most organizations have an ingrained inspection-based quality process that can be difficult to overcome. By partnering with your suppliers (or your customers if you're a supplier), you can drastically reduce the cost of possibly redundant inspection processes. If you can count on your supplier to send you a quality product, you don't have to spend time and money inspecting incoming material. In the following sections, we show you how to survey suppliers and outline your responsibilities as a buyer.

Verifying quality with a supplier self-survey

In dealing with the Soviets, Ronald Reagan famously said, "Trust, but verify" — you should adopt the same policy with your suppliers. Although you want to have a partnership with your suppliers to produce a quality product or service for your end customers, you must remember that you're still separate companies, with your own goals and objectives.

The best step you can take to verify the quality of your suppliers is to administer a supplier self-survey. The survey lets you know whether the supplier is using the appropriate quality processes in producing your product. The supplier fills out the survey and returns it to you, along with any necessary documentation (such as copies of any certifications, organization charts, and so on). You should send the survey to all prospective suppliers before you add them to your approved supplier list (see the following section for details about this list).

You can also use the survey whenever a supplier undergoes a major change that may affect product or service quality, such as the following:

- New or updated facilities
- New or updated equipment or capacity
- Key management personnel changes
- Change in the status of the business (such as its legal structure)
- Expansion or contraction of the business
- Changes in the product line (such as model changes)
- Changes in the company's financial situation (such as bankruptcy or a credit rating change)

When you send the survey to the suppliers, assure them that you'll treat all information in the survey as confidential, and you won't disclose the information to other parties except as required for quality assessment purposes. They'll want your assurance that you won't share any confidential information with their competitors.

So, what questions should you include on the supplier self-survey? The exact questions vary by industry and the requirements you place on your suppliers, but the survey typically consists of the following five parts:

1. Basic company profile information

2. Information about facilities and equipment

3. Documentation of their suppliers

4. Organizational structure and human-resource environment

5. Quality systems and certifications

See Figure 3-1 for an example of a supplier self-survey questionnaire. Review each section, and modify the questions to fit your situation. For example, you may need to add industry-specific certifications that your suppliers need to have.

In addition to using the supplier self-survey questionnaire, you can perform on-site audits at potential or existing suppliers to see for yourself that the appropriate quality controls are in place before you place orders for the supply of materials and services (that's the verify part). You should review the effectiveness of your suppliers' quality systems at regular intervals — and more frequently for more complex items or if the suppliers have experienced recent quality problems. The frequency of the audits depends on your confidence level in the supplier to provide you with a quality product. Your internal quality people are the most qualified people to audit your suppliers.

Knowing your responsibilities as a buyer

As a quality buyer, your job is to ensure that only quality parts and materials come into your process. You shouldn't just trust your suppliers like you trust hot-dog makers (you don't want to know what kind of parts they use). And how do you do your job? To start, you should follow these steps:

1. Continuously monitor quality and delivery performance of all suppliers, using a monthly supplier performance rating system. Develop a point system to rate suppliers on important areas such as on-time delivery, defect rate, and flexibility in meeting your production requirements.

2. Distribute the monthly supplier performance report to all affected departments.

3. Ask any suppliers you associate with poor quality performance to implement corrective actions and report these actions to you in writing. Suppliers should return their reports within two weeks of receiving notice of poor performance.

4. Remove suppliers from the approved supplier list if their performance continues to be inadequate and they show no signs of improvement. Establish a timeframe for removal from the list based on the importance of the supplier and the availability of suitable replacements.

Supplier Self-Survey Questionnaire						
Company survey team to complete this section:						
Supplier:				Product:		
Evaluation results:	☐ Approved ☐ Rejected ☐ Need more information ☐ Onsite audit required					
Reviewed by:					Date:	
The supplier to complete this section:						
Part 1 — Company Profile						
Company name:						
Address:						
Phone #:		Fax #:			Web address:	
Parent company:						
Type of company:	☐ Public ☐ Private ☐ Joint venture ☐ Other:					
Years/months in business:		Last year's sales (USD):			This year projected sales (USD):	
Major customers:						
Major competitors:						
Major shareholders:						

Management team:

Title	Name	Role	E-mail address
		CEO/President	
		Plant/Production	
		Human Resources	
		Sales/Customer Service	
		Engineering/R&D	
		Other	

Part 2 — Facilities and Equipment

Production locations:

Location:		Year opened:		Size in sq. ft.:	
Location:		Year opened:		Size in sq. ft.:	
Location:		Year opened:		Size in sq. ft.:	
Location:		Year opened:		Size in sq. ft.:	
Plans for expansion or relocation:	☐ Yes ☐ No	If Yes, location:			

Major production equipment:

Process/area	Equipment name	# of units	Years in service	Country of origin

Major inspection equipment:

Process/area	Equipment name	# of units	Years in service	Country of origin

Research and Development (R&D)

Does the company have its own in-house R&D team?	☐ Yes ☐ No
Does the company have its own in-house design team?	☐ Yes ☐ No
Is the production area under environmental control?	☐ Yes ☐ No
Are clean room facilities available?	☐ Yes ☐ No

Figure 3-1:
A self-survey helps ensure that you receive quality supplies.

Information Technology (IT)

Does your IT team have experience integrating your systems with those of your customers?	☐ Yes ☐ No
What type of system do you use for inventory control?	
Do you use EDI to communicate with partners?	☐ Yes ☐ No
Are your production systems available via the Internet?	☐ Yes ☐ No

Disaster Recovery (DR)

Does each major function have a DR plan?	☐ Yes ☐ No
Have you tested every DR plan within the last year?	☐ Yes ☐ No

Part 3 — Supply Chain

Major suppliers:

Material/service	Annual usage	Supplier name	Supplier location	DR plan
				☐ Yes ☐ No
				☐ Yes ☐ No
				☐ Yes ☐ No

Major customers:

Customer name	Product category	Customer type	Annual usage

Part 4 — Infrastructure and Human Resources

Total # of employees:		Average tenure:	
Function	**Head count**	**% of total**	**Average tenure**
Management			
Marketing/Sales			
Quality Control			
Production			
Other			

Do you have employee involvement programs in place?	☐ Yes ☐ No
Do you have standard shutdown periods?	☐ Yes ☐ No
Do you have any union agreements?	☐ Yes ☐ No
Have you had any strikes in the past 5 years?	☐ Yes ☐ No

Part 5 — Quality Systems and Certifications

Quality standard	Certified?	Certified by	Certification date
ISO 9001	☐ Yes ☐ No		
ISO 9002	☐ Yes ☐ No		
ISO 14000	☐ Yes ☐ No		
QS-9000	☐ Yes ☐ No		
	☐ Yes ☐ No		
	☐ Yes ☐ No		

Please describe your company's quality mission and goals:

Figure 3-1: (continued) A self-survey helps ensure that you receive quality supplies.

The quality manager at your company should maintain a list of all approved suppliers that affect the quality of your finished product or service (see Chapter 5 for more about the selection of a quality manager). The list should note suppliers that have completed the supplier self-survey questionnaire and those who have been audited by your firm (see the previous section). You should use only suppliers on this approved list when ordering materials and services. If you need to make an emergency purchase from a supplier not on the list, make it mandatory that the quality manager and your purchasing manager approve of the transaction in writing.

Make an updated approved-supplier list available on the company intranet, or print and distribute a list to all applicable employees at least monthly. And make sure you document any disputes or problems with the quality you receive from a supplier.

Here are a few more tips regarding the supplier-buyer relationship:

✔ The quality manager and purchasing manager should work together to ensure that all suppliers meet the quality requirements of the organization. Any problems with a supplier regarding the quality of supplied products or services should involve both of these managers.

✔ Keep communications open with your approved suppliers to facilitate quick identification and resolution of any quality problems.

✔ Identify who should get involved if the quality and purchasing managers can't resolve a quality problem with a supplier (usually someone such as the Vice President of Manufacturing or the Chief Operating Officer).

Focusing on the Process with Plan-Do-Check-Act

To make improvements in the quality of your product or service, quality assurance focuses on the processes you use to make the product or provide the service instead of only performing tests on the final product. Probably the most well-known technique used for identifying spots for improvement processes is called the *Plan-Do-Check-Act,* or the *PDCA Cycle.* In the following sections, we describe the main stages of the cycle and techniques you can use to complete each stage.

Walter Shewhart, a pioneering statistician who developed Statistical Process Control while at Bell Laboratories (see Chapter 10 for more about this technique), created the PDCA Cycle technique in the 1930s. Shewhart's friend W. Edwards Deming, a famous quality management guru, made the technique popular in the 1950s.

The major stages of the PDCA Cycle

The idea behind the PDCA Cycle is that process improvement isn't a one-time linear event; it's a continuous cycle of activities that make the process better and better over time (see Figure 3-2). The following list outlines each stage:

1. **Plan** to improve the process by identifying what's going wrong and coming up with ideas to make it better.

   The planning stage involves a few steps:

   - Make sure you clearly define the problem and have a measurable goal for the effort involved.

   - Identify the process or processes that impact the problem and select one to work on.

   - List the steps involved in the process, and review the steps to identify potential causes of the problem.

   - Collect and analyze data related to the problem to identify the problem's root cause. (See Chapter 8 for more on collecting data.)

   For example, suppose you're trying to reduce the number of reported bugs in a software program. You would review your software development process to look for areas that seem to have the biggest impact on the number of bugs created.

2. **Do** small changes a little at a time to minimize disruption to your normal activities, which allows you to clearly see the effects of the change.

   Establish criteria for selecting which solution to try, and implement the solution on a pilot basis to limit potential problems.

   In our software example, we may decide to add a code review process to see whether the bug count decreases.

3. **Check** whether the small changes are producing the desired result.

   To carry out the checking stage, you should

   - Gather the appropriate data on the solution you implement.

   - Analyze the data to see if you achieved the desired result; if not, go back to the Plan stage.

   After three months of performing code reviews, we look at the bug count for the software to see whether it's decreased.

4. **Act** on what you discover, and implement positive changes throughout the process.

   Identify the changes required to make what you've learned part of your process, and plan ongoing monitoring of the solution to make sure it doesn't cause new problems.

   If the bug count has gone down, you make code reviews a permanent part of the software development process. If the bug count hasn't gone down, go back to the Plan stage to look for other things to try.

5. After you solve the problem and improve the process, start over again to plan the solution to the next problem in a never-ending improvement cycle.

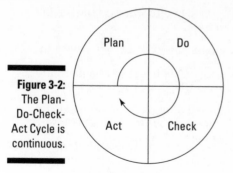

Figure 3-2:
The Plan-
Do-Check-
Act Cycle is
continuous.

Tools for working through each PDCA stage

At each stage of the PDCA Cycle, you have numerous tools and techniques at your disposal to complete the steps required for success in the stage; we discuss these items throughout this book. The following sections outline the tools and techniques in an easily accessible list format (if you haven't gathered it already, lists are to become a big part of quality control life).

Planning tools

You can facilitate the Plan stage by using any of the following tools:

- **Flowcharting:** Draw a diagram that shows the step-by-step progression of the product through the process.

- **Customer/supplier mapping:** Create a diagram of the interactions between all customers and suppliers in your supply chain.

- **Brainstorming:** Bring together a small group to brainstorm possible problem solutions.

- **Pareto analysis:** Use the 80/20 rule to narrow the problems you need to work on — look at 20 percent of your activities that cause 80 percent of your problems.

- **Evaluation matrix:** Develop problem evaluation criteria and relative weights to rank each problem.

- **Cause-and-effect diagrams:** Draw a chart that shows the problem and the reasons why the problem occurred to look for root causes.

Doing tools

The Do stage may require any of the following techniques:

✔ **On-the-job training:** You can train your workers while on the job in order to implement changes to a process.

✔ **Experiment design:** Design experiments and expected outcomes to determine the effectiveness of the change.

✔ **Small-group leadership skills training:** Help lead the team to make the required changes.

✔ **Conflict resolution:** Build the skills needed to resolve issues between the people and departments performing the process.

Checking tools

You can complete the Check stage by using any of the following tools:

✔ **Data worksheets:** Track important outputs from the process.

✔ **Control charts:** Measure data to determine whether the process is consistent.

✔ **Key performance indicators:** Identify the factors that directly and indirectly influence the effectiveness of the process.

✔ **Graphical analysis:** Graph the process results to highlight any changes.

Acting tools

The Act stage puts the process in place by using any of the following tools:

✔ **Process mapping:** Draw an updated diagram of the process for all to see.

✔ **Process standardization:** Compare the updated process to other existing processes to look for issues or opportunities.

✔ **Formal training for the new process:** Make sure everyone performs the new process correctly.

Getting What You Really Need with Product or Service Specifications

Just as a football team needs a playbook so that every player knows his role, a quality product or service needs a specification with every step in the process clearly defined so that everyone knows exactly what needs to be done. Your goal is to instill trust and confidence in your employees that the production process will create a quality product or service. This process doesn't happen by itself; you have to look at other required ingredients:

1. Create a specification that defines the requirements of the product or service. The design and production team should work together on this task.

2. Production follows the specifications.

3. Implement conformance-testing checks so that the quality team can confirm whether the requirements in the specifications have been correctly implemented during production of the product or in the execution of the service.

The three parts (specifications, production, and testing) are interrelated. You can look at the three processes as a three-legged stool. Each leg depends on the other two; like a stool, if one of the legs is broken, the stool keels over. The specification, however, is the key leg, because the requirements in the specification form the basis of production and are used as the basis of quality testing (which we cover in Chapters 7 and 8). Incorrect requirements can cause problems in production, testing, or both.

In the following sections, we explain how to craft clear specifications, and we warn you about the dangers of including extra info in specifications.

Creating clear specifications

To know what's required to produce a quality product or service, you must have clear specifications. The specifications must contain *all* the information you need to produce a quality product or service for the customer. If the requirements aren't correct, everything else that follows probably will be incorrect. Good specifications have the following attributes:

- ✔ **The desired final result is clearly defined.** You need to tie down the requirements to specifics, not in vague generalities. Use terms not subject to interpretation, such as 6.0 inches, 2.35 ounces, and so on.

- ✔ **They capture all the customer requirements.** Make sure that everything important to the customer is what the customer really wants. (See Chapter 6 for more about listening to the voice of the customer.)

- ✔ **They're precise, unambiguous, and measurable.** Clear, commanding words in specifications make what's expected very clear and don't leave anything to discretion. You may decide to use "shall," "shall not," "must," and "must not." For example, a good specification is "the hole must be 6.0 inches in diameter."

You can't clearly test words such as "should," "should not," "recommend," and "may," making them poor words to use in a specification. The worst words to use are "of best quality" and "good" because they're not precise or testable.

✔ **They define clearly what's expected of the production worker.** Production workers need to know exactly what you expect of them and how you'll measure their conformance to the specifications.

✔ **They're defined in a formal technical language — not English.** Most operations have a precise language that uses words with unambiguous meaning — use this language in place of plain English.

After the specifications are clear, make sure to train everyone involved in production on how to use the specifications. A formal training process that includes an assessment is the best way to ensure that everyone understands the specifications.

Avoiding extras in specifications

Just as important as getting what you need out of a process is not getting what you don't need. Anything added beyond what's required in the specification may seem like a good idea at the time, but overkilling the requirements may cause unintended problems later in the supply chain. Even if you don't cause harm later, adding aspects to the product that you don't outline in the specification just adds cost to the product. Your process should produce the product to meet the specifications — nothing more, nothing less.

For example, a supplier might decide to use a heavier gauge material to make a product stronger, which it thinks is an improvement. However, the original design might have been more than strong enough for your purposes, and the increased weight might cause your product to be too heavy for the customer's needs. Process and product improvements should be designed in, not added on a whim and without consideration for unintended side effects.

Chapter 4

The Role of Inspection in Quality Control

*I*n a perfect world, your product or service would always come out just right, but sometimes mistakes happen, and the only way to catch these mistakes is to inspect items before you ship them to consumers. In this chapter, we discuss the role of inspection in quality control: when it's appropriate, how to do it properly, and how it fits into your overall quality process.

Examining the Basics of Inspection

No matter the product you create or service you provide, you have to complete a series of steps before you can deliver to your customers. Errors can occur at any one of these steps, causing your product or service to fall short of your customers' expectations. How do you catch these errors before they reach the customer? Inspect the product or service at key points between major steps in production and remove or repair any bad items along the way.

Inspection is the analysis or examination of an item carried out to determine whether it's defective. Experts use the terms *conforming* to say that an item meets customer specifications and *nonconforming* if it fails. Quality control managers use two approaches to determine if a product conforms:

✔ Examine the item or the results of the service and compare it to some standard description or image.

✔ Measure some physical property of the item or service and compare the measurement with a customer specification.

In the following sections, we define the term "defect" and explain the importance of inspection so that you don't allow your customers to catch product errors before you do. We also introduce the basic concepts at the heart of inspection: measuring attribute and variable data.

The definition of "defect"

In Chapter 1, we define *quality* as conformance to customer specifications; so, is nonconformance the same as a defect? Well, not exactly. A *defect* is a glitch that prevents your product or service from being acceptable to the customer. *Nonconformance* means that you didn't match the customer or product specifications. They're not exactly the same. The bottom line is that every defect means the product doesn't conform to specifications, but not every nonconformance is a defect.

A defect may prevent the product from working 100 percent, or it may simply be a cosmetic blemish. If the hard drive in your laptop fails, it has a defect because the laptop is unusable. If your laptop has a scratch, it has a defect that makes the machine look less impressive, even though it still functions.

If the manufacturer of the laptop installs the wrong hard drive, but it has the same or larger capacity, the machine wouldn't have a defect. The laptop is perfectly usable, and you may not even notice the difference. However, the laptop doesn't conform to specifications because the manufacturer didn't build it as planned — in other words, the laptop is nonconforming.

The importance of catching bad products before your customers do

Why should you worry so much about catching defective products and services? Wouldn't it be cheaper to tell your customers that you'll replace any defective products and save yourself all the time and effort? The reality is that both are costly, but the cost of giving defective products to your customers is much more damaging than the cost you incur to replace the items. And you're not the only one to incur the costs; your customers incur them, too. The following list presents costs associated with producing defective products:

- ✔ Premature failure of a part, which damages the entire product
- ✔ Chasing down problems that occur when the customer uses the item
- ✔ Extra material required to repair the item
- ✔ Delivery costs to replace the defective item
- ✔ Customer charges for costs incurred

> ✔ Effort spent by the customer determining whether the item is conforming
>
> ✔ Potential loss of business due to poor reputation
>
> ✔ Costs to acquire new customers to replace lost ones
>
> ✔ Any safety margin designed into the process to allow for variation (see the next section for more about variation)

Your goal is for your product or service to meet your customers' requirements each and every time, with a minimum of variation between individual units. Achieving this goal lowers the cost to both the producer and the customer.

The heart of inspection: Attribute and variable data

To inspect for quality, you first must decide what product or service characteristics you want to inspect, and then you determine what values will signify that the product or service conforms to customer specifications. The following list presents two types of data used to measure an item's quality:

> ✔ **Attribute data:** Qualitative information about the product, such as "the label is in the correct place" or "the light is red." Attribute data clearly defines whether the product achieves conformance; either it does or it doesn't. For example, if a light must be red, either it is or it isn't.
>
> ✔ **Variable data:** Measures some physical characteristic such as length, width, temperature, time, and so on. Variable data is great when you have a desired target value and you can determine the amount of variation from the target. For example, a product may require a part to be 3.5 inches in length — you can measure the length of the part to see how close to 3.5 inches it falls. You may require your lawn service to cut the grass to a height of 2.5 inches. Your marketing consultant may guarantee to increase your sales by 10 percent.

You can turn variable data into attribute data by comparing it to specification limits for the product — it then conforms or it doesn't. For example, you may want a product to be 3.5 inches in length, but the customer will accept it as short as 3.495 inches or as long as 3.505 inches. If the part falls within this range, you can accept the part as conforming to the customer's specifications.

Although attribute data is very useful in clearly stating whether you've met the customer's requirements, you can't perform any analysis on attribute data other than counts. To do a more sophisticated analysis than simple counts, you must convert attribute data to variable data. You can turn attribute data into variable data by using a scale to describe the characteristic, called a *Likert scale*. A Likert scale typically has five values, although some companies use seven or nine. The following is an example of a Likert scale:

Statement: The color is uniform.

1. **Strongly disagree**

2. **Disagree**

3. **Neither agree nor disagree**

4. **Agree**

5. **Strongly agree**

You may decide that any score less than 3 is nonconforming, at which point you label the part as defective.

You also can track the value for each part by using this scale and then track changes in value over time. This tactic helps you determine whether the process is getting better or worse over time. (See "Tracking Defects to Improve Your Business," later in this chapter, for details about tracking.)

Recognizing and Addressing the Challenges of Quality Inspection

Although all this inspection stuff may look good on paper, it can be difficult to implement in practice. An effective inspection process requires a change in how your company normally manufactures a product or provides a service. In the following sections, we discuss human error in the inspection process and the financial costs of implementing an inspection process, and we give you ways you can change your production process to address these issues.

Getting a grip on the human aspect of inspection

One challenge in the inspection process is unavoidable: The more humans you have working in the inspection process, the greater the chance for human error. You must pay attention to two categories of errors people can make during the inspection process:

- **The inspection doesn't detect an error.** This category is called *Consumer's Risk,* because the consumer risks receiving a defective item.

- **The inspection reports an error that doesn't exist.** This category is called *Producer's Risk,* because the producer risks rejecting a good item.

One way to remove the human element from inspection is to use inspection equipment. Some machines may detect blemishes on an item (such as looking for insect damage on vegetables), while other machines can measure weight, size, color, and so on. (These examples illustrate attribute and variable data, which we discuss earlier in this chapter.) Some include machine vision that can visually inspect a part just like a person would, only much faster.

Even with machine inspection, an item can become damaged during packaging after it goes through inspection. With some operations, you can inspect and package items in the same process, which can eliminate defects that occur after inspection.

Totaling the expenses of inspection

You have many costs to consider when designing your inspection process. Some costs include the following:

- ✔ **Setting up inspection equipment:** Time and expense involved in setting up your inspection process

- ✔ **Labor costs:** Cost of inspectors and supervisors

- ✔ **Machine costs:** Measuring equipment, inspection machines, and so on

- ✔ **Space costs:** The space in the facility used by the inspection process

- ✔ **Time spent on bad parts:** Time wasted when inspectors assume that parts are correct — production continues, but you later find out that you must scrap some parts

- ✔ **Time spent waiting on inspection:** Parts sitting idle and not moving through the production process or being shipped

Of course, the cost of your quality processes, including inspection, should be less than the cost of poor quality (see Chapter 2 to find out how to calculate this cost). As with any other business investment, you need to calculate the total return on your inspection investment to help guide you.

Jumping over other inspection hurdles

Some of the additional challenges you should expect to face when implementing a quality inspection program include the following:

- ✔ **Developing processes for accurately measuring the product or service:** Each new product or service presents its own set of measurement challenges. Accurate measurement is important to avoid unnecessary waste and effort.

- ✔ **Inspection speed and accuracy:** In most cases, speed is the enemy of accuracy. You need to find the right balance for your process.

- ✔ **Employee awareness and training:** Employees require proper training to perform the inspection correctly.

- ✔ **Communication with customers:** Your customers, in many cases, require you to provide details about your inspection process as part of their evaluation of your quality (see the later section "Considering different factors as you select an inspection process").

- ✔ **Consistency in the inspection process over time:** As you add new products, machines, and people to the process, it becomes difficult to maintain consistency.

- ✔ **Maintaining consistency over multiple production sites:** You need to remain vigilant for local deviations from the corporate best practices.

- ✔ **Developing the skills to meet tighter specifications:** Your customers will require tighter specifications over time as they strive to improve the quality of their own products.

- ✔ **Focusing on the important issues:** Make sure you focus on the vital few issues and not the trivial many (remember the 80/20 rule; see Chapter 8).

- ✔ **Educating suppliers:** Keep suppliers in the loop about your inspection process and work with them to reduce the overall cost of inspection. Simple changes in their processes could pay big dividends in your inspection process.

- ✔ **Motivating people to take responsibility for their work:** The more people feel responsible for their work, the better the inspection process.

- ✔ **Getting reasonable requirements from the customer:** Just as you work with your suppliers, work with your customers to look for possible efficiency improvements between your process and theirs. (See Chapter 6 for more about the voice of the customer in quality issues.)

- ✔ **Management support:** Continued management support is critical in keeping everyone focused on improving quality.

- ✔ **Root-cause analysis of failures:** Getting to the real cause of quality problems can be difficult.

Choosing the Inspection Approach That Fits Your Company's Needs

Given your situation, how much inspecting should you do? The inspection process comes with three options:

- ✔ Zero inspection

- ✔ 100% inspection

- ✔ Acceptance sampling by lots

In the following sections, we provide you with different factors to think about when selecting an inspection process, and we give you brief overviews of different inspection processes.

Considering different factors as you select an inspection process

Before you implement an inspection program, you need to think about the following factors to determine the right amount of inspection:

- ✔ **Acceptable quality level:** Because it all starts with the customer, your first order of business is to determine the quality level required by your customers. We call this the *acceptable quality level,* or AQL. You express the AQL value as a percentage of defects that the customer will tolerate. The fewer defects your customers will tolerate, the more rigorous your inspection process must be.

- ✔ **Nature of the production process:** Do you produce your products one at a time in a continuous process, or do you produce them in batches?

- ✔ **Variation in the process:** The more consistent your process, the less likely you are to produce bad products. A stable process has very little variation between individual items.

- ✔ **Cost of inspecting a product:** The more inspection costs, the less inspecting you'll want to do.

- ✔ **Cost of shipping a defective product:** Is the product small and returned easily or big and difficult to return? How much does it cost your customer to receive a bad product from you? The more expensive the shipping, the more important it is to send an acceptable item the first time to avoid the expense of return shipment.

- ✔ **Value of the product:** You can afford to spend more on inspection if you produce a high-value product.

- ✔ **Probability that inspection doesn't detect an error:** The higher the probability, the more inspection you may need to do. If the result of not detecting an error is very costly (high cost in dollars or human life), you need to increase the level of inspection. If the cost is high enough, 100% inspection may be justified.

- ✔ **Probability that inspection reports an error that doesn't exist:** The higher the probability, the greater the cost incurred from rejecting an item that truly is acceptable.

Figure 4-1 is a simple chart that you can use to determine the best inspection process for your company.

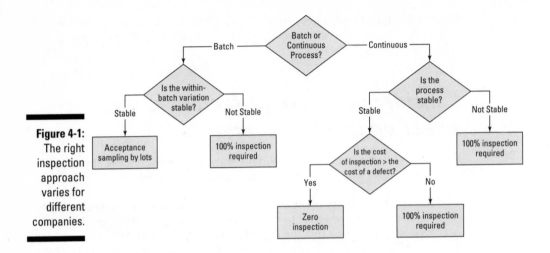

Figure 4-1:
The right
inspection
approach
varies for
different
companies.

Checking out zero and 100% inspection

If you know that your company produces more bad products than your customers will accept, zero inspection isn't an option. On the other hand, we can list several reasons why you likely won't inspect all the items that you produce (100% inspection):

- ✔ The testing process may be destructive. Testing rifle bullets or the amount of weight an item holds destroys the sample being tested.

- ✔ The cost of inspecting each product may be prohibitive. Items of low value, such as common nails, just aren't worth inspecting.

- ✔ The time required to inspect each product properly may be prohibitive.

Surveying lot sampling

In most cases, zero inspection isn't an option, and 100% inspection is too costly. So, what do you do? For most organizations, the most sensible approach to inspection is to inspect enough of the products to catch most of the bad ones, but not to inspect so many that you drive your costs too high. Instead of inspecting each product, you select a sample of the products for inspection. This process is known as *acceptance sampling by lots*.

In the following sections, we show you how lot sampling works and present several different types of lot sampling.

Reviewing lot sampling's job description

When you lot sample, you take a product sample from a "lot" of products and pass judgment on the lot based on testing from the sample — known as *lot sentencing*. The lot is made up of products that have something in common, such as the following examples:

- ✔ Produced by the same machine
- ✔ Produced by the same operator
- ✔ Produced from the same batch of raw materials
- ✔ Made at the same time

After you test the sample, you typically accept or reject the entire lot based on the results of the test. The tests you use can focus on attribute or variable data, which we discuss earlier in this chapter.

Perform any sampling entirely at random to avoid anyone gaming the system — you want to vary the time, day of week, machine number, and so on for picking the sample to inspect. Use a random number chart or generator to pick products from the lot for testing. You don't want to always pick from the same spot in the lot; an operator paid by the piece may be tempted to ensure that items he knows are good appear in the spot you pick from.

Hand-picking the best lot-sampling method

When it comes to lot sampling, you have three commonly used sampling methods to choose from. The following list presents them in detail.

To make the decision on which sampling method to use, compare the average sampling savings gained by the different sampling methods to the added cost and complexity of these methods. The use of software to calculate the sample size required, based on your quality goals, is critical to making this decision. Your industry's trade group or a search on the Internet can provide you with information on available software.

- ✔ **Single sampling:** You take a single sample from the lot and accept the lot if the number of defective products is less than a certain number (the *acceptance number*). You calculate the sample size and acceptance number based on the size of the lot, the acceptable quality level, and the amount of Producer's and Consumer's Risk you're willing to take (see the earlier sections "Considering different factors as you select an inspection process" and "Getting a grip on the human aspect of inspection" for info on the last two criteria). You must choose the samples randomly to reduce the chances of an error reaching the customer.

✔ **Double sampling:** You take a smaller sample for double sampling than you do for single sampling. You perform your tests, and if the products in the lot pass the tests, you accept the lot. If you don't accept the lot, you take another sample, retest, and combine the results of both samples to determine the fate of the lot. Double sampling works well if your process produces good products for the most part. This method can save you time and effort compared to single sampling; however, it's more complex to administer, and it may increase the opportunity for inspection errors.

✔ **Sequential sampling:** You keep testing products from a lot, and after you inspect each item, you make a decision to accept or reject the lot or to continue sampling. With sequential sampling, you could end up conducting 100% inspection on the lot. The advantage to sequential sampling is that the sample size can, on average, be much smaller, based on the number you decide must be good before you can accept the lot (in other words, the acceptance number). The disadvantage of sequential sampling is that it doesn't account for variation from one lot to another.

No matter which sampling method you use, you may want to consider using a *rectifying scheme,* where you subject all rejected lots to 100% inspection. Most companies use this tactic. You replace all defective products in the lot with good products. The customer receives two types of lots:

✔ Lots with some defective items that have passed inspection by sampling

✔ Lots that you've subjected to 100% inspection with no defective items

Tracking Defects to Improve Your Business

After you know a little bit about inspection, what should you do? Do you just inspect your products, removing the bad ones and sending the good ones to your customers? Can you do anything to actually prevent making more bad products in the future?

The smart thing to do is to learn from your mistakes to make fewer mistakes in the future. One good learning vehicle is properly tracking your defects. In the following sections, we explain why you should track trends in your production process, keep careful records, and calculate the cost of rework so you can better your business.

Following trends in your process

By tracking trends in your production process, you can create a process that's more stable and features a small enough variation that drastically reduces nonconformance (see the earlier section "Examining the Basics of Inspection"). You call processes that can do this *capable* — that is, they're capable of consistently producing quality products.

Performing a simple inspection allows you to determine whether a product is conforming or nonconforming. However, if you use variable data (covered in the section "The heart of inspection: Attribute and variable data"), you can use statistics to

✔ Detect when a process is getting worse and will soon cause a defect

✔ Reduce variation to improve quality

✔ Detect causes of variation

Using variable data in this way is called *Statistical Process Control* (SPC). We cover SPC in much more detail in Chapter 10. For now, you need to know that making SPC part of your inspection process allows you to track trends in your production process and to help find the cause of problems.

For example, say you need to drill a hole a half-inch in diameter. Your specifications say that the hole's diameter can be between 0.495 inches and 0.505 inches. When you first begin drilling holes, you see that they start out at 0.5 inch. But as you cut hundreds or thousands of holes, you begin to notice that the holes are getting slightly smaller and smaller. As the sizes of the holes start to reach 0.495 inches, you can safely bet that the drill bit is wearing down and needs replaced.

SPC is used in most types of quality control. With SPC, you can

✔ Reduce the risk of defective parts and the need for inspection

✔ Detect information on production trends and causes of problems that you can use in the future

✔ Minimize the cost caused by defects in your process

Keep in mind that you also can use SPC for services that might produce errors, such as creating legal documents or preparing tax returns. In these cases, you can track the number of errors categorized by the type of error.

Keeping careful records

Keep careful records of the defects that you detect during the inspection process and what you're doing to fix them and prevent them from occurring in the future. The ideal system for tracking defects does so automatically, with information available at all times in real-time. When your company is just getting started with inspection and quality control, a manual process works fine as you refine your data-collection process.

Figure 4-2 is an example of a manual form that can get you started. Your form will vary, depending on your industry; a defect form for a software company is much different than a form for a washing machine maker.

The following list presents some of the basic data you should collect:

- Product or service name
- The person or machine that detected the defect
- The date and time you detected the defect
- Description of the defect
- The impact of the defect

  You may want to have separate values for the impact on the customer and the impact on your production process.

- An assessment of the impact of the defect on other parts of the production process or the business as a whole

  List any risks or concerns here.

- The person responsible for correcting the defect

Defect Tracking Form			
Product:		Detected by:	
Date detected:		Defect impact:	☐ Urgent ☐ High ☐ Medium ☐ Low
Defect description:			
Defect assessment:			
Defect owner:			
Defect resolution notes:			
Estimated effort:		Actual effort:	
Description of modifications:			
Status of defect:	☐ Resolved ☐ Unresolved ☐ Reassigned		

Figure 4-2:
Track product defects to plan improvements to your production process.

✔ The estimated effort required to resolve the defect

✔ The actual effort required to resolve the defect

✔ The status of the defect

Have you resolved it, or have you assigned someone else to resolve it?

✔ The final solution to preventing reoccurrence of the defect

Keeping careful records makes it possible to see patterns that may develop and to see shifts in your process that you may be able to tie to some event (a new machine, a new employee, and so on). Customers also may require that you keep records so they can perform a quality audit of your organization.

Calculating the cost of rework

You've heard the saying: "If you have time to do something over, you have time to do it right." This stern suggestion is especially true when you build products or deliver services to clients. If the value of a part is low enough, you can just throw away or recycle a bad one. But for high-value parts, you usually attempt to fix the defect to make the bad parts good. This process is called *rework*.

Although it may make sense to rework valuable parts, rework is bad for business and a sign of a poor process. Rework is bad because

✔ It can be expensive.

✔ The cost wouldn't be there if your production process worked correctly the first time.

✔ It takes valuable resources away from the main production process.

✔ It slows the delivery of the product or service to the customer.

✔ It's bad for the morale of employees who want to do a good job.

Capturing all the costs associated with rework can be time consuming, but the task is necessary. You need to know the cost of rework so that as you make improvements to your production process, you can calculate the benefits of the improvements. This information is helpful when you evaluate different possible options for making improvements and select the improvement process with the best payback. Management also requires a cost/benefit analysis for changes made to the production process. When calculating the cost of rework, make sure to include the following costs:

✔ Labor/personnel (including administrative time used and training costs)

✔ Materials

✔ Equipment used for rework

✔ Space used for rework

✔ Scrap disposal

Check with your accounting department — it can provide you with "fully loaded" costs for labor and space used. Also, modify the worksheet in Figure 4-3 to fit your environment to help you calculate the cost of rework.

Cost of Performing Rework	
Personnel Costs/Hour	
Hourly wage of your rework personnel	
Hourly cost of rework personnel benefits	
Other hourly costs (temp-agency fees, for example)	
Hourly cost of supervision	
Hourly cost of quality training	
Hourly cost of production training	
Total Personnel Cost Per Hour (A)	Sum of above
Material Costs/Hour	
Hourly cost of workstation	
Hourly cost of replacement parts	
Hourly cost of repair materials	
Hourly cost of consumables	
Total Material Cost Per Hour (B)	Sum of above
Space Cost/Hour	
Sq. ft. per workspace × cost per ft. × work hours in year	
Total Space Cost Per Hour (C)	Sum of above
Total Hourly Cost of Rework (D)	A + B + C
Average number of units one operator can complete in one hour (E)	
Cost per component reworked (F)	D ÷ E
Scrap Costs	
Average production cost of item (G)	
Number of items scrapped during rework (monthly) (H)	
Number of items reworked (monthly) (I)	
Scrap rate (J)	H ÷ I
Scrap costs per component reworked (K)	G × J
Total Cost Per Component Reworked	F + K

Figure 4-3: A handy worksheet can help you calculate the cost of rework.

Part II
Putting Fundamental Quality Control Methods to Use

The 5th Wave   By Rich Tennant

"Our customer survey indicates 30% of our customers think our service is inconsistent, 40% would like a change in procedures, and 50% think it would be real cute if we all wore matching colored vests."

In this part . . .

*P*romoting quality within a company isn't hard; everyone agrees that quality is a good idea. However, getting workers to change their ways so that you can create high-quality products can be a battle. The key is to demonstrate why the changes are in their best interest; in this part, we cover this idea and others for starting down the road to quality.

Also in this part, we discuss how the customer defines quality through what's called the *voice of the customer*. If consumers dislike a product or service's quality, they won't buy it. Plain and simple!

Finally, we show you how to measure your current quality process and evaluate the results with the use of statistics and Statistical Process Control.

Chapter 5

Starting Down the Road to Quality

*Q*uality isn't a fixed destination; it's an exciting and action-packed journey. The demands of your customers will change over time, and your quality processes must adapt to continue to meet your customers' needs. You can't fix all your quality problems with one simple program; it requires constant correction, a little at a time, to get to where you want to go. In this chapter, we help you overcome the natural resistance to change that a new quality program creates, and we give you tips on keeping a pilot project on course through communication and training. The navigator on your quality journey is your quality control manager, but he or she needs help from other members of the quality team and from stakeholders who have a vested interest in the destination of your quality journey.

What's New? Introducing Change in Your Company

Few corporate changes are as disruptive to the status quo as the introduction of a quality control process into an organization that previously went without. Whether you plan to implement a change as minor as the reorganization of a single workstation or as major as the reengineering of your entire production process, you'll encounter some level of employee resistance to change. Change requires people to move away from what's familiar and routine and into unknown and potentially risky territory.

When your organization starts on the road to quality, it needs to have a map so that everyone involved knows where you're headed and how you're planning to get there. A quality roadmap encourages support among the employees and guides your organization toward your quality goals.

Any roadmap to quality should consist of the following four steps:

1. **Needs analysis.** An examination of the need for quality control. The quality control manager typically performs this step as a repeating cycle, involving the following tasks:

   a. Analyzing the current situation

   b. Negotiating with all the involved stakeholders (management, workers, customers)

   c. Defining the organization's needs

2. **Decision process.** The matching of defined needs for quality control with the available quality control options. (Parts III and IV of this book are full of specific quality control methods to consider.) If no existing quality control process meets the requirements determined in the needs analysis, the quality control team needs to develop a custom quality control process.

3. **Implementation.** Integrating your quality control strategy into your production process. Your new quality control process becomes part of how you do business. The company will refine its processes as it gains experience and as employees analyze the new process's impact on performance.

4. **Incorporation.** During this step, the new activities and behaviors required by the individuals who make up the production process take hold. A new quality control process requires that people change their old behaviors; the process won't be complete until the required new behaviors become a natural part of each individual's daily routine.

Implementing a quality program isn't a one-time-and-you're-done venture. The people involved in a quality control process need to perform the steps over and over again as your company moves away from where it is now to the desired quality destination. You may take a few detours along the way, but your quality roadmap will keep you moving in the right direction. Performance improvement happens in steps, one project at a time.

Having a Sponsor as a Champion of Quality Control

Every project starts with a sponsor — anything from motivating your friends to go to a movie to lobbying for a bill in Congress. A sponsor should be a person with enough organizational influence to give a project credibility, financing, and strategic direction. The sponsor also should be in a position to ensure the willing cooperation of all departments within an organization.

Implementing quality control processes involves changing people's attitudes and some of their tried-and-true business practices (see the previous section). So, to suppress the reluctance to change, the sponsor should have a stature lofty enough to overcome objections before they arise.

In the following sections, we describe the ideal sponsor for a new quality control process and the initial tasks handled by the sponsor.

Deciding on the sponsor

Ideally, the sponsor is the company's CEO or the vice president in charge of production. A person in either of these roles has the influence and credibility to motivate employees and enact change. However, a department manager may one day realize that something must be done about quality and ask to become a sponsor. Whoever assumes the role must remain involved with the project throughout its lifetime. As the sponsor's interest fades, so does the interest of the team.

Find out why the sponsor is interested in the project; the reasons will tell you how much support to expect. In some cases, the sponsor honestly believes the project is a good idea and is personally interested in seeing it through to completion. In other cases, the sponsor has to start the project due to a customer's complaint of poor quality. In the latter situation, the sponsor may want only the minimum amount of improvement to satisfy the unhappy customer. Spend some time early in the project digging around for the motivation behind the project.

By understanding what motivates the sponsor, you may be able to educate the sponsor on the many advantages of having a well-developed, company-wide quality program.

Understanding the roles of the sponsor

A sponsor of a new quality control process has several important duties, as we explain in the following sections.

Appointing a quality control manager

The sponsor's first task is the selection of the quality control manager (QCM). Most cynics say that the person who raises the issue gets the job (the sponsor, in other words). QCM by default isn't a bad way to assign the responsibility because only people who believe in something raise the issues. Still, the selection of the right QCM helps make the project a success; selecting the wrong person will make success much more difficult to attain.

The quality control manager is responsible for improving the quality process as the organization becomes better at quality. Traits of a good QCM include

✔ Good leadership skills

✔ Good project management skills

✔ An understanding of the organization's political landscape

To garner the support of everyone in the organization, the quality control manager should be assigned to this task with the sponsor's unqualified support. You need to overcome internal politics and let everyone know that the QC team needs their assistance. As the project moves forward, regular public displays of support are required if you want to produce a complete and usable plan.

Figure 5-1 gives you an example of a letter appointing the quality control manager. The letter should not only announce the sponsor's support for the quality control manager, but also outline the quality control manager's responsibilities and the criteria that will be used to measure the success of the quality control efforts.

Securing approval for the process

The sponsor has additional duties on top of nominating a quality control manager (see the previous section). The list includes the following:

✔ Approving the plans created by the quality control team and ensuring that the plans meet the objectives for the project

✔ Reviewing the scope of the quality efforts to ensure that they fit within what the sponsor has in mind

✔ Checking that any assumptions made in any plans created by the quality control team are correct

The sponsor also must obtain approval for funding if needed.

Hiring a consultant

Some sponsors begin the quality control process by hiring outside consultants. A consultant can be useful in mentoring someone in the organization to assume the QCM position. Generally speaking, it takes more time, effort, and expertise to organize and develop the quality control process than it does to keep it going. As you put the process into place, the consultant can teach the QCM the ropes and move the project along faster. Talk to companies similar in size and operations (in your industry if possible) to find a consultant who has successfully helped with other quality control projects.

TO: Al Wallace
FROM: Michael Webber, Chief Operating Officer
DATE: 01 November 2006
SUBJECT: Quality Control Manager appointment

Dear Al,

You are appointed as the **Quality Control Manager** for Widget Manufacturing.

Implementing quality control is a logical progression in our efforts to improve the performance of our business. As the manager for quality, you will be the key player in ensuring that our facility's quality control plan is complete and workable. Your initial responsibility is to assist in the plan's development and then assume the role as the plan's ongoing champion.

Your responsibilities include:

- Ensuring that all departments have a quality plan.

- Ensuring that new processes and equipment are implemented to support our quality plans.

- Scheduling ongoing testing by department and by product.

Here are the criteria for success:

- Every department's quality plan must provide for meeting customer requirements and for continuous improvement.

- Each department's quality plan must be understandable to anyone familiar with that type of equipment or technology.

- A quality control plan will be submitted for every process in the facility.

- At the end of the project, the project manager will submit a list of known problems in our processes or equipment along with long-term recommendations to address them.

- All quality control plans will be tested (by someone other than the plans' authors) and certified by the department managers as suitable for their purposes.

- This project shall commence on December 1st and be completed by June 30th. By that time, all plans will be complete, tested, and approved by the department managers.

An e-mail will be sent to all associates announcing your new position. Please be sure to provide me with monthly status reports of your progress. Feel free to contact me at any time if you need assistance in working with any department.

Sincerely,

Michael Webber
Chief Operating Officer
Widget Manufacturing Company

Figure 5-1:
Appoint
the quality
control
manager
in a letter.

The consultant's responsibility is guiding the project, and that's it; the consultant shouldn't assume the role of quality control manager. Every company, every facility, and every production line is unique. The creation of a quality product is the result of the key people at each step of the production process doing the right thing. An outside consultant can provide considerable insight into the quality control process, but he or she lacks in-depth experience at your company. The consultant doesn't know your business processes and doesn't understand the pulse of your business and what its key elements are.

Talk About It: Quality Communication within an Organization

Effective communication is critical for the success of any new change in policy within a company. How the entire quality process unfolds depends on how well the sponsor and the quality control manager communicate to the rank and file the importance of the quality process — not only to the organization, but also to them personally. In the following sections, we explain the different types of quality-related information your company needs and show you how to craft two important tracking documents.

The creation and instillation of a communications plan encompasses more than just memos floating around the office. It should include meetings within the various teams, meetings with the sponsor, and presentations to the various departments. Another important communications task is to raise the awareness of employees and how the quality control plan impacts them. Posters, newsletter articles, and open meetings all serve to answer their questions and instill a quality culture in your organization.

Listing the types of information to communicate

Each member of your organization has different information requirements and preferred formats for receiving information. The president doesn't require or want the details of every meeting. A department manager wants the specific details of what's happening in his or her department, and only a general idea of what's happening in other departments. So, when implementing a quality control process, a proper communication plan provides the right level of information to the right people at the right time.

Having an effective communication program becomes more critical the larger the organization becomes.

Information that you need to communicate to your organization falls into three main categories:

- ✔ **Mandatory communications:** Tasks that must be done, such as status reports to the sponsor, meeting minutes to the team members, and so on. Skipping a piece of mandatory communication may affect the quality control project's support or credibility.

- ✔ **Informational communications:** Includes reports to the interested and curious. Many people will see the quality control process under development within the organization and believe that it directly or indirectly affects their jobs. Informational communications pass on project accomplishments, testing schedules, and so on. They can help to shape expectations so that interested people understand what's coming next instead of being surprised or disappointed.

- ✔ **Marketing communications:** With these, you build a positive image of your quality control project to the rest of the company. Marketing communications educate the company as a whole on quality control principles (customer requirements, measuring quality, continuous improvement, and so on) and how they relate to each employee's work processes. This type of communication helps keep everyone motivated to support the quality control efforts.

One effective communication method is to give a presentation on quality control to each of the various department staffs. The more employees understand quality control, the greater your support will be across the company.

Determining who communicates different types of information

The quality control manager must develop a communications plan that addresses a wide range of audiences. Be sure to identify the person responsible for generating each type of communication and its major focus.

Make sure you evaluate every report and every meeting in your communications plan to make sure they're worth the effort. Some reports may require too much research, and some meetings are just wastes of time (we've all been in one of those!). Effective communication is important for focusing a team on a goal, but you must strike a balance between efficient communication and wasted time.

You can use Figure 5-2 to plan out who's responsible for creating certain communications. Start by making a column for each of the important communications; we used Project Plan, Status Meeting Minutes, Budget Report, and Plan Testing Schedule in our example. (List the ones used in your organization.) In each row, list the important positions that need to create these communications and the names that go with them. By checking off which communication is created by which person, you create an at-a-glance reminder of who creates what information.

Creating a stakeholder reporting matrix

After the quality control manager develops the communications plan (see the previous section), he or she needs to create a plan that details which employees need to receive information and when. For example, who should receive project status reports (the sponsor, perhaps)? Who needs copies of the team meeting minutes (the department manager, maybe)? Who needs to know about minor project delays or accomplishments (the facility's employee newsletter)? To manage this communication structure, you can build a matrix — a *stakeholder reporting matrix* — that accounts for the information needs of all stakeholders. A sample stakeholder reporting matrix is shown in Figure 5-3. In this matrix, you identify the following:

Figure 5-2: Keep track of people providing certain information with a communications plan.

Communications Plan					
Stakeholders		**Project Plan**	**Status Meeting Minutes**	**Budget Report**	**Plan Testing Schedule**
Sponsor	(names go here)	✓	✓	✓	✓
Quality Control Manager		✓	✓	✓	✓
Assistant QC Manager		✓	✓		
Production Manager			✓		✓
Facilities Manager			✓		
Purchasing Manager			✓		
Controller			✓	✓	
Data Processing Manager			✓		

✔ People requiring different documents

✔ The documents they should receive

✔ The amount of detail to include in the documents

✔ The best format (hard copy, PDF, and so on)

✔ How frequently these people should receive the documents (daily, weekly, on demand, and so on)

The stakeholder reporting matrix also should indicate the best way to deliver information. Do some of your executives ignore their e-mail? Do some require face-to-face reports? Always indicate the methods of delivery to which important people are most receptive.

Stakeholder Reporting Matrix						
Role	Name	Reports to Receive	Amount of Detail	Frequency of Reporting	Best Format	Delivery Mechanism
Sponsor						
Data Processing Manager						
Controller						
Plant Manager						
Employees						
Production Manager						
Security Manager						
Facilities Manager						
Purchasing Manager						

Figure 5-3: A stakeholder reporting matrix shows who needs to stay informed.

Class Is in Session: Training Employees

The key to having a predictable and repeatable process that consistently churns out a quality product or service is well-trained employees. Your organization's employees must have the skills, knowledge, and confidence needed to perform their duties correctly each and every time; the responsibility for making sure this is the case falls on the organization. Employees who have confidence in their jobs and who receive recognition for jobs well done will produce more, in both quality and quantity, than employees who don't feel so certain about their assigned tasks.

Confidence in the ability to do your job can come only from knowing exactly what to do — a knowledge cultivated by training. No amount of fancy marketing can make up for dissatisfied customers or missed sales opportunities due to poor product or service quality.

Employee training comes in many flavors, depending on what works best for your organization. You can provide training either formally or informally:

- **Formal training** is most effective for getting employees up to speed quickly and consistently. Use your in-house training department, if you have one, or use an outside firm or remote program to administer formal training to your employees.

- **Informal training** often provides the deepest and richest learning experiences, because this type of training is what occurs naturally in our everyday lives. Informal training occurs within the organization, with employees learning from one another and from executive-administered materials.

All organizations use a combination of formal and informal training methods. Experience with training in other areas can guide you when choosing the best approach to quality training in your organization. We describe both types of training in the following sections.

Training, of course, has to fit into your production schedule; some organizations find that short training sessions (one or two days) work best.

No matter what training combination you use, be sure, as a quality control team and a quality organization, to recognize the efforts of your employees and provide feedback to reinforce positive behavior. Make sure that supervisors praise their people for doing their jobs well. Any requests for improvement that an organization submits must be tied to measurable performance standards so that employees know how you'll measure them.

Ensuring consistency with formal training

If you need to ensure that your employee training is consistent and done on your schedule, formal training is the way to go. With a formal curriculum, you make sure that employees are exposed to the information they need. In the following sections, we guide you through the steps of formal training, explain when to use it, and show you how to find the right help.

Walking through the steps

Formal training is based on a standard format (almost as rigid as those formal dances from way back when). It usually includes the following steps:

1. **Developing a specific set of learning objectives.** It's important to identify learning objectives and to compare the objectives to the class curriculum. Learning objectives may include proper measurement technique, recording data correctly, or how to adjust a piece of equipment.

2. **Using a variety of learning methods to reach your objectives.** You could go with a combination of the following delivery options:

   • Instructor-led classroom training

   • Instructor-led remote training (over the Internet, for instance)

   • Electronic learning (or e-learning), such as Web-based seminars (or Webinars) or CD/DVD-based training

   From past experience with other types of training, you should know what works best for your employees.

3. **Applying evaluation activities at the end of the training periods to determine the amount of knowledge gained.** The evaluation process should be closely associated with the learning objectives to ensure that employees learn what needs to be learned in the training. A formal evaluation performed as a written test allows you to track the quality of the instruction.

4. **Developing individual training plans, with the assistance of supervisors.** This step helps to ensure the achievement of individual employee development.

5. **Tracking employee performance.** You want to be positive that the training is improving employees' overall performance and the achievement of company and/or division goals.

Knowing when to use formal training

Your organization should use formal training in the following situations:

✔ When the skills needed for jobs are very complex and require detailed instruction.

✔ When your budget for training is generous; formal training is more expensive than informal training.

✔ If you find that your employees aren't highly motivated within your quality program; a formal training program forces their participation.

✔ When you need your employees to acquire the skills quickly; formal training is the fastest method to acquire new skills.

✔ When job roles change frequently; formal training is the fastest way to get up to speed on a new role.

✔ When consistency of training is critical; formal training provides a well-defined structure to the training process.

Finding help

Look to the following sources of formal training when you decide to implement a training program:

✔ **Training firms:** These firms have their own classrooms and instructors, or they may take their shows on the road to your location. Use the Internet, or talk to other companies in your area or industry for referrals to good training companies.

✔ **Consulting firms:** These firms can help you develop your own in-house training program tailored specifically to your needs. Again, use the Internet, or talk to other companies in your area or industry for referrals.

✔ **Suppliers:** These folks may have training sessions that your employees can attend to become familiar with their processes.

✔ **Customers:** If you're selling to other businesses, some of your larger customers may have in-house classes on quality that your employees may be able to attend. Customers have an interest in helping you provide quality products. Employees will find it helpful to learn firsthand how customers use your products and services and what issues they face in their production processes.

✔ **Local governments:** Job training programs are sometimes available through local government. You may be eligible for financial assistance or access to trainers and materials in exchange for retaining or creating new jobs.

Rounding out skills with informal training

Although formal training can go a long way toward getting employees up to speed on what they need to know, it isn't the only training method you should use. After all, your knowledge isn't complete until you actually spend time putting what you discover into practice. No amount of formal training can cover all the little nuances of the job like informal, on-the-job training can. On the other hand, although informal training can be a powerful tool, by its informal nature you have less control over how, when, and what's communicated. So, some amount of formal training is necessary. But for now, we take the following sections to discuss when and how to use informal training to round out the skills you need for an effective quality control process.

Examining different types of informal training

Informal training can take many forms, but no matter the form, it can be an effective way to bring your employees up to speed in your quality process. Here are some of the ways you can implement informal training:

- **Senior staff members:** These employees have intimate knowledge of their jobs. They may hold nonproduction jobs, but they still have valuable knowledge about your production process that they could share with others. Make them part of your employee orientation process and have them serve as mentors during an employee's first few months on the job.

- **Cooperative training:** Create opportunities for employees to work together and learn from each other. Moving people around to learn different parts of the production process helps employees gain an appreciation of how the quality of their work impacts others. You can encourage cooperation by making their participation in this process part of their annual performance evaluations.

- **Experimentation:** Don't punish employees for trying new things to improve the production process; make sure to encourage experimentation and the sharing of lessons learned. An organization should create an environment where employees aren't afraid to try new things and fail. Create a process in which employees can make suggestions and see their suggestions tried out.

- **Self-motivated training:** Be generous in providing self-study materials (such as manuals and instructional videos) for employees to use, either on the job or during off hours.

Figuring out when to use informal training

Your organization should consider using informal training in the following situations:

- When the necessary job skills are easy to understand.

- If your organization has little or no budget for training.

- If your employees are highly motivated and eager to learn on their own.

- When employees can acquire the necessary skills over a long period of time.

- If job roles don't change frequently.

- If you find other aspects such as camaraderie developed from mentoring important.

Testing the Waters with a Pilot Project

In many cases, the best approach to implementing a quality control process is to launch a pilot project. A *pilot project* is a test or trial run of a process on a small scale, conducted so an organization can evaluate the quality control process's effectiveness and its impact on the product being created or service being delivered. A good pilot project allows an organization to try new things with a minimal amount of risk. In the following sections, we show you how to select a stellar pilot project and ensure its success as it takes off.

Choosing the right pilot project

Your organization's quality control team needs to choose the right pilot project in order to collect the proper information and to minimize the damage if the pilot project goes bad. Here are some questions to ask of your organization before you choose a pilot project:

✔ What are your primary reasons for implementing a new quality control process?

- To reduce costs

- To increase revenue

- To reduce defects

- To improve customer satisfaction (see Chapter 6)

- To achieve greater flexibility

- To obtain certification (see Chapter 2)

✔ What are the short-term improvements you hope to see?

- Getting real-time data on your process

- Satisfying customer demands

- Achieving regulatory compliance

✔ What are your long-term objectives for the new process?

- More flexible production process

- Faster new-product rollout

- Access to new customers

As you evaluate potential pilot projects, use your list of reasons to determine the one to pick first. Of course, you probably have many reasons for implementing a new quality control process; your pilot project should address one or two of the most important reasons. Don't try to fix too many things at once; it'll be more difficult to determine which part of what you did fixed which problem.

For example, say your main goal in implementing a new quality control process is to reduce the number of service complaints that come back to your landscaping business. You should design your pilot project to collect data on the reasons for the service calls and then implement changes to see their impact on the level and type of service complaints you receive.

When looking for a proper pilot project, seek out "low-hanging fruit" — look for areas where you think you can get the biggest return for your effort.

Succeeding early with results from the pilot project

One of the goals of performing a pilot project is to create early quality successes that encourage everyone involved with the organization to support the process and be enthusiastically involved. Here are some objectives to keep in mind as you attempt to succeed early on in your quality process:

✔ Create a quality process that can be effective in multiple departments within the organization. You want to quickly take the lessons learned from the pilot project and spread them throughout the organization. For example, effective measurement techniques learned in a pilot project can most likely be used in other parts of the organization.

✔ Publicize early successes to clearly illustrate to the rest of the organization the benefits of the quality control process. See the section "Talk About It: Quality Communication within an Organization," earlier in this chapter, for details on communicating with employees.

✔ Understand the tasks and challenges involved in implementing a quality control process and the activities required to manage it once it's in production. This objective includes determining realistic time frames and budgets for a particular type of project within your organization.

✔ Demonstrate to the organization that the quality control team can successfully integrate a quality control process into your production process. Political capital earned during the pilot project can help overcome objections to larger projects down the road.

✔ Assess the organization's readiness for quality control and gaps in the areas of skills, technology, and process. It's important to formally document what you discover in the pilot project and apply those lessons to future projects.

Multiple pilot projects may be required to adjust your quality control process to work best within your organization. After all, Thomas Edison conducted more than 3,000 experiments before he perfected the light bulb. Understand that success on the first try isn't guaranteed, and that you shouldn't use failure on the first attempt as a reason to abandon the effort.

Conquering Obstacles as Your Company Implements Change

Make no mistake, all companies encounter obstacles to the changes required to implement quality control programs. How you deal with these obstacles may determine how successful your quality control program will be. In the following sections, we show you how to anticipate potential problems, steer the quality control process back on track when an obstacle derails it, and stay positive no matter what you encounter.

Staying ahead of potential problems

To keep ahead of potential problems in your quality program implementation, you must identify and manage the risks that can negatively affect your quality project. Although you can't always prevent problems from occurring, by thinking ahead you can minimize the damage and prevent huge train wrecks.

Here are the four basic steps to evaluating and managing risk:

1. **Identify risks.** Review the plan for implementing your quality control process to look for tasks that could cause problems. Look for factors such as

    - **Aggressive budgets or time schedules.** You'd rather underpromise and overdeliver. If your organization has a history of being overly aggressive on budgets and/or schedules, watch this factor closely.

    - **Areas with limited resources.** Important resources may become unavailable just when you need them the most.

    - **Areas with limited expertise.** The less expertise you have in an area, the less accurate the schedule is likely to be.

    - **Tasks with a lot of resources or long durations.** The longer the task, the more likely something will go wrong.

Another step you can take is to seek out experts who have implemented similar projects — either inside or outside your organization. People with experience may be able to help you identify risks that you would never think of on your own.

2. **Quantify risks.** Calculate the costs for each risk you identify in Step 1. A simple formula you can use to compare risks is to take the potential cost of the risk if it occurs and multiply it by the probability that the risk will occur. This calculation gives you an expected cost that you can use to compare risks to determine which ones you need to worry about the most. *Note:* The cost unit can be dollars or time, and you can determine the probability by taking the best guess from your team.

   For example, if the cost incurred when the risk happens is $1,000, and your best guess of the probability of the risk actually occurring is 50 percent, the cost of the risk is $500 ($1,000 × 0.50).

   A spreadsheet program, such as Microsoft Excel, is a great tool for keeping track of risks — especially in quantifying the risk to your project.

3. **Plan for risks.** Now that you've identified risks to your quality control project and quantified their potential impact, you're ready to plan for their prevention. For each risk, determine any early warning signs that you can watch for, and then create plans either to prevent the risk from occurring or to mitigate the damage if you can't prevent it.

4. **Monitor and manage risks.** As your quality control project progresses, report to important stakeholders any risks that you've identified and how you handled them. Talk regularly with your quality control team about risks to the project, and make any needed adjustments to your risk plan.

Getting back on track

Even the best quality control projects can get off track, due to organizational politics or budgetary issues. You can get your quality control project back on track if it loses its way by following one or more of these steps:

- ✔ **Review your goals.** Make sure you're working on what's really important to your quality control sponsor and other stakeholders (see the section "Having a Sponsor as a Champion of Quality Control" for more on sponsors). A budget can always be found for projects considered important to the organization.

- ✔ **Evaluate where your project really stands.** Perform an honest assessment of what you've achieved and where the project is having problems.

✔ **Review your risk plans (see the previous section).** You may be able to find out if you can adjust them to give you better warning on problems before they get out of control. Install an early-warning system to keep your project from backsliding after you get it back on track.

✔ **Get professional help.** An outside expert may be able to break through political or technical logjams that are preventing progress.

✔ **Learn from your mistakes.** Although you can't change the past, you can prevent the same mistakes from happening in the future.

✔ **Determine the minimum acceptable goals of your organization.** Sometimes, the best way to right the ship is to make it more manageable by reducing its scope. Adjust your project to meet its reduced objectives.

Chapter 6

Detecting the Voice of the Customer in Quality Issues

• •

In This Chapter

▶ Identifying what's really important to your customers

▶ Measuring your customers' level of satisfaction

▶ Asking customers for their opinions on products and services

• •

*Y*our organization doesn't exist to provide you with a paycheck (although you may think it does) or to give you something to do during the day. Your organization exists to provide some product or service to your customer!

Without customers, your organization would cease to exist. Any number of competitors are just waiting for the chance to swoop in and take your place if you don't meet your customers' needs and expectations. Identifying your customers' likes and dislikes so that you can continue to provide them with the products and services they need is critical to the survival of your organization (and to the delivery of your paycheck).

In quality control, the phrase *voice of the customer* (VOC) describes the customers' needs or requirements. This phrase embodies both the needs and requirements that customers have explicitly stated and those they may not have told you about. Actively seeking the voice of the customer provides benefits beyond your immediate quality concerns, including the following:

✔ Demonstrating to your customers that you care

✔ Gaining important intelligence about what your competitors are doing, both right and wrong

✔ Providing information about products or services your customers didn't know you provide

✔ Reinforcing the importance of the voice of the customer to your employees

✔ Making your customers feel that you're more than just a vendor; you're a partner that helps them meet their needs

In this chapter, we discuss quality issues that are critical to customers; explain how to take stock of customer satisfaction with products and services; and show you how to gather information from and about your customers so you can improve your organization's overall quality.

Identifying Critical-to-Customer Quality Issues

Because the customer is critical to the survival of a business, you need to provide your customers with products or services they're willing to pay for. Your customers' concerns should become essential parts of everything you do. What customers want, you provide. You and your competitors have educated consumers on the importance of quality through your sales and marketing efforts, and being quick studies, the customers are now using quality as an important factor in choosing who they buy from.

When you boil down your customers' desires, you discover that they fall into three major categories, which we discuss in the following sections:

- They want the product or service to be perfect.
- They want it when they want it — usually now.
- They want a great price.

In other words, they want it good, fast, and cheap. The reality is that having all three at the same time is extremely difficult, so you have to choose the right balance in your products or services. These aspects, taken together, represent the quality of your product or service in the eyes of your customers.

Product or service performance: I want it perfect!

The quality control movement that started in the last century has raised the bar on what customers expect in terms of quality. And as we mention throughout this book, quality is directly related to customer expectations. All else being equal, a customer will buy the product or use the service with the highest perceived quality. Performance, in many cases, causes a customer to pay a little more for a product or service or is the reason for buying a product or using a service again and again.

If what you sell is a service, you generally measure quality by how well you do the job. Of course, with some services, customers can't judge the quality of the service with authority. For example, most people don't know enough about medicine to know for sure whether their doctors are any good; they base their judgments mostly on how well they "feel" about the services provided. Studies have shown that doctors who make their patients "feel" better by using good listening skills and spending a little more time with the patients are far less likely to be sued for malpractice. The customers perceive the extra attention as better quality. Customer service, therefore, is a big part of determining whether what you deliver is "perfect."

Delivery: I want it fast!

Customers usually take their time deciding whether to buy from you, but as soon as they decide, they usually want results fast. When's the last time you bought something and had to wait a long time to receive it? People used to order cars to be built and delivered in several weeks; now they drive them home the same day. People used to go to computer stores or use mail order to buy software; now they can download software over the Internet and have it up and running on their computers in minutes. In this time of next-day delivery and the always-available Internet, customers are no longer willing to wait to receive the products they buy.

Always look for ways to reduce the time from when the customer decides to make the purchase to when the customer gets to enjoy the product or service. Quick delivery increases the quality of your product or service in your customers' eyes. With many products and services (such as a retail purchase or a hair cut), you can deliver at the point of sale. With others, you may have to get very creative to get at least something in the customers' hands as soon as possible. For example, you may provide some part or sample of the product or service, or you may hand out a token to signify a purchase, such as a special key for a customer who orders a car.

Cost: I want it cheap!

No matter what anyone tells you, price always matters. Customers won't pay much beyond the going rate for any product or service, regardless of the quality. The key is to get customers to focus on the real cost over time, not only on the price of the item or service at the time of purchase. You may spend less for a poorly made chair, but you'll have to replace the chair much sooner than you would a high-quality chair. The challenge you may face is conveying that a higher-priced item may actually be cheaper in the long run.

If your product or service is of higher quality but costs a little more upfront to purchase, you need to motivate customers to focus on the cost of the item or service over its useful life. For example, you could advertise to customers that your high-quality product may have lower service costs or won't require the frequent upgrading that a low-quality product commands. This low overall cost, which is sometimes referred to as the *total cost of ownership*, increases the perceived quality of your item or service.

Total cost of ownership includes not only the purchase price, but also factors such as the following:

✔ Maintenance and repair costs

✔ The cost of energy to operate (such as gas for your car)

✔ The amount of training required

✔ The cost of consumable supplies (such as ink for a printer)

The focus should be on value rather than price alone; that's how companies such as Gucci stay in business.

Gauging Current Customer Desires with the Kano Model

Keeping existing customers satisfied is more profitable than finding new ones. Many organizations spend so much time looking for new customers that they neglect the ones they already have. Marketing studies have found that 50 to 70 percent of customers abandon companies because they feel ignored. Only 10 to 20 percent leave due to problems with the products or services, and less than 10 percent leave for competitive reasons (such as price).

Competitors can lower their prices or copy your products or services, but they can't steal your relationship with your customers. Strong customer relationships may be your only competitive advantage. Don't give it away by ignoring your current customers.

Attention to quality in your product or service says a lot about your concern for the customer. Just as important as your product or service's initial quality is how you handle quality problems. Because quality is directly related to customer requirements, understanding what will satisfy your customers is essential for maintaining quality in their eyes.

One popular technique for organizing and prioritizing your customers' desires is the Kano Model. Professor Noriaki Kano first developed this approach to analyzing customer needs in the 1980s. The model is based on the concept of customer quality, and it provides a simple ranking scheme for organizing customer desires. In the following sections, we show you the different categories of customer desires in the Kano Model and explain how to apply the Kano Model in your organization.

Surveying the Kano Model's categories

The Kano Model divides customer desires into three categories:

- ✔ **Must-Haves:** These features are necessary conditions or qualities that your product or service must have before a customer even considers doing business with you. The inclusion of these features doesn't necessarily cause customer satisfaction, but their absence automatically causes the customer to be dissatisfied. The customer assumes that the Must-Haves are included. An example of a Must-Have is brakes on a car. Must-Haves are also called *Threshold Attributes* or *Basics*.

- ✔ **Performance attributes:** These features satisfy the customer based on how well they function. If the performance of the product or service is high, the customer is satisfied; if the performance is low, the customer is dissatisfied. Customers usually know they need these features and tend to look at them closely. An example of a Performance attribute is engine horsepower for a sports car. Performance features are also called *Linear* or *One-Dimensional Attributes*.

- ✔ **Satisfiers:** If present, these features increase the customer's contentment with your product or service, but they don't cause dissatisfaction if you don't include them. If you can include them, you have an opportunity to "delight" the customer, which can separate you from your competitors. An example of a Satisfier is good gas mileage for an expensive sports car. Satisfiers are also called *Attractive Attributes* or *Exciters*.

Of course, customer expectations change over time. Cup holders in cars were initially Satisfiers, but they became a Performance attribute over time as customers discovered how useful they are. These days, cup holders are a Must-Have — most people won't buy cars without them. You need to constantly monitor which category your customers put your product or service into to know which product attributes are most important to your customers.

Using the Kano Model in a few easy steps

To use the Kano Model, follow these steps:

1. **Determine the main attributes of the product or service you want to analyze.**

   You have many ways to determine which attributes of your product or service are most important (see the following section for info on collecting data, for example). Example attributes may include ease of use, durability, flexibility, size, weight, speed, completeness, and so on.

2. **Create a questionnaire that contains pairs of questions for each attribute at different possible levels of quality; ask one question in the positive (for example, "How do you feel about X being present?") and one in the negative ("How do you feel about X being absent?").**

   The answers should use a 0–5 answer scale:

   - 0 — I'm not interested.
   - 1 — I really don't like it.
   - 2 — I don't like it.
   - 3 — I feel neutral.
   - 4 — I like it.
   - 5 — I really like it.

3. **Sum the answers for each attribute in your survey, using the number scale from Step 2.**

4. **Plot the answers on a graph, as shown in Figure 6-1.**

   The X-axis represents the perceived quality of the product or service in functionality or features. As you move to the right, the perceived quality or functionality gets higher. The Y-axis represents the customer's satisfaction with your product or service; the higher the satisfaction, the higher you are on the graph.

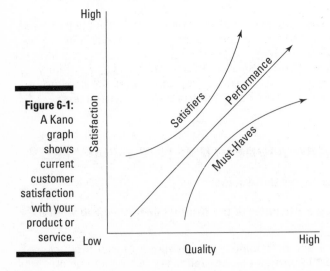

Figure 6-1:
A Kano graph shows current customer satisfaction with your product or service.

The three categories of customer desires usually appear on a Kano graph in the following ways:

✔ Performance attributes plot pretty much in a 45-degree angle; that is, the quality is proportional to the customer's satisfaction.

✔ Satisfiers show a dramatic increase in customer satisfaction for small improvements in quality.

✔ Must-Haves show only slight increases in customer satisfaction as quality increases, but they show dramatic decreases in satisfaction for small decreases in quality.

To apply the Kano analysis to your product or service, and to increase its quality in the eyes of your customers, you should now

✔ Make sure your product or service has all the Must-Haves. You may have to remove attributes in the other two categories to do so, but if you don't include these necessary features, you're done before you start.

✔ Look at the Satisfiers to see whether you can add more or improve the quality of the ones you have. Satisfiers give you the opportunity to rise above the competition.

✔ Maximize the Performance attributes within other constraints, such as cost, to maximize the customer's satisfaction.

✔ When possible, remove any attributes for which customers didn't care one way or the other.

Digging Up Data from (And about) Your Customers

The destiny of your product or service (read with a movie-trailer voice, of course) is to satisfy the needs of your customers. And how do you know what your customers want? You ask! You do some research! In the following sections, we explain how to gather information from your customers in many popular ways, including conducting surveys and gathering focus groups. We also provide you with some rules to follow when digging up info on your customers, no matter which method you choose.

Following some important rules

No matter how you collect data on your customers, you need to follow certain rules to make sure you get the information you really need:

- ✔ **Define your objectives.** Know what you hope to accomplish before you begin. Some techniques work better than others, depending on what you want to find out.

- ✔ **Select the customers to research.** Unless you have a small customer base, you need to choose a subset of your customers to gather information from. Gather the maximum amount of information you can from the most customers within the constraints of your budget. If your customers are all very similar in needs and wants, you can use a smaller sample size. If your customers' needs vary quite a bit, you need a larger sample representing each type of customer.

- ✔ **Think about how you'll analyze the data.** Consider budget and time constraints, as well as your objectives. Your method of analyzing data affects the kind of information you can collect. If you want the process to be highly automated, you're limited to asking questions that have a small set of possible answers. Closed questions (such as multiple choice and true/false) are easier to analyze. Open questions (where customers can answer any way they want) are much harder to analyze but may provide information about topics you hadn't thought about.

- ✔ **Use good questions.** If your technique involves asking questions, make sure the questions you ask fit with the objectives you've defined and the analysis method you plan to use. Good questions are easy to understand, use the language of the customer, and aren't leading in any way.

- ✔ **Keep the data-collection process simple.** Keep things as simple as possible to keep errors to a minimum. If you plan to enter the data into a spreadsheet program, such as Microsoft Excel, design the form to look like the spreadsheet to make entering the data easier.

- ✔ **Use an unrelated party to collect the data.** You may want to consider hiring an outside firm to collect the data to prevent bias from creeping into the answers. You don't want your data collector to be someone who may take the answers personally.

- ✔ **Train the data collectors.** Just as training is important for your quality control people (see Chapter 5 for details), proper training of those collecting customer data is important to ensure consistency and accuracy. Make sure the data collector's name is on any forms in case you need to follow up later. You may discover trends that show answers varied according to who asked the questions.

- ✔ **Perform a trial run.** Test your data-collection process on a small subset of your customers to work out any bugs in the process. You may realize that certain questions are a waste of time, but you may also discover new questions you want answered. You could find that some questions need to be reworded because they're difficult for customers to understand. Pay close attention to any questions the customers ask, taking them as clues to what changes you need to make. A trial run also is a good test of any instructions for the person performing the data collection.

These rules should help you design the right data-collection process to hear the voice of the customer. The most important points to remember are to ask the right questions and to listen carefully to what the customer has to say.

Putting surveys to work

Having the customer fill out and return a survey is a common technique for hearing the voice of the customer. A survey can be a great way to get customers to open up about problems, especially if people complete the survey anonymously. Surveys also are great for market research and for pointing out the availability of products and services the customer may not know about. Your organization can conduct a survey the old-fashioned way with pencil and paper; you can contact customers over the phone; or, as is becoming more common, you can post a survey on the Internet.

Here are three main steps to follow to create a successful survey (for general information, see the preceding section):

1. **Determine the survey's objective(s).**

   Staying focused and developing the right questions is easier if your objectives for the survey are clear. Take advantage of the opportunity not only to focus on quality issues, but also to promote your business. Asking questions that cover the entire range of products or services you provide may alert customers to items they didn't realize you featured.

   Objectives can include looking for quality gaps, uncovering desired features, or finding out what's important to a new demographic.

2. **Develop the questions and conduct the survey.**

   Keep the questions short and to the point. Don't include any unnecessary questions, because shorter surveys are more likely to be completed. Examples of good questions include the following:

   My top priority in buying a new car is

   a. Styling

   b. Gas mileage

   c. Horsepower

   What's the maximum number of minutes you're willing to wait for service?

   How many widgets have you purchased in the last 12 months?

3. **Analyze the results.**

Be careful how you analyze the data. Take sample size into account — the smaller the sample size, the larger the potential error. Try not to force fit the data into a pre-existing point of view. You don't want to read too much into small differences in data (such as saying customers really want Product A when they chose it over Product B by a small percentage).

Customers can complete the survey in person, or they can fill out the survey and send it back. In-person surveys are more expensive but make follow-up questions easier. On the other hand, some people are more honest when filling out an anonymous survey. You can also use an Internet survey. Think about whom you're going to survey to determine which method is best.

Keep the following tips in mind to encourage high-quality responses:

✔ **Keep the length of your survey to a minimum.** The longer the survey, the less likely customers are to complete it. Respect your customers' time by keeping the questions short and relevant.

✔ **Give people taking the survey a good estimate of how long it will take to complete.** This way, they can plan to take the survey when they have time to complete it in one sitting.

✔ **Use multiple pages for long surveys.** Splitting up a long survey makes people more likely to complete it, because long single-page surveys tend to scare people off.

✔ **Let survey respondents know about your privacy policy and how you'll use the information you collect.**

✔ **Offer some kind of reward for completing the survey, such as a gift card or a chance to win a valuable prize.** At the very least, let customers know how the survey will benefit them.

Figure 6-2 shows a sample customer survey.

Using focus groups properly

A focus group can be an extremely useful tool for finding the voice of the customer. *Focus groups* are basically interviews with several people at the same time (usually 6 to 12 people). The interaction between the members of the group can be much more informative than interviews done one at a time. Conducting a focus group has four major steps:

1. **Plan for the focus group.**

   Based on the major objectives of the focus group, determine who should be in the group. When you ask a consumer to participate, be sure to let him know how his input will help you create a better product. Plan for the meeting to be no more than one or two hours long. Make sure you have a comfortable location such as a conference room. Prepare nametags for the participants and provide appropriate refreshments.

2. **Develop the questions.**

   Create no more than five or six questions. Review beforehand what issues each question addresses. The questions should be open-ended to encourage answers that you may not have considered. Make sure that the questions aren't leading or biased in any way. Examples of good questions to ask include the following:

   - What need did you have that caused you to buy from us in the first place?
   - How did our products or services help you meet your needs?
   - What do you currently like about buying from us?
   - How could buying from us be better?
   - What other related products or services do you buy from other vendors?

3. **Perform the interviews.**

   Review the purpose of the focus group with the participants and make sure they understand the ground rules. Consider the following guidelines:

   - Stay focused on the objectives.
   - Keep on the agenda to maintain momentum.
   - Get closure on all the questions.

   Record each session, and make sure the participants know that you're recording. Also, call on members who are less talkative to ensure that one or two people don't dominate the meeting. Be sure to thank everyone for participating after all the questions have been answered.

4. **Analyze the data.**

   Review the collected data to look for answers that didn't provide useful information or that brought up questions that you should address in the next session (usually with a different group). Pay careful attention to data that challenges assumptions that you had before; it may prove valuable in pointing out erroneous assumptions you had about your customers' wants and needs.

Sample Voice of the Customer Survey

You are invited to participate in this Voice of the Customer survey for The Sample Widget Company. We will use this information to improve the quality of the products we provide our customers. The survey takes just two to four minutes to complete. All information about you will be kept confidential and will not be given to any third parties. If you have any questions or concerns, please contact: George Jenkins, President, The Sample Widget Company; e-mail: gjenkins@samplewidgets.com. Thank you for your participation!

Below are some statements about the products of The Sample Widget Company. Please indicate your level of agreement with each statement:

	Totally Disagree	2	3	Neutral	5	6	Totally Agree
I am satisfied with the quality of the products I receive from The Sample Widget Company.	O	O	O	O	O	O	O
The quality of the products I receive from The Sample Widget Company is important to me.	O	O	O	O	O	O	O
I am satisfied with the reliability of the products I receive from The Sample Widget Company.	O	O	O	O	O	O	O
The reliability of the products I receive from The Sample Widget Company is important to me.	O	O	O	O	O	O	O
I am satisfied with the value of the products I receive from The Sample Widget Company.	O	O	O	O	O	O	O
The value of the products I receive from The Sample Widget Company is important to me.	O	O	O	O	O	O	O
I am likely to provide enthusiastic referrals to The Sample Widget Company.	O	O	O	O	O	O	O

Do you have any additional comments or suggestions?

Thanks again for participating in our survey. Please don't hesitate to contact me if you have any questions or comments.

George Jenkins
President, The Sample Widget Company

Figure 6-2:
A customer survey is great for gathering feedback about your product or service.

Tracking with a CRM system

Most organizations have a process for tracking their interactions with prospects and customers. Typically called a *customer relationship management* (CRM) system, this process can provide you with a wealth of information on the wants and needs of not only your customers, but also potential customers. A good CRM system can help you track and analyze the VOC (voice of the customer) intelligence derived from the hundreds or thousands of contacts your organization has with customers and prospects.

Most organizations implement CRM systems to track sales-related information such as leads and prospects. These systems are designed to help the marketing and sales teams manage the sales process from the initial contact with the customer to when a sale is made. Because a major part of their job involves talking to the customer, sales or marketing employees should collect as much information as possible about the customers' wants and needs. Marketing and sales teams can then share information with the design and production teams to ensure that your products and services more closely meet the needs of the customer.

By purposely tracking customer quality issues at the point of interaction with the customer, an organization can

- Provide quick feedback on quality issues that arise in the field
- Track feedback on issues that may not have resulted in a service call but are irritating to the customer
- Track customer buying patterns to see possible changes in customer needs
- Collect information on competitors' offerings

Borrowing from what competitors got right

Although plagiarism is a bad thing in writing books, there's no shame in incorporating the best practices of your competitors into your quality process. You should never break the law or do anything unethical, but being on the lookout for ideas that you can use to improve your business is always a good idea. Sam Walton, the founder of the largest corporation in the United States, has been quoted as saying that "stealing shamelessly" from competitors was key to Wal-Mart's success. What he meant was that he had to be constantly on the lookout for good ideas wherever he could find them.

Check out these ways to find out what your competitors are doing right:

- Talk to customers who've looked at your competitors' products.
- For retail organizations, shop at their stores.
- Purchase your competitors' products to analyze how they're made.
- Review their marketing material — some companies, in their desire to impress prospects, tell more than they should.
- Use some of the same suppliers your competitors use.

Examining other ways to seek feedback and information

You can hear the voice of the customer by using a number of different tools and techniques. In addition to the techniques in the previous sections, some common methods include the following:

✔ **Customer complaints:** If you have a process that customers use to document complaints, you have a great source of information about what your customers want. Although complaints can be difficult to take, the sooner you hear about them, the sooner you can act.

✔ **Field reports:** Anyone who comes into contact with customers should have a way to report back any tidbits of information learned. This group includes salespeople, support technicians, and even executives.

✔ **Observation:** Observing customers in the act of using your product or service is a great way to find out about your quality. Ask a customer if you can watch while he or she uses your product. Customers may not tell you everything in an interview or survey — not because they mean to leave anything out, but because they just can't think of everything. You may not think to ask the right questions until you actually see customers in action. As processes change over time, people use products and services in ways that differ from the original intended use. The most important question you can ask while observing is *why?*

✔ **One-on-one interviews:** Sometimes all you have to do is ask. Some customers are too shy or too busy to contact you with problems, but they can turn into fountains of information if you just take the time to sit down and talk to them. Interviews can be highly structured, with a list of predetermined questions, or they can be informal chats. Your questions will be similar to those you present to a focus group but possibly tailored to the individual whom you're interviewing.

Tap into all your resources. Make sure you talk with any employees who share demographics similar to those of your end customers.

✔ **Specifications:** Good specifications, of course, can tell you exactly what customers need. Look for ways to be part of your customers' specification-development process; you may find that some difficult-to-meet specifications aren't really necessary and that inexpensive solutions can give the customers what they need. Ask whether the customers can work with your design department to help you do a better job.

✔ **Warranty data:** Review problems covered under warranty to look for problem areas in your quality process. Look beyond the repair itself for glitches in other parts of the production process — glitches that may be the root causes of the problems.

No matter how you hear the voice of the customer, don't let what your customers tell you fall on deaf ears. Incorporate what you discover by reviewing your design and production processes and making any changes necessary to better meet your customers' needs — your paycheck depends on it!

Chapter 7

Preparing to Measure Your Current Quality Process

In This Chapter

▶ Figuring out what (and how) to measure

▶ Discovering the role of hand tools, gauges, and coordinate measuring machines

*H*ow can you prepare to meet your quality control goals? How do you conduct the measurement process? Glad you asked! Just like with any other journey, you need to know three things: where you're going, how you plan to get there, and where you are when you start the journey. In this chapter, we help you figure out where your company is today as you start your journey down the road to quality by preparing to measure your current quality process. We discuss the items you need to measure and the processes and tools available to you to make the journey possible. (Check out Chapter 8 for details on actually collecting data on your quality process.)

Mapping Out Metrics and Measuring Processes

Measurement is the compass you use on your organization's journey to quality. A proper measurement process tells you where you've been, warns you if you get off the right track, and lets you know when you hit your goal. The old management saying "You can't manage what you can't measure" is especially true in quality control.

Before you can measure your current quality process, however, you must decide on the definitions of the terms you'll use and how your measurement process will relate to customer specifications; these definitions are called *metrics*. You also must decide on the decision process you want to use to accept or reject items that you inspect. You have two basic decision processes you can use: go/no go and measurement against specifications. We explain all these topics in the pages that follow.

Making sense of metrics

How do you determine what to measure within your organization, and what processes should you use to measure after you decide? The items or processes that you decide to measure are called *metrics*. A metric is simply a measured value; in the quality world, a more precise definition of metric is a standard measurement of a customer specification to which you can apply a quality standard. Examples of metrics include the following:

- Dimensions such as length, width, height, and depth
- Number of items produced per hour
- Number of phone calls made in a given period
- Average number of pages written per day
- Lines of code written per hour

A good metric has the following characteristics:

- Someone is ultimately responsible for the outcome of the metric (in other words, someone is the owner of the metric).
- It's clearly defined and understood by everyone involved.
- It's a measurable part of the process.
- It gives clear indication of whether it's getting better or worse.
- It's meaningful to management goals.
- It has meaning to the customer.

Generally speaking, the best metrics to use are those usually considered "standard" within an industry. (Chapter 2 has more information about quality standards.) The following list presents the main advantages of using industry standards as your quality metrics:

- The hundreds of other companies in your industry have worked out the bugs in the standard. Don't reinvent the wheel if you don't have to.
- Their definition and standard of use are well defined and understood by every veteran in your industry. New hires may require less training if they have experience in your industry.
- Your customers are likely to use the metrics because they *are* the "standard."
- They make handy benchmarks to compare your performance to others in your industry. Many trade groups, for example, collect information from members and make aggregate data available.

Using the appropriate metrics is critical in relaying information about the quality of your products or services to the customer. For example, if your customers require that an item be tough, what does that mean? Should the item be able to support a certain amount of weight? Over what period of time should it remain tough? Must it resist chemicals or other environmental hazards? The metrics you use should clearly communicate the customer's requirements.

How do you discover the requirements of your customers? Just ask them! See Chapter 6 for details about the customer's role in quality issues.

To determine the appropriate metrics for your organization, ask yourself and your customers the following questions:

- ✔ Why is the measurement required? Some attributes are more important than others; some may have legal ramifications, such as government-mandated standards.

- ✔ What are we going to measure? Length, width, height, diameter, strength?

- ✔ How will we measure the item? By hand? By machine?

- ✔ What amount of accuracy do we require? We don't want to be any more perfect than we need to be, as more accuracy usually equals more cost.

- ✔ What will we do with the measurement after we make it? Are there reporting requirements for the customer or for government agencies?

- ✔ How much will it cost to measure? Some measurements cost more than they're worth.

- ✔ Who will use the measurement? The customer, our quality department, the design team?

Working with your customers on the answers to these questions will most likely generate even more questions. You have to take the questions and their answers into consideration when you design your measurement process. The goal is to produce a quality plan and to measure the appropriate metrics to achieve progress on your quality journey.

Putting measurement processes under the microscope

After you determine the appropriate metrics for your organization, your next step is to select the right measuring process. You have two main choices:

- ✔ **Go/no go:** You compare the item or process to a standard, and it either matches the desired standard or doesn't. For example, say you want to find out if a bolt fits within a drilled hole. Either the bolt goes into the hole *(go)* or it doesn't *(no go)*. Go/no go measuring is also known as a *pass/fail test*.

✔ **Measurement against specifications:** You measure an item to see where the measurement falls between the largest acceptable size (called the *upper limit*) and the smallest acceptable size (called the *lower limit*). The measurement results in a value that you can use mathematically to make judgments about an item or process. For example, you can measure the number of days it takes to complete a particular tax return.

In the following sections, we provide the details about these processes and help you select the best process for your organization.

No matter which measurement process you choose, however, it must be

✔ **Reliable:** The same measurement tool should give the same results, no matter who does the measuring or when it takes place. (See "Equipping Yourself with Tools of the Measurement Trade," later in this chapter, for more about measurement tools.)

✔ **Valid:** The measuring tool you use must be capable of measuring what you desire it to measure.

✔ **Standardized:** The metrics you use and the data you collect should follow the norms for your industry so that you can benchmark your process against others in your industry.

Go/no go measurement

A go/no go measurement test is usually quick and easy, so it's excellent for high-production speeds and requires minimal operator training. However, although go/no go measurement can tell you whether an item conforms to some specification, it can't tell you other important information you may need, such as the following:

✔ By how much is the item or process off from specification?

✔ Why doesn't the item or process meet specification?

✔ How close is a passing item or process to being unacceptable?

The basic problem with the go/no go test is that it just doesn't give you enough information to make improvements in your processes. Because you can't use the information mathematically other than for counting bad items (the only value you have is whether it passed or not), you can't do statistical quality control, which we talk about in more detail in Chapter 10.

Therefore, most companies use the go/no go measurement process to check noncritical specifications, such as the length of a common nail. In these specifications, the company believes the process works well and the customer's requirements are easily met.

Beware of relying on error counts

One of the most basic quality measures is to count the number of errors that occur in your production processes or during a particular service. Although errors are simple and easy measures to collect, there are several downsides to relying on error counts for quality control:

✔ An error count is dependent on how long (and how hard) operators look for errors.

✔ Multiple factors can cause a single error count.

✔ An operator can count a single problem multiple times.

✔ An error count gives little or no information on the cause of a problem.

✔ Error counts may not relate a defect to the value of the loss caused by the defect.

A high error count prompts you to examine your process (assuming the high count isn't due to operator issues). You can attribute an error to poor design, material failures, requirements that aren't understood or well defined, or human issues with the production process. You need to do much more work if you're going to make good progress on your quality journey.

Measurement against specifications

To avoid producing products or services containing defects (items not conforming to specifications; see Chapter 4), you need to understand your customers' specifications and agree within your quality control department on how to measure successful production. The customer's requirements are normally expressed as the attributes to be measured and the tolerance of the measurements. If the customer's tolerance is too tight, it may not be cost effective to manufacture the item or provide the service. If the tolerance is too loose, the item or service may not meet the customer's needs.

You can determine the tolerances to focus on in your measuring process in one of two ways:

✔ Use the experience of your product designers and manufacturing team to determine what will work best for you and the customer. Your manufacturing team has experience in what types of measurement processes work best in your environment; your design team can work with the customer to ensure that the product design meets the customer's requirements in the most efficient manner.

✔ Calculate the cost of quality at different tolerance levels to find the optimum cost. (See Chapter 4 for items to include in your cost calculations.) Typically, the lower the tolerance level, the higher the cost.

Selecting the right process for your needs

You have many factors to consider when selecting a measurement process for your organization — we present a sampling of these factors in the following list:

- **Measurement speed required.** Go/no go measurement is much faster than measuring against a specification value.

- **Amount of precision required from the measuring tool** (see the next section for more about tools). It's best to use go/no go when you require low precision. You typically measure against specifications when you require higher precision.

- **Cost of the measuring equipment.** Go/no go measurement devices are less expensive.

- **Skill requirements of the operator.** Go/no go measurement devices typically require less operator skill.

- **Ease of use.** The easier the measuring process, the more likely busy production people will perform it correctly.

- **Versatility of the measuring device.** If you're making lower-volume, higher-value items, you want a measuring process that can be adjusted easily for each different part. High-volume items usually can justify a unique process for each item because the cost of the measuring process is spread out over more items.

- **Uniqueness of the item or process to be measured.** A very unique item may require a very unique measuring process.

- **Volume of items or processes to be measured.** Go/no go measurement devices are capable of higher speeds.

- **Value of each item or process to be measured.** Low-value items are better suited to go/no go measurement because the cost of being wrong is less than it is for high-value items.

Equipping Yourself with Tools of the Measurement Trade

If you're going to measure something, you'll need some sort of device with which to measure. The quality of your quality control process will be only as good as the tools you use for measurement. Measurement tools are most common when making products, but they're sometimes used to measure the end result of a service (for example, the depth of a trench, the height of cut grass, or the color of paint on a house). Types of measuring devices available include the following:

- ✔ Hand tools
- ✔ Gauges
- ✔ Coordinate measuring machines

We discuss all these tools in the following sections.

Getting a handle on hand tools

The oldest and most common way to measure anything is with a hand tool. We've all used hand tools to measure something in our lives: a tape measure to measure a piece of wood, a measuring cup to measure ingredients, a scale to measure our weight, or a bolt-size gauge for measuring what size bolt we need for a project. Similar hand tools are used in a production environment to measure all kinds of product attributes. Hand tools tend to be easy to use and cheap to operate, and they're appropriate for many types of quality measurements. They're best suited for general-purpose applications that require individual measurements of many different items.

Hand tools come with some disadvantages, however. Their precision can be less due to human error. The measurements usually take longer to perform as the operator adjusts the device for each measurement. The tools also require some amount of skill to operate properly.

Allowing a gauge to do your measuring tricks

A common tool used for measuring products is the *gauge* (or gage). Gauges are measuring devices designed for a more specific measuring purpose than hand tools. The term *gauge* is used for most any device that measures a physical property such as length, diameter, thickness, pressure, and so on. You can apply the use of gauges either during the production process or as part of an inspection process after production.

You can use gauges by hand, or they can be part of an automated process. They require less skill than hand tools, because the operator usually sets up the gauge so he can quickly put the part into place for measurement. Once constructed, the gauge allows the operator to record data quickly and with a high degree of accuracy.

In the following sections, we present different kinds of gauges, help you select the best gauge for your needs, and explain how to set up a gauge.

Surveying types of gauges

You can utilize a gauge for just about any application you can think of. Common types of gauges include the following:

- **Air (or pneumatic) gauges** measure changes in air flow or pressure to provide measurements such as thickness, internal or external diameter, roundness, bore, and taper. You can use air gauges in high-volume production environments where accuracy and speed are important.

- **Bore and ID gauges** measure the internal diameter of holes or cylinders; they can be mechanical, electronic, or pneumatic.

- **Calipers** measure the distance between two points — usually for determining thickness, length, or diameter. You can also use calipers to measure the distance between teeth on a gear.

- **Depth gauges** measure the depth of indentations or holes in a product.

- **Electronic gauges** use an electronic probe to measure the distance or displacement by physical touch using a contact or stylus.

- **Fixed gauges or fixed-limit gauges** have fixed dimensions that you compare to the product being made. The product either passes or fails based on the comparison; you don't use fixed gauges to make actual measurements. You can use these gauges to measure thickness, inside or outside diameter, length, width, and so on. Fixed gauges work best in situations that require a quick and cheap inspection of items.

- **Gauge blocks** are tools that calibrate gauges. They're made of special material, such as hardened steel or ceramic, and built to various tolerances, dependent upon the intended application.

- **Mechanical gauges** measure the movement of a sensor — such as a spindle, stem, or slide — to determine a measurement.

Picking the right gauge for your products

As you can see from the list in the previous section, you have a tremendous number of gauges available; so, how do you pick the right one for the job? Consider the following questions when selecting a gauge:

✔ **What is it that you need to measure?** You first need to select a gauge that can perform the measurement you need. Measuring length requires a different gauge than measuring the inside diameter of a cylinder, for example. You may want a gauge capable of several different types of measurements, but the more functions a gauge has, the less well it will probably do each one.

✔ **How important is speed?** The greater the number of items produced, the faster the assembly process. An automated gauge allows for faster production but comes with additional cost.

A general rule of thumb is that if an inspection using a manual gauge requires more than 30 to 40 seconds, you should look at an automated gauge.

✔ **How important is accuracy?** This question relates directly to the tolerances required in your customer specifications (see the section "Measurement against specifications," earlier in this chapter, for more about tolerances). The rule of thumb commonly used is that the measuring device must be ten times more accurate than the specification tolerance. Factors such as the speed of the operation, the operator's skill, and the environment in which the gauge functions affect accuracy. Gauges should be calibrated by a lab capable of certifying them to required tolerances (required by ISO 9001:2000, which we cover in Chapter 2, and many industries where safety is critical, like aviation).

✔ **What type of environment will you expose the gauge to?** If used on a production line, the gauge may be exposed to dirt and temperature extremes that can affect its performance.

✔ **Must the gauge go to the item, or can the item go to the gauge?** If the product is large and/or heavy, you may have to take the gauge to the item. A gauge that's fixed in place is more stable than one that constantly moves around.

✔ **What kind of material is your product made from?** If you make your product out of a soft material, you want a gauge that's gentle or that doesn't physically touch the part, such as an air gauge. You don't want the measurement process to change the part in any important way.

✔ **How much can you spend on the gauge?** Like anything else you want in this world, your budget plays a large role in what gauge you select. The more valuable the item being made or the larger the quantity, the more you can justify spending on a gauge.

✔ **How skilled are your operators?** If you have skilled and motivated operators, you can implement more complicated gauges. You can improve skill with training, but motivation can be a tough problem to solve and is beyond the scope of this book!

Setting up a gauge

You can set up gauges to perform go/no go testing or to provide measurement values to compare against specifications (we cover both processes earlier in this chapter). To set up a gauge, use the following basic steps:

1. **Start with the desired value in the customer specification and the variation allowed.**

   For example, say that your customer wants a 1/2-inch diameter hole drilled into a part where the hole can be up to 0.06 inches larger. So, the largest acceptable hole size is 0.50 + 0.06 inches.

2. **Follow the rule of thumb that the measuring device must be ten times more accurate than the specification tolerance.**

   In our example, the tolerance is 0.06, so the measuring device must be capable of measuring to 0.06 × 10 percent = 0.006 — the measuring tolerance.

3. **Take the measuring tolerance and divide it in half. You subtract this value from the largest acceptable value, and add the same value to the smallest acceptable value.**

   For this step, you take 0.006 ÷ 2 = 0.003. You subtract from the largest acceptable hole — 0.560 – 0.003 — and you add to the smallest acceptable hole — 0.500 + 0.003.

4. **Any value smaller than the smallest acceptable value or larger than the largest acceptable value is a no go.**

   For our example, any hole smaller than 0.503 or larger than 0.557 inches is a no go.

Your calculations will differ depending on the type of product you want to measure and the industry you're in. You can receive standard calculation instructions from organizations such as the American National Standards Institute (ANSI) to apply to your situation (see Chapter 2 for more about ANSI and other quality organizations).

Here are a couple key things to remember about setting up a gauge:

✔ The product tolerance determines the gauge tolerance.

✔ Use gauges and tools that support the product specification required by your customers, not the other way around.

Checking out coordinate measuring machines

If you decide that hand-held devices and gauges can't give you the performance you need, you should turn to *coordinate measuring machines* (CMMs). They're expensive, but they can handle much higher volumes of items than hand tools or gauges.

CMMs are three-dimensional electronic rulers that can accurately measure in all three dimensions. You use a CMM to measure a product along several surfaces by using a probe to determine the coordinates of points along the surface. CMMs are usually computer controlled and consist of the following four components:

- The CMM itself
- A measuring probe
- A control or computing system
- Measuring software

You use CMMs in situations that require more flexibility and accuracy than a simple gauge can provide. These tools are also easier to automate than a gauge. They come in a variety of designs and sizes and use a wide array of probes. They're best used for dimensional measurement, depth plotting, imaging, and profile measurement. They're commonly used in the automotive, aviation, and electronic industries, where high-value parts requiring strict tolerances are made.

In the following sections, we explain when to use CMMs and what to look for when you buy one for your organization.

When should you use coordinate measuring machines?

When you need to measure a product, along its surface areas, a CMM may be your only choice to quickly and accurately take measurements. If your product has contours or curved surfaces (such as car exteriors, furniture, and hand tools), a CMM *is* your only choice for measuring along the entire surface. Measuring contoured surfaces requires that you record a massive amount of data points, which you can't do efficiently with a hand tool or gauge.

A CMM also provides an additional level of quality assurance. Although many machines used to make products have the capability to perform measurements on the products they make, a CMM can provide an independent check of the quality specifications of the products.

The main disadvantages of a CMM are its cost and the training required for configuration and operation. CMMs are much more expensive than simple gauges and require specialized training to be set up correctly and operated effectively. These disadvantages limit CMM use to high-value or high-volume items; the extra expense over other options is justified due to the value of the item or because the cost can be spread over lots of items.

How do you select the right coordinate measuring machine?

The criteria for selecting a CMM aren't complex; you should look for a CMM that does the following actions or has the following properties:

- ✔ Measures quickly enough to keep up with your production process. Be sure to think about future growth in production rates.

- ✔ Is flexible enough for use with the most complex products you manufacture. Review the products you make and compare their requirements to the capability of the CMM.

- ✔ Can handle the largest products you make. Again, consider future requirements.

- ✔ Can interface easily with other computer systems you already have.

- ✔ Is appropriate for the material your product is made of. You don't want the measurement process to damage your products.

- ✔ Has reverse-engineering capabilities. In other words, you can easily determine how it works with basic engineering skills. This capability can save a lot of time if appropriate data isn't available to set up the machine.

- ✔ Can handle any environmental issues within your facility. You may need to provide a controlled environment.

You have other options to consider, too, such as the configuration of the probe arms, the material used to support the CMM, and the cost of support for the machine. Compare features from different vendors to see what's available; your industry trade association may have information on the options that work best for your type of operation.

CMMs usually last for many years because upgrades to probes and software can extend their useful lives. Look to buy the best and biggest you can afford today because it will probably be around for a long time.

Chapter 8

Collecting Your Quality Data

· ·

In This Chapter

▶ Walking through the data-collection process

▶ Searching for the meaning of your data

· ·

*H*ow do you know if your organization's quality is good or bad? Do you know if it's getting better or worse? Are you meeting your customers' expectations? The key to answering these questions is collecting and analyzing data. Collection of quality data is critical to developing a quality system that addresses these questions. You must have data to analyze in order to determine the effectiveness of your quality process.

Data is valuable because it represents important information about your processes — factual information, used to reason or make decisions. Data may give you information about the speed of your process, such as units per hour or hourly usage of raw material. It may tell you information about the popularity of your product, such as units shipped per week or average inventory on hand. But what should really interest you is what the data tells you about the quality of your production or service-delivery process, such as first-time quality or defects per million units produced. With the right data, you can zero in on problems in your production process that cause you to make bad items, waste resources, and disappoint your customers.

Data also can surprise you or clarify a situation that was previously unclear. Many times, casual observations become accepted facts when repeated enough times, with no scientific analysis to validate their accuracy (known as *anecdotal evidence*). Without good data, you may think your quality is fine when it's actually getting worse.

In this chapter, we show you how to collect and analyze the data you need to improve the quality of your product or service and your production or service-delivery process. With the information you find here, you can manage with facts instead of guessing based on anecdotes and assumptions.

Check out Chapter 7 for details on preparing to measure your current quality process; it contains information about metrics, measurement processes, and measurement tools. Chapter 9 discusses the importance of sampling in data collection.

Planning and Instituting a Data-Collection Process

How do you start collecting data about quality? How do you know what data to collect? You not only want to collect the right data for your organization and industry, but also minimize the time and cost required to collect it. Data collection can be time consuming and expensive, so a little planning up front can save you time and money in the long run.

To start your organization's data-collection process, identify the business goals and objectives you intend to meet by collecting the data. Here are some important questions to ask of your organization before getting started:

- ✔ What data will you collect? What data do you have now that your organization can use?

- ✔ Why are you collecting the data? Are you acting in response to a customer's issue or as part of a business goal to serve more demanding customers? (See Chapter 6 for more about the customer's involvement in quality issues.)

- ✔ Who will collect the data? Is training necessary for existing employees? Do you need to hire new people to collect the data?

- ✔ Where will you collect the data, and how will you report it?

- ✔ How frequently will you collect and report the data? Do you need to collect and report the data in real-time?

- ✔ How will you verify the quality of the data?

- ✔ How much will the data collection cost?

We cover these questions and more in the following sections.

Knowing exactly what data you're looking for

The first phase of the data-collection process is figuring out what data you need to collect for your production or service-delivery process. You have many options for getting started, some of which are more effective than others, depending on your organization and industry. The following list presents some options you may consider to figure out what data to collect:

- Gather anecdotal evidence
- Enact one-change-at-a-time testing
- Perform a design of experiments
- Create a SIPOC map

The goal of this phase is to determine the specific metrics you're going to measure so you know which tools you need to perform the data collection (see Chapter 7 for more about metrics and tools).

Anecdotal evidence

As you might imagine, guessing isn't an effective way to determine what data you need to collect for your organization. Even using anecdotal evidence (a form of guessing) to determine what data to collect causes you to spend time on processes that really aren't problems or on factors that are out of your control. For example, you may have a suspicion (anecdotal evidence) that the delivery time for the service you provide is an important metric to measure. Maybe no one bothered to ask the customers, who are really more concerned about the accuracy of the service than the delivery time.

The only good use for anecdotal evidence is as a "sanity check" for the data you *do* collect, not as a process for determining *what* data to collect. Past experience may alert you to data that doesn't "smell" right, which should be a signal to dig deeper into the process to see whether the data collected is correct.

One-change-at-a-time testing

A simple method you can use to determine what data to collect for your organization is to set up small experiments that allow you to change possible quality factors one at a time to see what affects they have on quality — a process called *one-change-at-a-time testing.* When an experiment identifies an attribute of your process that affects quality, you can begin to measure that attribute as part of your quality control process. For example, you might add more yeast to your pizza-dough recipe to see whether you can improve the quality of the dough. If the small change in the amount of yeast has an impact on the quality of the dough, the amount of yeast included is a good candidate for a quality measure.

Although only slightly better than guessing, one-change-at-a-time testing can provide useful information on what factors have the biggest impact on quality, and at a reasonable cost. The factors with the biggest impact are the factors you want to spend time and money on to measure.

With this method, the temptation is to stop the experiments when you iden-tify the first significant affect on quality. If you stop too soon, however, you may not identify situations where changing one attribute has a significant effect on a different attribute; the two attributes may work together in some way to impact quality.

The design of experiments

A *design of experiments* (DOE) process improves upon the one-change-at-a-time process (see the previous section) by planning out all possible depen-dencies in advance. By defining in advance what experiments to perform in the DOE process, you put yourself in a position to catch multiple attributes that work together to affect the quality of your product or service.

Inexpensive software packages for performing a DOE are available. Use your favorite Internet search engine to see what you can find.

To perform a DOE, use the following steps. For this process, we stick with the pizza-dough example from the previous section. You want to sell your pizza dough as a mix for consumers to use at home, and, of course, you want to make the best possible mix. Many factors may affect the production of your pizza dough mix, but for this example, you're concerned only with the recipe.

1. **Identify the input and output factors that the experiments will measure.**

   Start with a limited number of factors that you think will impact the quality of your pizza dough mix: flour, yeast, and salt.

2. **Define for each input value a number of levels for which the output value is known.**

   Your current standard recipe calls for 500 grams of flour, 30 grams of yeast, and 2.5 grams of salt. You then need to decide how to vary each of these factors. For example, you can vary flour from a low of 400 grams to a high of 600 grams; yeast from 20 grams to 40 grams; and salt from 1.5 grams to 3.5 grams.

3. **Create an experiment plan that includes the input-level values defined.**

   In this case, you try different combinations of flour, yeast, and salt, mix and bake the crust, and then have a taste tester judge the quality of the crust on a scale of 1 to 10 (with 10 being best).

4. **Perform the experiments for each input level and measure the output.**

   In other words, you create a matrix of the selected combinations of input values and levels. For instance, Mix 1 — with 400 grams of flour, 20 grams of yeast, and 1.5 grams of salt — yields a quality score of 7. Mix 2 — with 500 grams of flour, 20 grams of yeast, and 1.5 grams of salt — yields a score of 6. Mix 3 — with 500 grams of flour, 40 grams of yeast, and 2.5 grams of salt — yields a score of 8.

5. **Look for differences between the output values for the different levels of the input changes.**

   These differences are due either to the input value by itself or to the input value acting in combination with another input. Mix 3 received the best score, but you may want to do more experiments to determine whether other factors play a role in the quality of the dough.

Make sure that each department involved in the process of creating your product or developing your service is involved in identifying the input values and levels (design, production, shipping, service, and so on). For the DOE method to work, you must perform an experiment for each possible combination of input values and levels. If this seems impractical for your business, you may need to focus on the values you think are most critical; however, the fewer experiments you do, the closer you get to guessing.

The SIPOC map

Creating a *SIPOC map* allows you to determine which data to collect by identifying all the key stakeholders and activities for which you should be collecting quality data. A SIPOC map, short for "suppliers, inputs, process, outputs, and customers," forces you to consider each important area of your business so that you don't overlook any opportunities for quality improvement.

To create a SIPOC map, follow these steps (we stick with the pizza dough example we've used in the past couple sections):

1. **Diagram the top five to ten steps required to create your product or service.**

   In the pizza dough example, these steps may be the following:

   - Receive the raw materials from suppliers.
   - Measure the ingredients.
   - Mix the ingredients together.
   - Fill the mix boxes.
   - Prepare the mix boxes for shipping.
   - Ship the mix boxes to the customer.

2. **Make a list of all the outputs of the process.**

   In the example, the output is simply the filled box of pizza dough mix.

3. **Make a list of all the inputs required for the process to operate.**

   You need the raw ingredients, boxes for the mix, and shipping cartons.

4. **Make a list of all the customers that receive the outputs of the process.**

   Your customers may include retail stores, distribution centers, and restaurants.

5. **Make a list of all the suppliers that provide the inputs to the process.**

   List the firms that supply the ingredients, boxes, shipping cartons, and so on.

6. **Review the map with all your stakeholders to verify that what you've created is correct.**

   Show the map to customers, suppliers, and employees for verification.

A completed SIPOC map allows you to manage expectations and clearly communicate the answers to the following questions to your team:

✔ What are the inputs required for the process to be successful?

✔ Who provides the inputs that you need?

✔ What are the steps required to create the product or service?

✔ What's the end result of the process?

✔ And, most importantly, who is the process for?

With the answers to these questions, you can focus on measuring the critical parts of your production process — in other words, you know what data to collect!

Working out the data-collection details

Important questions to answer are who should collect the data, when to collect the data, and how to collect the data. Although details vary from industry to industry, the following guidelines apply to most situations:

✔ Employees closest and most familiar to the process — typically the people producing the item — should collect the data.

✔ Collect the data as quickly as possible to avoid changes in subsequent processes. For example, if an item isn't measured until after packaging, and the item gets damaged during packaging, how will you know what caused the item to be defective?

✔ Look for the tools you have available to determine how you collect the data (see Chapter 7 for more about measurement tools). If the process can justify the expense, a fully automated data-collection system is usually your best choice (see the later section "Absorbing the costs of data collection" for details). For many processes, however, simple pencil-and-paper collection can be very effective.

Ensuring that everyone measures the same way

The purpose of a quality control process is to detect and eliminate variations in the production process. You also want to make sure that each person involved in the quality process measures quality in the same manner. But how do you make sure that any variation you detect isn't in the measurement process itself?

The process of ensuring that everyone measures in the same way is called *gauge* (or *gage*) *repeatability and reproducibility,* also known as *gauge R&R.* The process, which you can use with any type of measurement process and device, is a statistical tool that allows you to measure the amount of variation caused by the production process or the measurement process. It considers both the tool used for measuring (repeatability) and the people performing the measurements (reproducibility).

You should perform a gauge R&R

- ✔ Before putting a new measuring device into production (see Chapter 7 for more about measuring devices)
- ✔ Whenever a new operator or inspector begins performing measurements
- ✔ As part of your data-collection training and certification processes
- ✔ At least once a year to make sure your measurement process is still valid

In the following sections, we go into detail about what gauge R&R examines; we show you the importance of taking samples; and we walk you through the steps of actually performing the process.

Examining the elements of a consistent collection process

You have six ways to look at your measuring processes to judge how well they work:

- ✔ **Repeatability:** Can the same operator measure the same item multiple times with the same measurement device and get the same result each time?
- ✔ **Reproducibility:** Can different operators measure the same item with the same measurement device and get the same result?
- ✔ **Stability:** Will the measurement process produce the same result over time with the same sample?

- ✔ **Bias (or accuracy):** How close are the operators to the actual value?
- ✔ **Discrimination:** Do you have the ability to tell things apart?
- ✔ **Linearity:** How consistent is the measuring process over the entire range of possible values? In other words, is the accuracy the same for both large and small measurements?

When you talk about measurement, you also must consider the difference between accuracy and precision. In your quest to improve your organization's quality measures, you should aim to improve both accuracy and precision in your data-collection process. *Accuracy* is how close you are to a true value; *precision* is the number of digits used to express a number.

Four combinations of accuracy and precision exist:

- ✔ Accurate but not precise
- ✔ Precise but not accurate
- ✔ Accurate and precise
- ✔ Not accurate and not precise

See Figure 8-1 for an illustration of the differences.

Figure 8-1:
Accuracy
and
precision
are crucial
in a data-
collection
process.

Accurate but not precise   Precise but not accurate   Accurate and precise   Not accurate and not precise

How sensitive should your measurement tool be? The rule of thumb is that the measuring tool should measure 10 times the precision called for in the specification. For example, if the spec calls for the item to be 5.2 inches long (measured to the tenth of an inch), the measuring tool must be able to measure out to hundredths, or to 0.01.

Taking standard samples

To prepare for a gauge R&R test, you need precisely measured samples that you can use to test operators who will use the measuring devices in your organization.

An expert operator should perform the sample measurements under ideal conditions. After the collection of these samples, you'll have what's known as a *standard measurement.* You should use a minimum of 30 samples; somewhere between 30 and 100 samples gives you good results (see Chapter 9 for more about sampling).

Testing the data collectors

To carry out the gauge R&R, you test your measurement operators by having them measure the samples multiple times to see how close the results come to the standard measurements and how consistent the operators are in the measuring process (see the previous sections). You look for four results when implementing the gauge R&R test:

✔ How consistent the operator is in measuring the same sample

✔ How often the operator gets the standard measurement

✔ How consistent multiple operators are amongst themselves

✔ How often the operators as a group get the standard measurement

Use Figure 8-2 as a starting point for developing a chart to perform a gauge R&R test. The example is set up for attribute data (such as pass/fail or yes/no), but you can easily modify it to use variable data (quantitative data, such as 1.4 or 25.343). See Chapter 4 for a discussion of attribute versus variable data and how to convert attribute data to variable data.

A spreadsheet program such as Microsoft Excel makes the calculations of a gauge R&R test much easier and less prone to error.

Have each operator measure each standard sample at least twice. Make sure you randomly select the samples so that the operators don't know which samples they're measuring. Record the measurements by using your gauge R&R form.

After the operators measure all the samples and you have the form filled out, you're ready to make your calculations:

1. **Calculate the variation for each operator by counting the number of samples for which the operator gets the same measurement value and dividing this number by the number of samples.**

   For example, in Figure 8-2, Operator #1 has different results for samples 1, 6, and 22. You calculate his variation by dividing the number of similar measurements (22) by the total number of samples (25). His operator score is 88 percent, or a 12 percent variation.

Known Measurements		Operator #1		Operator #2		Operator #3		All operators agree within and between each other (Y/N)	All operators agree with Standard (Y/N)
Sample #	Standard	Test #1	Test #2	Test #1	Test #2	Test #1	Test #2		
1	pass	pass	fail	pass	pass	pass	pass	N	N
2	pass	pass	pass	pass	pass	pass	pass	Y	Y
3	fail	fail	fail	fail	fail	fail	fail	Y	Y
4	pass	pass	pass	pass	pass	pass	pass	Y	Y
5	pass	pass	pass	pass	pass	pass	pass	Y	Y
6	fail	fail	pass	fail	fail	fail	fail	N	N
7	pass	pass	pass	pass	pass	pass	pass	Y	Y
8	pass	pass	pass	pass	pass	pass	pass	Y	Y
9	pass	fail	fail	fail	fail	fail	fail	Y	N
10	pass	pass	pass	pass	pass	pass	pass	Y	Y
11	pass	pass	pass	pass	pass	pass	pass	Y	Y
12	pass	pass	pass	pass	pass	pass	pass	Y	Y
13	pass	pass	pass	fail	fail	pass	pass	N	N
14	fail	fail	fail	fail	fail	fail	fail	Y	Y
15	pass	pass	pass	pass	pass	pass	pass	Y	Y
16	pass	pass	pass	pass	pass	pass	pass	Y	Y
17	pass	pass	pass	pass	pass	pass	pass	Y	Y
18	pass	pass	pass	pass	pass	pass	pass	Y	Y
19	pass	pass	pass	pass	pass	pass	pass	Y	Y
20	pass	pass	pass	pass	pass	pass	pass	Y	Y
21	pass	pass	pass	pass	pass	pass	pass	Y	Y
22	fail	pass	fail	fail	fail	fail	fail	N	N
23	fail	pass	pass	pass	pass	pass	pass	Y	N
24	pass	pass	pass	pass	pass	pass	pass	Y	Y
25	pass	pass	pass	pass	pass	pass	pass	Y	Y
Operator versus Self		88%		100%		100%			
Operator versus Standard		80%		88%		92%			
Operators Agreed								84%	
Operators Agreed w/Standard									76%

Figure 8-2: Complete your gauge R&R analysis with a detailed form.

2. **Calculate the variation for each operator versus the standard by counting the number of samples for which the operator gets the standard measurement value and dividing this number by the number of samples.**

   Operator #1 has different results for samples 1, 6, 9, 22, and 23. You divide the number of standard measurements (20) by the total number of samples (25). His operator score versus the standard is 80 percent, or a 20 percent variation.

3. **Calculate the variation between the operators by counting the number of samples for which the operators get the same measurement value and dividing this number by the number of samples.**

   In Figure 8-2, the operators have different results for samples 1, 6, 13, and 22. You divide the number of similar measurements (21) by the total number of samples (25). The variation between operators' scores is 84 percent, or a 16 percent variation.

4. **Calculate the variation between the operators versus the standard by counting the number of samples for which the operators get the same standard measurement value and dividing this number by the number of samples.**

   The operators have different results from the standard for samples 1, 6, 9, 13, 22, and 23. You divide the number of standard measurements by the total number of samples (25). The variation between operators' scores is 76 percent, or a 24 percent variation.

Analyzing the gauge R&R

What do the values from the gauge R&R test mean? A rule of thumb is that a variation of up to 10 percent means that the collection process is working fine and that the production process is to blame for any variation. If the variation between measurements is greater than 10 percent but less than 30 percent, the data may be acceptable, depending on the costs involved and the importance of the collection being performed. Variation between operators is probably due to differences in skill and/or training gaps that your organization needs to address.

Confirming the quality of your data

Just as the production of your product or service has a quality control process, so must your data-collection process. Think of it as this book's quality-in-quality screen, much like a television's picture-in-picture screen. The quality of your data has a major impact on actions you take as a result of your quality control process, so you need to make sure that your data goes through a review process to ensure its accuracy. Although you have no way to guarantee that your data will always be 100 percent correct, you can take comfort in the fact that a little quality control goes a long way toward catching errors before your organization uses bad data to make quality control decisions.

Poor decisions based on inaccurate or out-of-date data have serious consequences for your quality control effort. Alas, errors happen as long as human beings are involved in the data collection process. Some common data-collection errors include the following:

- ✔ Measurement taken incorrectly
- ✔ Value misread from the measuring device
- ✔ Numbers transposed as they're recorded
- ✔ Miscounting
- ✔ Handwriting that's hard to read
- ✔ Values entered incorrectly into the computer
- ✔ Data processed too late to make corrections to the process

Some of these errors simply require more care on the part of the collector, but you can't always rely on people taking great care. Therefore, we provide you with additional options for ensuring that you have the correct data during and after its collection in the following sections.

Checking out check sheets

One tool you can use to ensure that you get the right data is a check sheet. A *check sheet* is a structured form used for collecting and analyzing data. It can be as simple as a tally sheet, where you make tick marks to record a count of when an error happens, or it can be as complex as a chart of the data that forms as data collectors gather it.

To create and use a simple check sheet, perform the following steps:

1. **Determine what event you want to count.**

   You may perform a simple pass/fail test (is the label in the right spot?), or you may check to see whether a measurement is within specifications.

2. **Define what warrants a check mark.**

   In most cases, you're counting the number of failures.

3. **Decide when you'll collect the data and for how long.**

   For instance, you may collect data for ten minutes during each shift.

4. **Design the check sheet to collect the data.**

   Be sure to make it simple to use, and include space for all the data you need to collect. Each sheet should be uniquely identified and should record information such as the date, time, person collecting, process under review, batch number, check-sheet number, and so on.

5. **Record the data by making simple check marks.**

Make sure that your data collectors are trained and understand the process. Don't assume that anything is obvious.

Check sheets can take many forms:

- ✔ A simple check sheet, as shown in Figure 8-3, records each error as it occurs. List the errors you want to record in the column labeled "Error" and place a tick mark in the column labeled "Tally" each time the error occurs. When you're done collecting data, count the number of tick marks in the Tally row and put that number in a row under the column marked "Total." Divide the value in the Total column by the number of items made during the time you collected the data, and place that value in the column labeled "Percentage."

- ✔ Some check sheets allow you to record not only when an error occurs, but also where the error occurs.

You can make a diagram of the item a collector is checking and create space for the user to place check marks at the locations of the errors. You also can have a column for each possible location on the check sheet, as shown in Figure 8-4. The "Total" column notes the total number of errors that occurred at the different locations.

Date:		Check Sheet #:		
Process:		Operator:		
Error	Tally		Total	Percentage

Figure 8-3: A simple check sheet tallies data on errors made during a process.

Date:		Check Sheet #:	
Process:		Operator:	

Error	Front	Back	Left	Right	Top	Bottom	Total

Figure 8-4:
A more detailed check sheet notes the location of errors.

Taking time to compare and review

You can perform simple compare-and-review checks to confirm the quality of your data:

- ✔ **Have someone other than the person collecting the data review the data.** Anyone familiar with the quality process can perform this role.

- ✔ **Compare your data with data generated by other processes or systems.** For example, production quantity should make sense when compared to the amount of raw material or parts purchased.

- ✔ **Perform some basic statistics on the data to see whether it falls in line with data previously collected.** This can work for characteristics such as minimum and maximum values, averages, frequencies, and so on.

- ✔ **After you load the data into whatever system you use to analyze it, have a person involved in collecting the data review the analysis to see if it matches what the person collected.**

Anything you find outside of what you expected requires further investigation. If a result points to a quality problem, you have a head start on doing something about it. If you identify bad data, you have time to correct the data before it causes problems of its own.

Cowering at the cost of poor data quality

Erroneous data costs you money, so the sooner you can correct an error, the less negative impact the error will have. To scare you straight, we'll introduce the *cost of poor data quality* (COPDQ), which is similar to the cost of poor quality (COPQ; see Chapter 2). Here are some factors that determine your COPDQ:

✔ Cost to find the error

✔ Cost to fix the error

✔ Cost of wasted effort due to bad data

✔ Lost production of workers fixing data problems rather than producing products

Although the COPDQ can be difficult to calculate, doing so gives you a better idea of how important good quality data is to your organization. A good way to determine your COPDQ is the "rule of ten": A task costs ten times more when the data isn't perfect compared to when it is perfect. For example, if a task costs $1.00 when the data is perfect, you can assume it will cost $10.00 if the data is flawed.

Absorbing the costs of data collection

After you get excited about all the data-collection opportunities out there and how they can improve your quality control processes, you find yourself back at the dreary hangout of your company's financial executives: the bottom line. There is, of course, a cost associated with collecting quality data. If you collect data manually, the majority of the cost is in labor. The quality control manager may designate one employee to collect quality data and assign an additional person as required, or he may use production employees, which makes them less productive in their primary jobs of producing items (see Chapter 5 for more on the quality control manager). If you key the data into a software program for analyzing purposes (see the previous section), you add time and cost. If you use an automated data-collection system, you incur a cost in equipment and training.

Factors to look at when calculating the cost of a data-collection process or system include the following:

✔ Labor (don't forget to include benefits, taxes, and other costs)

✔ Materials (such as raw materials that go into a product)

✔ Operating expenses (such as electricity, water, and gas)

✔ Machine costs (for the machines used to make a product)

Know where your data comes from!

Never forget that your quality effort is only as good as the data that goes into it. No matter how sophisticated your analysis process is, it still relies on good source data to work properly. A quote from the book *Some Economic Factors in Modern Life* (Lond), written by Sir Josiah Stamp and published in 1929, sums up the problem nicely:

"The government are very keen on amassing statistics. They collect them, add them, raise them to the n'th power, take the cube root and prepare wonderful diagrams. But you must never forget that every one of those figures comes in the first instance from the village watchman, who just puts down what he damn well pleases."

Some things never change!

Like any other cost, the cost of your quality control process needs to be figured into the cost of your products. When done correctly, the cost of quality control is less than the cost of selling poor-quality products.

An automated data-collection system may save you money in the long run. You get a break with labor costs, and you gain from having more timely data and possibly higher-quality data. (Machines with jobs such as barcode reading are much more accurate at recording data than humans writing down or keying in data.) Additional benefits of automation include

- Improved efficiency in the production and quality control processes
- Higher employee morale due to a reduction in menial tasks
- Increased accuracy of the data collected
- Higher customer satisfaction because you can give customers better visibility into the process

Making Sense of Your Data

We doubt that you're planning on collecting quality data just for fun; if so, we're sure you'll find a few companies at your doorstep with lists of tasks for you to jump into. More likely, your goal is to turn the data you collect into meaningful information that you can use to improve the quality of your production processes or service deliveries. In the following sections, we discuss different techniques you can use to whip your data into shape and begin turning it into useful information. Keep in mind that coding may require you to do some work before you even collect your data. (For more information about fully evaluating your data with different statistical methods, see Chapters 9 and 10.)

Coding the data

Coding data as you collect it helps you identify patterns or problems in your data. Coding is a way to organize and categorize raw data into useful information. It allows you to put data into buckets so you can analyze it in such a way that you compare apples to apples. Codes can be numbers, letters, or tags of three or four letters such as LNG, SHT, SCR (long, short, scratch).

To code your data, you need to define the coding units for each characteristic that you're measuring. (See the section "Knowing exactly what data you're looking for," earlier in this chapter, to figure out what to collect.) You may use a scale of numbers such as one through five or simply a pass/fail code. The different types of scales you can use include the following:

✔ **Binary:** One of two values (pass/fail, true/false, and so on)

✔ **Nominal:** Names or numbers given to label something (colors, model, and so on)

✔ **Ordinal:** A rank order where the distance between any two values can vary (for example, you can rank your machine operators in order of percentage of parts made right the first time, but the difference in the percentage between each operator will vary)

✔ **Interval:** A rank order where the distance between any two values can't vary (a ranking such as 1, 2, 3, 4)

✔ **Ratio:** A measurement such as weight or length

You can set up your coding scheme after you review your data to see what sort of coding makes sense, or you can set up the coding scheme in advance (as you would in a survey). Either way, you'll make adjustments to the coding scheme as you gain experience with collecting the data.

Using pivot tables

A simple, yet powerful, technique for analyzing quality data is the pivot table. A *pivot table* allows you to summarize and analyze large amounts of data in lists and tables. You call it a pivot table because you can rotate the row and column headings around the main data area in order to analyze different views of the data.

You also can use a pivot table to quickly identify which quality problems occur most often; this is called a *Pareto analysis* (see Chapter 9 for more about this type of analysis). It makes sense to identify these problem children and focus your resources on fixing them.

To create a pivot table, you enter different dimensions of the data in question as rows or columns of a table. You total and display the remaining dimensions as numbers in the cells of the table. You add cross-tabulations and summaries to the resulting table of numbers and generate graphs of your conclusions. A pretty bone-dry process, huh? Allow us to incorporate some technology.

Pivot tables are inexpensive to use because most firms already use Microsoft Excel. The tables are available in Excel 5.0 or later, and you can find them in most other spreadsheet software. You can create a typical quality control pivot table with Microsoft Excel by using the following steps:

1. **Enter your data into the spreadsheet, with each row representing a single defect and each column representing an attribute of the defect.**

   For example, you may record the date, the workstation, and the type of defect in a single row for each defect found.

2. **Select a single cell in the data.**

3. **From the menu, select Data ‡ Pivot Table ‡ Pivot Chart Report.**

4. **Follow the instructions in the wizard to create the pivot-table template.**

5. **Drag and drop the fields onto the pivot table.**

You can now look at the data from different perspectives. You also can create graphs from the pivot table by using the charting feature in Excel. See Figure 8-5 for an example of data you can enter into Excel and a pivot table you can generate from this data.

Figure 8-5: You can summarize large amounts of data with a pivot table.

Developing useful data charts

Charts and graphs can be very powerful means of communication. You can use them to spot relationships within your collected quality data that may not be obvious (we cover spotting relationships in data later in this chapter). Otherwise, quality charts are useful for spotting relationships or patterns in the data that may give you insight into the quality of your production process. A pattern may alert you to an issue with a particular machine operator, for example, or a reduction in productivity at a certain time of the day. Charts give you a visual representation of data to help you see trends, outliers, and frequency.

You have several different types of charts at your disposal to help you manage your quality process. In Chapters 9 and 10, we get into the details of quality charts; in the following sections, we give you an overview of the types of charts used in quality control.

Histograms

A *histogram* is a commonly used graph for showing frequency distributions. A *frequency distribution* shows you how often each unique value in a set of data occurs. Therefore, a histogram can show you how consistently a production process stays within a desired range of values; the more the high-frequency attributes fall within customer specifications, the better. You can use a histogram to discover whether your production process is capable of meeting customer specifications consistently. It works best when you use it to summarize large amounts of data that you've collected over a period of time.

In addition to showing the relative frequency of each data value, a histogram shows

   ✔ The overall shape of the data (is the data bell-shaped or flat?)

   ✔ The variation in the data

   ✔ The distribution of the data

To create a histogram, follow these steps:

   1. **Decide what you want to measure.**

      Your data can be attributes such as size, time, weight, temperature, or speed, for example.

   2. **Collect a large set of data — at least 50 to 100 data samples.**

      Be sure to collect the data as randomly as possible. Chapter 9 has full details on sampling.

3. **Plot the data.**

   The Y-axis should show the frequency and the X-axis should show the different attribute values. Figure 8-6 gives you an example of a histogram that focuses on the frequency of defects.

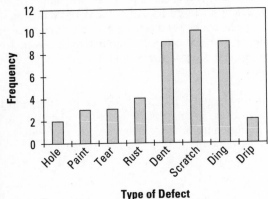

Figure 8-6:
A histogram shows frequency distributions.

Pareto charts

A *Pareto chart* is a specialized histogram (see the previous section) used to group and organize your data so you can quickly identify the best opportunities for improvement. Its main usefulness is to display the relative importance of each problem in a quick, simple, visual format. In other words, a Pareto chart helps you find the "low-hanging fruit" that you can easily pick to make improvements to your quality process.

A Pareto chart works by showing you the relative size or frequency of a quality problem, which allows you to focus on the things that will have the greatest impact if fixed. Its value is based on the *80/20 rule:* 20 percent of your production inputs cause 80 percent of your quality output problems (see the nearby sidebar for more about this "Pareto Principle").

To create a Pareto chart, follow these steps:

1. **List the quality factors you're interested in.**

2. **Measure the quality factors by using the same unit of measure for each factor (such as defects per 1,000 items).**

3. **Order the quality factors according to their measurement from the smallest to the largest, and plot the data.**

4. **Work on the quality factor that has the biggest impact on the final quality of the product.**

The Pareto chart we present in Figure 8-7 shows a range of quality factors for defects in truck cabs, including scratches, dings, rust, and paint drips. As you can see, the biggest quality problem is scratches, so you would address it first. Because scratches, drips, and dings all are pretty high relative to the other quality issues, you should review the production process to see whether a common problem in the line is causing them.

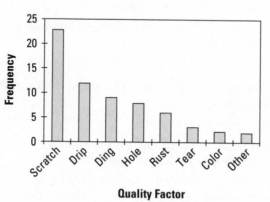

Figure 8-7:
A Pareto chart highlights the biggest issues in your quality process.

Scatter diagrams

A *scatter diagram* is designed to find a pattern in data or a relationship between two variables:

✔ You can record values for a single value, taking samples sequentially over time. You're really comparing the measured value with the variable time. For example, you can record how the size of a hole being drilled changes over time.

✔ You can discover if two production variables are related. For example, you may measure the strength of a wood joint versus the amount of glue used.

Meet the inventor of the Pareto Principle

The *Pareto Principle* is named after Vilfredo Pareto, a 19th-century Italian economist. He observed that 20 percent of the population controlled 80 percent of the wealth in Italy during his time. Many people later observed a similar phenomenon in other areas of study. Joseph Juran, a quality management pioneer in the 1930s, referenced Pareto's theory in observing that 20 percent of something is responsible for 80 percent of the result. The 80/20 rule has been known ever since as the Pareto Principle.

A scatter chart that shows how a value changes over time can graphically depict things such as the effect of a tool wearing out and help you determine how frequently to replace the tool. If two variables that you're comparing are related, you can see their effect on quality and their optimal values.

To create a scatter diagram, follow these steps:

1. **Determine the two variables you want to compare.**

2. **Plot the value for the variable that you changed (known as the *independent variable*) on the X-axis.**

   In Figure 8-8, this value is the amount of glue, measured in drops.

3. **Plot the value for the measured value (known as the *dependent variable*) on the Y-axis.**

   This value is joint strength in Figure 8-8.

4. **Look for a relationship between the two variables by seeing if you can draw a relatively straight line through the points.**

   In the sample scatter diagram in Figure 8-8, you find a fairly good relationship between the amount of glue used and the strength of the joint; the more glue used, the stronger the joint.

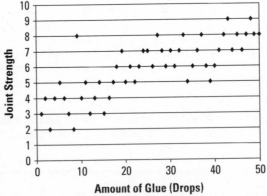

Figure 8-8: A scatter diagram shows the relationship between two variables.

Control charts

The most commonly used chart in quality control, by most accounts, is the *control chart* — an important tool used in statistical quality control (which we cover in much more detail in Chapters 9 and 10). A control chart is a variation of a scatter diagram (see the previous section) that you use to see how a process changes over time.

The process involves determining how large an attribute value can be (called the *upper control limit* [UCL]) and how low the attribute value can be (called the *lower control limit* [LCL]) and still be acceptable to the customer. After you test the limits, you measure the attribute over time to see how it fluctuates between the upper and lower control limits. You can use control charts with any quality attribute that's important to the customer.

An attribute can be either in control or out of control:

✔ If the attribute stays between the upper and lower control limits on a consistent basis, the process is said to be *in control.*

✔ If the attribute goes above the upper control limit or below the lower control limit, the process is said to be *out of control.* (The process also can be out of control if the data exhibits some nonrandom pattern, which we cover in Chapter 10.)

The two most common control charts are known as the *X-bar* and *Range* (or *R*) *charts.* They both work by plotting attribute values that result from samples of multiple measurements taken at a given point in time. A sample typically consists of measurements of two to ten samples. The X-bar chart plots the average (arithmetic mean) of the samples, and the R chart plots the range between the lowest and highest measured values of the samples.

In the sample X-bar chart in Figure 8-9, you can see the UCL and the LCL with the averages for each sample taken over time. The attribute value measured in the chart is the diameter of a hole being drilled, and time is measured in minutes. In this example, the process is staying in control.

Figure 8-9:
A control chart notes whether data falls within certain limits.

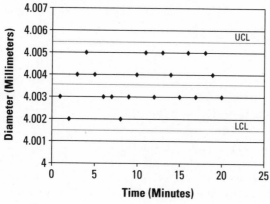

Chapter 9

Evaluating Quality with Statistics

The old management saying "you can't manage what you can't measure" holds just as true in the world of quality control. Statistics are the measurement tool you need to manage the creation of your product or service. In this chapter, we explain how you can use statistics as the language to measure and evaluate the quality of your product or service. We discuss the following statistical concepts in relation to quality control:

✔ **Sampling:** The idea that you don't have to measure every item you produce to be able to judge the overall quality of your production process.

✔ **Pareto analysis:** A *Pareto chart* is a visual tool you can use to gain a general understanding of your production process (see Chapter 8 for an introduction to Pareto charts).

✔ **Correlation:** A measure of how two values you measure in your production process are related.

✔ **Regression analysis:** A tool for predicting the value of one measurement when you already know the value of another one.

✔ **Variance:** A measure of the variability of your production process. You examine variance to determine whether a variation you discover is due to chance or to a problem in your process.

For details on preparing to measure your quality process, head to Chapter 7. Chapter 8 has the scoop on gathering data to evaluate. And you can check out *Statistics For Dummies,* by Deborah Rumsey, PhD (Wiley), for a crash course in basic statistics.

By the Numbers: Discovering the Basics of Statistics in Quality

Statistics permeate throughout the business world, from entry-level workers who crunch numbers to CEOs who forecast for the future. Although you don't need to be an expert in statistics to improve the quality of your processes, you do need to have a basic understanding of statistics to undertake a quality improvement process (or to even know you need one). You need to understand how statistics are useful as part of your quality control process and how to interpret and apply them. In the following sections, we explain the information you can gather from statistical evaluation and go over some basic statistical terms.

The most commonly used tool for collecting and evaluating quality statistics is Microsoft Excel. Most people have Excel (or a similar spreadsheet program) installed on their work computers. We use Excel throughout this chapter to do the heavy math lifting for the statistics work you'll use in quality control. We spend our time focused on how to interpret and apply the results to the quality control process. It helps to have a basic understanding of how to use Excel when working through this chapter and implementing a quality control process; the latest edition of *Excel For Dummies* for your version of Excel is a good place to start.

The story that statistics can tell you about quality

Statistics is the language you use to talk about the quality of your production processes. It allows you to communicate the critical attributes of your processes and gives you critical insights into how your processes are functioning. By quantifying your quality control efforts, you can put a dollar figure on the value of your proposed improvements and translate your efforts into something that the leaders of your organization can understand. Statistics also highlight the quality of the work you do so that your customers can see.

"There are lies, damn lies, and statistics." This quote, often attributed to Mark Twain, is a reminder that some people may use statistics to tell whatever story they want. People should be suspicious of statistics when it isn't clear how the data was collected and how the statistics were calculated. A great example in history is the 1936 American presidential election. A famous poll of the day predicted that Alf Landon would defeat Franklin Roosevelt in a landslide. Of course, the opposite was true. How did the poll get it so wrong?

Well, the people polled were selected based on phone numbers and car regis-
trations. Many Roosevelt voters were too poor during the Great Depression
to have either. Also, you should beware of allowing preconceived ideas to
creep into and skew your quality statistics.

The statistics terms that you need to know

A thorough understanding of the statistics in this chapter is beyond the
scope of this book, but you should be familiar with the following terms and
the equations behind them when implementing a quality control program:

- **Mean:** What most people call the average. To calculate a mean, you sum
  all the appropriate values and divide by the total number of values. For
  example, if your values are 1, 5, and 6, you add the values together (a
  total of 12) and divide by 3 (the number of values) to get 4 as the mean.

- **Range:** The distance from the largest value to the smallest value. For
  instance, if the mean of your customer satisfaction is 95 out of 100, but
  your range is 80, it means at least one client rated you at a 20 or below.
  What if it was your largest client that gave you a 15! You're in trouble
  regardless of the mean!

- **Variance:** A measure of the spread, or the dispersion of a variable
  around the mean of all the concerned data. You calculate variance by
  taking the sum of the squares of the deviations — that is, the sum of the
  difference between the measurement value and the mean value of all the
  values — and dividing by the number of samples minus one. Continuing
  with the example from previous bullets, if your values are 1, 5, and 6,
  and the mean is 4, you calculate the variance as follows:

  - One has a difference of 3 from the mean of 4. The squared value of
    the difference is 9.

  - Five has a difference of 1 from the mean of 4. The squared value of
    the difference is 1.

  - Six has a difference of 2 from the mean of 4. The squared value of
    the difference is 4.

  - The sum of the squares (9, 1, and 4) is 14. Because the number of
    samples is 3, you divide 14 by 2 (the number of samples minus 1),
    for a variance of 7.

  The problem with variance is that because it's the sum of the squared
  values, it isn't in the same unit of measure as the original measurements.
  If your original measurements are in inches, for example, the variance is
  in inches squared, which isn't very helpful. To fix that, you can use the
  standard deviation.

> ✔ **Standard deviation:** The square root of the variance. Because the variance involves squares of the data, you get a value that appears in the same units as the sample values when you use standard deviation. The standard deviation is effectively a mean or an "average" of these deviations. Using the previous example, the standard deviation is the square root of 7, or 2.65. If your original measurements are in inches, the standard deviation is now in inches (rather than inches squared). Standard deviation is a critical concept in Six Sigma — see Chapter 17.

Just One of Many: Delving into the Details of Sampling

In Chapter 4, we introduce the idea of using sampling as part of your inspection process. Sampling allows you to test a small number of the items you produce to get information about the quality of the entire population of items produced. In the following sections, we discuss why sampling works well when handling statistics about your quality control process, and we go into detail about how you include sampling in your quality process.

Understanding why sampling is a smart idea

We can list a number of good reasons why you should use sampling in quality control:

> ✔ Testing every item you produce at every stage of the production process can get very expensive, very quickly. If you make 500 items each day, it's cheaper to test 10 items rather than all 500.

> ✔ The testing process can be destructive, so you can't test every item you produce. For example, you can't test each bullet you make by firing it.

> ✔ For most processes and situations, using a sample can tell you just as much as an exhaustive testing system. If 2 percent of the million items you make have a problem, you have a good chance of finding one or two bad ones by testing 100 or less. You can then figure out why those items are bad to try to prevent the problem from occurring again.

Most people are familiar with the use of polls, especially during presidential election years; however, you may not be aware that they work on the same principle as sampling for quality control. Although you hear about the occasional poll being wrong, the very fact that a wrong poll is newsworthy suggests that sampling for quality control or for predicting election outcomes is prudent most of the time — as long as you sample correctly.

Examining the factors related to selecting a sample size

How large should your sample be when testing for your quality control process? The bulk of the statistics behind calculating most sample sizes is beyond the scope of this book; however, it's very common to use 30 as a sample size for many processes. This number is the generally accepted rule of thumb for the minimum sample size.

You have a number of tools available to help you calculate sample size. Several tools are available on the Internet; just type Sample Size Calculator into your favorite search engine and wait for the results to pop up. However, make sure you're familiar with the following terms before you use any of the tools you find:

- **Population:** The total number of items that you're evaluating. You take a sample of the population to perform your quality statistics.

- **Confidence interval:** The familiar margin-of-error figure you see in published opinion polls and surveys. It represents the range that the value would fall in if you surveyed all possible people. For example, if survey results say that 62 percent of persons polled answered yes to a question, plus or minus 3 percent, the 3 percent is the confidence interval for the sample. Statistically, you can be certain that if the researchers had surveyed everyone, the actual number who answered yes would've been between 59 and 65 percent. Usually, the larger the sample size, the smaller the confidence interval.

- **Confidence level:** Tells you how sure (confident) you can be in your results. The level is the true percentage of the population who would've picked the answer that falls within the confidence interval. A 95-percent confidence level means that you can be 95 percent certain that the real answer is within the confidence interval. Most quality people use a 95-percent confidence level.

Three factors determine the size of the confidence interval for a given confidence level:

- ✔ **Sample size:** The larger the sample, the closer it reflects the true value of the population, meaning the confidence interval is smaller. (**Note:** This relationship isn't linear; doubling the sample size doesn't shrink the confidence interval by half.)

- ✔ **Range between values:** The larger the range between the values, the less the chance for error. For example, if the possible values have a range of 50, it's more likely that your sample will accurately reflect the population than if the range is only 5.

- ✔ **Population size:** The larger the population, the more accurate the sample. The mathematics of probability prove that population is important only when the total population is relatively small. It's more likely to have a sample that doesn't reflect the total population for a population of 100 than it is for a population of 100,000.

Recognizing the importance of random sampling

For the sake of your quality control process, you must choose your samples randomly. The statistics we discuss in this chapter count on random samples. Whenever you use sampling, you run a risk that the sample won't be sufficiently representative of the population from which it was drawn; this is known as *sampling error*. Confidence intervals are especially sensitive to errors when the sampling isn't random.

Random sampling also avoids influence by people involved in the process; for example, the supervisor of a department that makes widgets may be tempted to provide samples from his best worker if he's asked to provide sample widgets to test. To avoid this situation, you must ensure that the samples provided are randomly selected. Although you can use a coin or playing cards to randomly select samples to test, most people use a random-number table or software to generate random numbers.

Some flaw in the data-collection process usually causes nonrandom samples (see Chapter 8 for more on data collection). An example of a poor sample would be taking a sample from only one shift and using the data to make judgments about products made on other shifts.

More Bang for Your Buck: Using Pareto Analysis

A *Pareto chart* is a specialized histogram — a commonly used graph for showing frequency distributions, which illustrate how often each unique value in a set of data occurs — that you use to identify issues that cause a disproportionate amount of your quality problems (see Chapter 8 for more discussion of the chart). The chart provides a process to help you group and organize your data in a manner that helps you focus your time and resources on the problems that matter most. You'll find the chart simple in its design and construction, but able to provide powerful insights into your processes.

A properly constructed Pareto chart can help your quality control effort in many ways, including the following:

✔ Tracking down the source of problems

✔ Assisting in setting priorities

✔ Determining the root cause of a problem

✔ Focusing your efforts where they'll have the biggest impact

A Pareto chart is effective only when the data you gather follows the Pareto Principle — when approximately 20 percent of the issues cause 80 percent of the problems (see Chapter 8 for details).

In the following sections, we explain how to draw and evaluate a Pareto chart for your quality process. As an example, we use a pizza parlor that's having a problem with customers returning too many pizzas. The manager of the parlor is concerned about the number of returns, both from a cost perspective and how they affect customer satisfaction. A Pareto chart can help him focus on the most critical issues that cause customers to be unhappy with their pizzas.

Creating a Pareto chart

Creating a Pareto chart isn't difficult, but you must do it correctly to get results that you can use for your quality improvement process. In the following sections, we explain how to create a Pareto chart successfully.

Selecting categories and gathering information

Before you create the actual Pareto chart, you need to perform the following preparatory steps:

1. **Determine the problem or process you need to evaluate.** Use techniques such as brainstorming, reviewing anecdotal data, or conducting interviews with stakeholders to select the problem or process that you should tackle first (we cover interviews with customers in Chapter 6). A pizza parlor may decide to look for sources of pizza quality issues, such as under- or overcooked pizza, incorrect toppings, or pizza served cold.

2. **Select the time frame to collect the data and the data-collection process you should use.** The data should be as accurate and timely as possible. (Chapter 8 has all the information you need to collect your data.) If most of the pizza quality problems occur during lunch, the manager can start his data-collection process during the lunch rush.

3. **Define the categories to use.** By placing the data you collect about a quality issue into categories, you can quickly determine a solution to prevent a problem.

Your organization or industry may already have defined quality categories that you can use (see Chapter 2 for details on quality standards). If not, you need to define the overall type of category (such as location, subject, or cause) and then create standard phrases to describe each category. Be as consistent as possible in the scope and naming of each category. You must also define how you assign a problem to a category and whether you can place a problem in more than one category.

Some examples of quality problems for which you can easily create categories include

- Customer returns

- Errors on college applications

- Workplace injuries

- Part defects

- Software bugs

In the pizza-parlor problem, some quality-issue categories include

- Undercooked pizza

- Overcooked pizza

- Too few toppings on the pizza

- Wrong toppings on the pizza

  • Cold pizza

  • Pizza delivered late

4. **Define what you want to measure.** Are you going to count the frequency of a problem or its impact? For example, the manager of the pizza parlor could measure the impact of returned pizzas in dollars lost (due to production and labor costs) or in time lost (for labor).

5. **Create a data-collection sheet to collect your data.** List each of the quality factors (such as under- and overcooked pizza, wrong toppings, and so on) on the check sheet.

6. **Collect the data.** For the pizza parlor, a count of each error will provide the necessary data.

Be sure to train your data collectors so that they collect the data in a correct and consistent manner. You should have at least 50 total points of data or observations, though more is usually better (see Chapter 8 for specifics).

Forming the chart

After you finish your preparatory work and collect the necessary data (see the previous section), you can form the Pareto chart by using the following steps:

1. **Total each category for the time period you select.** See Figure 9-1 for a sample chart for the pizza-parlor example.

2. **Determine the percentage for each category.** This isn't necessary, but it's helpful for determining when you reach the 80 percent mark of the Pareto Principle (see Chapter 8).

3. **Put the categories on the chart as bars, placed side by side as in a histogram (see Chapter 8 for more about histograms).** You place the categories on the X-axis (the horizontal); you note the frequency (or counted value) on the Y-axis (the vertical).

   The height of each bar represents the value for that category (such as count, cost, time, and so on). The largest bar should go on the left, and you should place the remaining bars in descending order of height so that the smallest bar falls on the right.

   You make a placement exception if you use the category "Other"; you place it to the extreme right, regardless of its height. See Figure 9-1 to check out the bars for the pizza return problem.

4. **Analyze the data, using the chart as your guide (see the following section for details).**

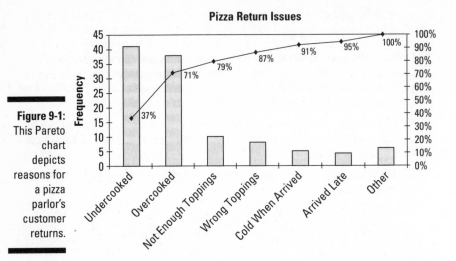

Figure 9-1:
This Pareto
chart
depicts
reasons for
a pizza
parlor's
customer
returns.

In addition to creating the category bars on a Pareto chart, you may want to add a line that shows the cumulative percentage of errors as you add each category. You calculate the cumulative percentage by starting with the lowest percentage and adding it to the next lowest percentage. Repeat until you reach the last attribute, which should have a cumulative percentage of 100 percent. This action helps to identify the categories contributing to 80 percent of your problem within the Pareto Principle. In Figure 9-1, you can see that 71 percent of the issues stem from only two categories.

Interpreting a Pareto chart

A Pareto chart helps by graphically showing the issues that contribute the most to your problematic product or process. After you create a Pareto chart, you can work with what the chart is trying to tell you by focusing your quality efforts on the bars to the left (the tallest ones) in order to maximize the results from your efforts. In most cases, it takes the same amount of effort to reduce a tall bar by 50 percent as it does a smaller bar. Occasionally, you can easily eliminate a small bar, but more often you get the biggest benefit by working on the larger bars. A Pareto chart helps you to separate the critical few from the insignificant many. We show you what to look for in your Pareto chart in the following sections.

Recognizing possible patterns in your Pareto chart

You can achieve three different outcomes when creating a Pareto chart:

✔ **A good Pareto chart.** The chart clearly shows that your process follows the Pareto Principle, where the majority of your problems fall in the top two or three categories. Figure 9-1 gives you an example of a good Pareto chart. If your chart looks like this, focus on the categories that make up close to 80 percent of your problems. You may want to create another Pareto chart based on the possible causes of the top categories to determine root cause(s) of the problems.

✔ **No clear winners.** The chart in Figure 9-2 shows a slow decline from left to right — not really a Pareto effect. The chart doesn't follow the 80/20 rule; it may take six or eight categories to reach 80 percent. You can still focus on the highest categories first, but you won't get as dramatic an improvement as you will with a good Pareto situation.

✔ **An evenly distributed chart, which doesn't show the Pareto Principle.** The chart in Figure 9-3 is an example. You can see that 76 percent of the issues fall across the first five categories, and that the bars representing the categories are roughly the same height. Focusing on any one of the categories has no added value. You may need to create new categories from a different perspective and try again. Sorry!

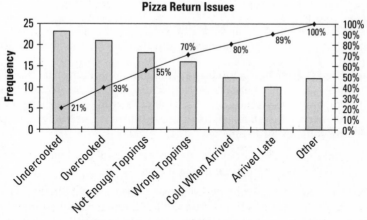

Figure 9-2: You can see no clear winners (or problems) in this Pareto chart for pizza-parlor customer returns.

Putting Pareto results to good use

After you define a category on a Pareto chart as a problem primed for fixing (see the previous sections), ask yourself who, what, where, when, how, and why to try to determine possible solutions. Looking at the Pareto chart for the pizza problem in Figure 9-1, you can see that 71 percent of the problem pizzas have cooking-time issues. The quality manager of the pizza parlor should now look at how cooking time is determined to see if the pizza makers can consistently cook the pizzas for the correct amount of time.

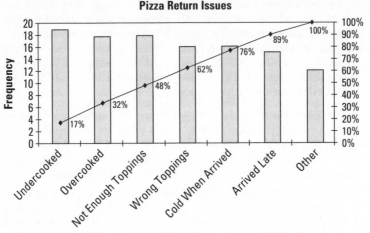

Figure 9-3:
This Pareto chart for pizza returns is evenly distributed — not a good sign.

You should apply obvious solutions, even for small categories. Anyone familiar with the process should be able to come up with some obvious solutions to try after a problem has been identified.

Potential problems that may pop up

Problems you may encounter with your Pareto chart include the following:

- ✔ **The "Other" bar is too large.** This bar should never be the tallest bar; if it is, you need to break down the category into new categories because you can't work on issues you haven't identified. The category doesn't have to be the smallest, however, because it's useful for grouping insignificant problems.

- ✔ **Bad data.** If the data is old, or based on invalid opinions or assumptions, you may reach the wrong conclusion.

- ✔ **Too little data.** A rule of thumb is to have at least 50 observations. The key is to continue to get data until you reach a point where the shape of the graph doesn't change with the addition of more data (see Chapter 8 for info on data collection).

- ✔ **Bad categories (or counting the wrong thing).** You may want to look at cost or time rather than frequency, for example. Just because a problem occurs most frequently doesn't necessarily make it the most expensive problem. It pays to look at a problem from several angles.

The most frequent problem isn't always the most important! Be aware of the impact of all the problems you identify on your customers or organization. When looking at or adjusting categories, think about other factors that may influence the data. For example, in the pizza problem, the graph may be evenly distributed at first. If the parlor manager changes the way observers look at the data by creating a graph for just Monday through Friday and another for the weekends, rather than one overall graph, he or she may discover different problems for each graph that exhibit the Pareto Principle. Such a discovery would merit the need for separate solutions for the weekday shifts versus the weekend shifts.

The Positive and the Negative: Coming Up with Correlations

In many production processes, the value of one measurement is related or connected to the value of another measurement. For example, what effect might temperature or humidity have on your production process? Can the education level of a call-center employee predict his or her average call time? Do years of experience really make a difference in production output level? You can use statistics to answer these and other questions that involve the search for a relationship between two values (or variables) in a process.

The degree of the relationship between two or more values in statistics is called *correlation*. If a relationship exists, you can implement changes to one value that have a desirable effect on the other value and that make a big difference in the quality of your product. In the following sections, we explain the details of correlations and how to determine a correlation between two values.

What exactly is a correlation?

A *correlation* exists between two values if a change in one value causes a change in another value. If the value of one measurement increases and, at the same time, the value of another measurement increases, a *positive correlation* exists between the two values — in other words, the values move in the same direction. A *negative correlation* exists when the values move in different directions: If one value increases, the other decreases.

If you suspect that a relationship exists between two values in your production process, you can measure the correlation to see how much of a relationship really exists. Technically, what you're testing for is the "statistical significance" of the relationship. You find the significance by calculating what's known as the *correlation coefficient* (we show you how to calculate the coefficient later in this chapter). The correlation coefficient is simply a number between −1 and 1 that measures how closely two values are related. A positive correlation coefficient (between 0 and 1) means that the values move in the same direction (a positive correlation); a negative correlation coefficient (between 0 and −1) means that the values move in the opposite direction (a negative correlation).

You also must look at the degree of the relationship; the closer the values are related, the closer the correlation coefficient gets to 1 (or –1).

- ✔ If the correlation coefficient is close to 1 or –1, the values are strongly related.

- ✔ If the correlation coefficient is exactly 1 or –1, the values are perfectly related.

- ✔ A correlation coefficient close to 0 means the values are weakly related.

- ✔ A correlation coefficient of 0 means that no relationship exists between the two values.

Use Table 9-1 when evaluating a correlation coefficient.

Table 9-1	Strength of a Correlation
Correlation Coefficient	*Interpretation*
0.0 to 0.3	Little or no correlation
0.3 to 0.5	Low correlation
0.5 to 0.7	Moderate correlation
0.7 to 0.9	High correlation
0.9 to 1.0	Very high correlation

Technically, you're just looking at the linear relationship between two variables when examining correlation. A linear relationship is one where the variables move together in a straight line on a graph. The relationship could take other shapes, such as a logarithmic (shaped like a hockey stick), a sigmoid (curved like the letter "S"), or any number of other forms.

How do you determine and use a correlation?

So how do you calculate correlation, and what do you do with it to improve quality? In the following sections, we explain how to use a scatter diagram to see a correlation, how to calculate the correlation coefficient to determine the strength of the relationship, and how to use the results of the diagram.

Plotting data on a scatter diagram

The first step in determining a correlation, after collecting your data, is to graph the values you want to analyze on a standard coordinate plane and examine the result to see if a relationship seems to exist. You create what's called a *scatter diagram* (we introduce scatter diagrams in Chapter 8). A scatter diagram gives you a general clue as to the relationship between two values.

Draw a graph with one variable on the X-axis and the other on the Y-axis.

Figure 9-4 shows a sample scatter diagram, where you compare the temperature of a surrounding area to the diameter of a part being made. Looking at the chart, you can see that as the temperature rises, the diameter of the part gets larger. You can see a positive correlation when the points on the graph go from the lower left to the upper right. If the opposite situation occurred — the diameter of the part got smaller as the temperature rose — the points on the graph would start on the upper-left portion of the graph and go to the lower right (what a negative correlation looks like).

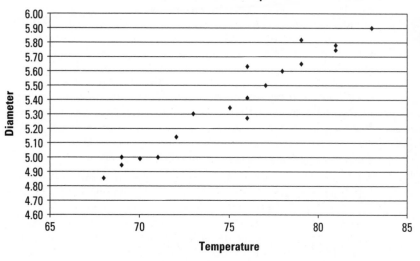

Figure 9-4: This scatter diagram shows a positive correlation between temperature and part diameter.

In Microsoft Excel, you can right-click on one of the points of the scatter diagram and have the program draw a trend line (see Figure 9-5). The line makes the correlation between the variables even clearer. You also can draw the trend line by hand.

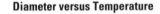

Diameter versus Temperature

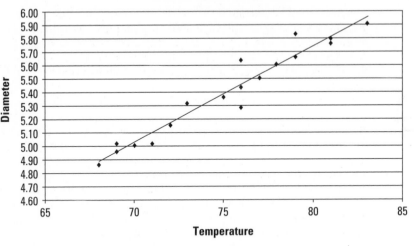

Diameter

Temperature

Figure 9-5:
A scatter diagram with a trend line clearly shows the relationship between temperature and part diameter.

Although you may see a general correlation between two values when you plot them on a plane, you still have to watch out for exceptions to the overall trend. Correlation is about an entire set of data, and some values may not fit the overall trend of the data. For example, in Figure 9-5 you see a couple of points in the middle that don't fit as neatly on the trend line as most of the other values. Also, be very careful about using the trend line to make predictions outside the range of the data on the graph. Most trends don't hold forever in either direction. For example, increasing the oven temperature will decrease the cooking time of a pizza, but you can't decrease the cooking time to less than zero.

Calculating the correlation coefficient

Although a scatter diagram and a trend line give you a general clue about the relationship between two values (see the previous section), they may not illustrate the strength of the relationship. Your next step is to calculate the correlation coefficient to get a more accurate picture of the relationship. You could calculate the value by hand, but being the tool-using animal you are, you can use Microsoft Excel to calculate the value for you. Find out how in the following steps:

1. **Place the data for the first value (whatever you placed on the X-axis in the scatter diagram) in column A and the corresponding data for the second value (whatever you placed on the Y-axis) in column B.**

2. **Go to the main menu at the top and select Tools and then Add-Ins. Review the list of add-ins that appears to make sure the Analysis ToolPak is checked. If not, check it.**

3. **Close the list and go back to the main menu; choose Tools and then Data Analysis.**

4. **Select Correlation from the list of analysis tools. Click OK, which should start the coefficient wizard (see Figure 9-6).**

5. **Select the input range of your data by highlighting the data in columns A and B. Be sure to select the "Labels in first row" check box.**

6. **Select the output range to tell Excel where to place the results and click OK.**

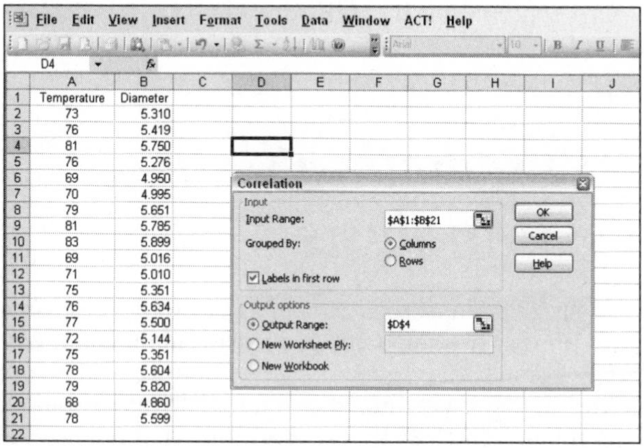

Figure 9-6: Use the wizard in Microsoft Excel to calculate a correlation coefficient.

You now have a small chart that shows the correlation coefficient for the two values. In Figure 9-7, you see that the correlation coefficient is 0.969953. Using the rule-of-thumb chart in Table 9-1, you know that the temperature of the surrounding area and the diameter of the part in question are very highly correlated.

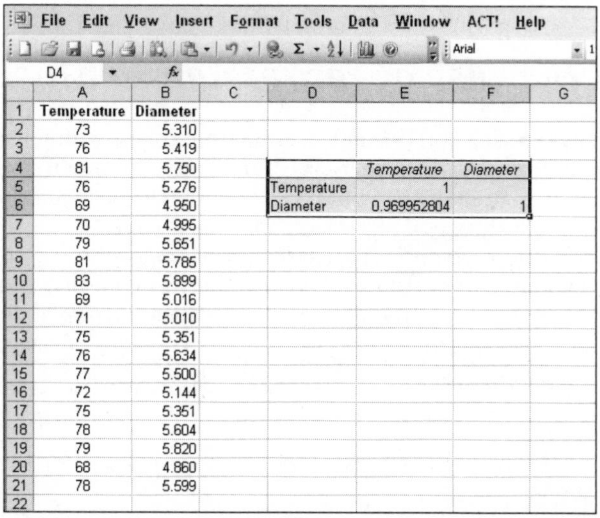

Figure 9-7: The correlation coefficient displayed in Excel for the relationship between temperature and part diameter.

Moving forward with your results

After you know whether two values are correlated, and you've identified the strength of that relationship, you can use this information to make adjustments in the process to improve your quality. You should be most interested in relationships where the correlation coefficient is close to 1 or –1. From the example in the previous sections, you can see that as the temperature increases, the diameter of the hole increases. So, if the hole is becoming too big, you know you can reduce the size of the hole by reducing the temperature of the piece when you drill the hole. Conversely, you can raise the temperature if you need a bigger hole.

Let Me Guess: Predicting Values with Regression Analysis

You can use a process known as *regression analysis* to develop an equation that allows you to predict the value of one measurement when you know the value of another. Becoming clairvoyant is useful in quality control because you can determine what and how much to change if you have a quality issue. In our example in the previous section on correlation, it may be helpful to be able to predict the diameter of the part if you know the temperature. This can help you determine what temperature to keep the work area at to ensure that the part is the diameter you want.

We don't go into all the statistics that make regression analysis work, but in the following sections, we show you how to use Microsoft Excel to perform regression analysis and how to use the results of your analysis in your quality control process.

Getting the gist of regression analysis

Regression analysis takes you beyond showing that the measurements of the values you've taken in the past are related by allowing you to predict what the value of one measurement will be if you know the value of another measurement. The simplest type of regression analysis is called *linear regression*. Linear regression exists when you can draw a straight line through a scatter diagram of two variables. For example, you can perform linear regression in the previous section by drawing a trend line on the scatter diagram in Figure 9-5. Statisticians may point out that you have to make a number of assumptions when you use linear regression, but for our purposes it will work just fine.

Performing a regression analysis

To perform a regression analysis, you must first define the value that you want to measure — the independent variable — and the value that you want to predict with the measurement — the *dependent variable*. The labels make sense if you think about it: The value that you want to predict is dependent upon the value you get when you measure the first variable.

When you draw your graph, you usually plot the independent variable on the X-axis and the dependent variable on the Y-axis. Referring to Figure 9-5, you see the temperature on the X-axis and the diameter of the part on the Y-axis. So, temperature is the independent value that you can use to predict the part diameter (the dependent variable).

After you define your measurable values, you collect data on your values. At that point, you can use Microsoft Excel to perform a regression analysis to get an equation you can use to predict the part diameter when you know the temperature. Follow these steps to perform the analysis:

1. **Go to the main menu in Excel and select Tools and then Data Analysis.**

   If you don't see this option, be sure that the Analysis ToolPak is installed by going to Add-Ins in the Tools menu and checking Analysis ToolPak.

2. **In the list of options that appears, click Regression and then click OK; you see the dialog box that appears in Figure 9-8.**

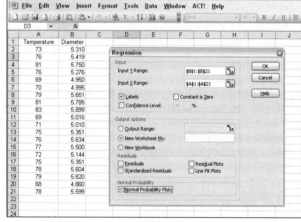

Figure 9-8:
You can use Excel to perform a regression analysis.

3. **For the Input Y Range, select the data for your dependent variable; for the independent variable, use the Input X Range.**

   Check the boxes marked Labels and Normal Probability Plots.

4. **Click OK; Excel will open a new worksheet with the results of the regression analysis (see Figure 9-9).**

Figure 9-9:
The results of your regression analysis appear in an Excel worksheet.

	A	B	C	D	E	F	G	H	I	J
1	SUMMARY OUTPUT									
2										
3	*Regression Statistics*									
4	Multiple R	0.969952804								
5	R Square	0.940808441								
6	Adjusted R Square	0.937520021								
7	Standard Error	0.080214359								
8	Observations	20								
9										
10	ANOVA									
11		*df*	*SS*	*MS*	*F*	*Significance F*				
12	Regression	1	1.840849018	1.840849	286.0974	1.70022E-12				
13	Residual	18	0.115818182	0.006434						
14	Total	19	1.9566672							
15										
16		*Coefficients*	*Standard Error*	*t Stat*	*P-value*	*Lower 95%*	*Upper 95%*	*Lower 95.0%*	*Upper 95.0%*	
17	Intercept	0.057384762	0.316146234	0.181513	0.857993	-0.606813828	0.721583352	-0.606813828	0.721583352	
18	Temperature	0.070900601	0.004191727	16.91441	1.7E-12	0.06209411	0.079707092	0.06209411	0.079707092	
19										

Don't get overwhelmed by the amount of information on the worksheet because you won't be using most of it. What's important for your purposes are the values you need to create a regression equation. You can find these values listed at the bottom left of the worksheet under the heading Coefficients.

The regression equation for determining value y when you know the value of x is as follows:

$$y = bx + a$$

In this equation, b is the slope of the line (how quickly the line goes up or down) and a is the intercept (the point where the line crosses the Y-axis). You can get these values from the worksheet you just created in the previous list: The first value under the Coefficients heading is a and the second value is b. Looking at the example in Figure 9-9, your regression equation is (rounding to three decimal places)

$$y = 0.071x + 0.057$$

You can now use this equation to predict the value of one of the variables when you know the value of the other.

Using the results of a regression analysis

After you have an equation that describes the relationship between the two values, you can predict the value for one variable when you know the value of the other. To use the previous section's equation to predict the diameter of the part in question when you know the temperature (the example that appears in previous figures and sections), you simply solve the regression equation by substituting the temperature for x. For example, if the temperature is 74°F, the equation becomes

$$y = 0.071(74) + 0.057$$
$$y = 5.311$$

The prediction for the diameter of the part when the temperature is 74°F is 5.311. If you look at the graph with the trend line in Figure 9-5, you see that this figure looks about right.

If you want the diameter of your hole to be exactly 5.000, you can use the following equation to determine what the temperature should be:

$$5.000 = 0.071x + 0.057$$
$$4.943 = 0.071x$$
$$69.6 = x$$

So, to make the diameter of the hole as close to 5.000 as possible, you should try to keep the temperature as close to 69.6°F as possible.

Consistency Counts: Analyzing Variance

You don't want variation in the process that produces the product or delivers the service for your customers. A consistent product or service is the Holy Grail, because a consistent product or service is more likely to meet your customers' needs. You can't eliminate variation, but you can make an effort to control it. In the following sections, we discuss how you can determine whether variation is something you need to worry about and how you can measure variation between two or more processes.

Identifying a variance issue

The statistical process you use to measure the variation between two or more processes is called *variance*. To analyze the variation in your processes to find out if you should be concerned about it, you use a process called *analysis of variance,* or ANOVA. Using this process, you can determine if a difference exists in the output of the processes — a difference that goes beyond what you'd expect due to random chance. If you discover a variation between the processes that isn't random, you know to look for the cause of the variation.

Businesses use ANOVA throughout many industries to help identify the sources of potential problems in the production process. They want to find out whether variation is due to differences within the process itself or due to differences between two or more processes. With this information, you can vary the factors in your production process to determine the cause of the variation.

The information produced by the ANOVA test is called the *F ratio,* named after its inventor, Sir Ronald A. Fisher. You can use the ANOVA test to evaluate the differences between any number of data sets, not just two. You can measure the data from any process; the number of measurements in each sample doesn't have to be the same. The number of samples measured can be as little as three and as large as infinity.

Calculating and using variance

You can use Microsoft Excel to calculate the values for your ANOVA test to analyze variance. This allows you to spend more of your time interpreting and using the results. As an example here, we look at a production process that consists of two different machines (Machine A and Machine B) used to make a part. We've collected data on the diameter of 20 different parts made by each machine. In Figure 9-10, you can see the values entered into an Excel spreadsheet. We use columns for the different machines and enter the values for each time we measure in the same row.

	A	B
1	Machine A	Machine B
2	5.310	5.234
3	5.419	5.765
4	5.750	5.342
5	5.276	4.960
6	4.950	4.993
7	4.995	5.012
8	5.651	5.454
9	5.785	5.933
10	5.899	5.888
11	5.016	5.218
12	5.010	5.101
13	5.351	5.432
14	5.634	4.894
15	5.500	5.555
16	5.144	5.934
17	5.351	5.483
18	5.604	5.693
19	5.820	5.931
20	4.860	4.943
21	5.599	5.601

Figure 9-10: You can enter data for two different machines into Excel to perform an ANOVA test.

Follow these steps to use Excel to calculate the values for your ANOVA test:

1. **Go to the main menu in Excel and select Tools and then Data Analysis. In the list of options that appears, click ANOVA: Single Factor and then click OK.**

   If you don't see the data-analysis option, be sure that the Analysis ToolPak is installed by going to Add-Ins in the Tools menu and checking Analysis ToolPak.

2. **For the input range, select both columns of data. Check Labels in First Row if you've selected the row with the names of the machines. Select the Output option to create the table where you want and click OK.**

   Excel will now create your ANOVA table, as shown in Figure 9-11.

Figure 9-11:
This ANOVA table is for two different part-producing machines.

	A	B	C	D	E	F	G	H	I	J	K
1	Machine A	Machine B									
2	5.310	5.234		Anova: Single Factor							
3	5.419	5.765									
4	5.750	5.342		SUMMARY							
5	5.276	4.960		Groups	Count	Sum	Average	Variance			
6	4.950	4.993		Machine A	20	107.924	5.3962	0.102982			
7	4.995	5.012		Machine B	20	108.366	5.4183	0.131848			
8	5.651	5.454									
9	5.785	5.933									
10	5.899	5.888		ANOVA							
11	5.016	5.218		Source of Variation	SS	df	MS	F	P-value	F crit	
12	5.010	5.101		Between Groups	0.004884	1	0.004884	0.041597	0.839478	4.098172	
13	5.351	5.432		Within Groups	4.461771	38	0.117415				
14	5.634	4.894									
15	5.500	5.555		Total	4.466656	39					
16	5.144	5.934									
17	5.351	5.483									
18	5.604	5.693									
19	5.820	5.931									
20	4.860	4.943									
21	5.599	5.601									
22											

A few items on the table should be easy to interpret; the Summary section contains the following information, for example:

- The count of measurement values
- The sum and mean of the measurements
- The variance for each machine

You can see from the table in Figure 9-11 that the mean diameter for the parts made with Machine B is slightly larger than the mean of those made with Machine A, and the variance between the parts also is slightly larger for Machine B. The next question you want to answer is whether the variation between Machine A and Machine B is something you need to worry about.

To answer this question, you need to interpret the ANOVA output by evaluating the F ratio (the information produced by the ANOVA test):

✔ If the F ratio (marked in the F column in Figure 9-11 in the ANOVA table) is larger than the F critical value (*F crit*), a statistically significant difference exists between the processes. Therefore, you need to examine the processes to see what's causing the difference.

✔ If the F ratio is smaller than the F critical value, the differences between the machines are best explained by chance.

Looking at the example in Figure 9-11, you can see that the F ratio is smaller than the F critical value, so you can assume that any difference between the two machines occurs strictly by chance.

Chapter 10

Assessing Quality with Statistical Process Control

In This Chapter

▶ Digesting the basics of Statistical Process Control

▶ Becoming familiar with the role of the control chart in SPC

▶ Building control charts to evaluate and correct a process

▶ Determining whether a process is capable

The following quote is from the "father" of Statistical Process Control (SPC), Walter Shewhart. Shewhart pioneered the idea that all manufacturing processes produce some variation that's natural to the processes and that quality problems arise when abnormal variation occurs. Shewhart was the first to use statistics to measure the natural variation of a process and detect the occurrence of unnatural variation.

> *Bringing a production process into a state of 'statistical control,' where there is only chance-cause variation, and keeping it in control, is necessary to predict future output and to manage a process economically.*
>
> — Walter Shewhart

In this chapter, you find out how to use simple statistical techniques to, as Shewhart said, bring your production processes into a state of "statistical control" by eliminating variation. With this control and variance elimination, you can produce a quality product or service for your customers.

Grasping the Basics of Statistical Process Control

Statistical Process Control (SPC) is defined as the use of statistical tools and techniques to measure a production process in order to detect change. To produce a quality product, you must have a process that's consistent. SPC helps you detect any changes in the process, because change is more times than not a bad thing. SPC is a philosophy that embraces the idea of continuous improvement brought on by using an assortment of statistical tools. The basis of the philosophy is that problems within a system cause most of your process issues, not problems with individual people. When done correctly, SPC puts data about a process in the hands of those that are best able to improve the process.

Even though the term "Statistical Process Control" sounds complicated, the general idea behind SPC is really pretty simple: You collect samples from a production process and use charts to plot the variability of the samples against target specifications. With SPC, you can catch and fix problems before you have a chance to make bad products or provide bad services.

SPC consists of the following four basic steps:

1. Measuring a production process (which we cover in Chapter 8; see Chapter 7 for information on preparing to measure a process)

2. Making the process consistent by eliminating variability (see the later section "Using Control Charts Effectively")

3. Monitoring the process

4. Improving the process to get as close to the target value — what the customer wants — as possible (see the later section "Calculating Process Capability")

SPC builds on the statistics we discuss in Chapter 9 and applies those statistics to the activity of monitoring a production process. By monitoring your process, you can detect whether a change has occurred and track down the reason for the change before you start making bad products or delivering bad services.

In the following sections, we explain the basic concepts and tools of SPC and go over its advantages and disadvantages.

Don't limit your use of SPC to simple manufacturing processes. Businesses can use SPC both on the factory floor and in an office environment. It not only improves a manufacturing process, but also reduces problems with any business function. Within an office setting, SPC can reduce errors and improve the efficiency of administrative tasks such as data entry, invoice generation, order processing, and the creation of purchase orders.

The importance of the normal curve

Traditional quality control involves inspecting products after their creation and making judgments as to whether the items are suitable for customer use (see Chapter 4 for more about inspection). Statistical Process Control, on the other hand, uses statistical tools to monitor the performance of a production process over time to detect problems before the process can create products that don't meet customer specifications. The main assumption is that any process that produces a product will have some variation built in. No combination of machine and human can produce a product that's exactly the same each time.

For example, say you're drilling a hole that's designed to be 13.5 millimeters in diameter. Using a new drill bit and a calibrated drill, you start out making holes exactly 13.5 mm in diameter. But are the holes really 13.5 mm? If you measure to a greater precision than one decimal place, you may find that the diameter falls within a range, with 13.5 in the middle. For instance, a hole that you measure to three decimal places may be between 13.490 mm and 13.510 mm. As long as the holes stay within this range, though they're acceptable to the customer (see Chapter 6 for more about customer specifications).

However, over time, the drill bit may wear down (causing you to drill smaller holes), or the drill itself may start to go out of alignment (causing the holes to get bigger). Using traditional quality control inspection, you'd continue to drill holes until the diameter changed enough to where it no longer measured 13.5 mm, at which point you'd scrap any parts made with bad holes.

If you plot the frequency of the measurements in a histogram (we cover histograms in detail in Chapter 8), you end up with a chart similar to the one in Figure 10-1. You can see that most values are close to the average; fewer values occur the further you get from the average. We call this occurrence a *normal process.*

Figure 10-1: This frequency histogram depicts a normal process.

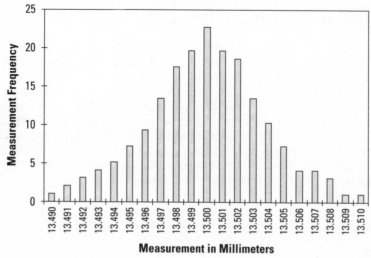

REMEMBER

If you connect the values in the histogram with a line, you create a curve, shown in Figure 10-2. The curve is called the *normal distribution curve,* or the *normal curve.* The normal curve is an important tool because it graphically shows the variation in a measured process. The wider the curve, the more a process varies, so, naturally, you want to make your curve as skinny as possible. You also want the average, or middle, part of your curve to be as close as possible to your customers' desired value for whatever it is you're measuring. Keep these goals in mind as you discover more detail about the SPC process in this chapter.

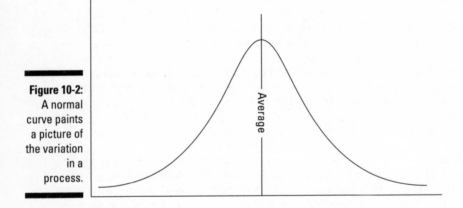

Figure 10-2:
A normal curve paints a picture of the variation in a process.

Average

Useful tools for calculating and plotting within SPC

Statistical Process Control isn't a single process-measuring tool; it's a collection of tools and techniques you use to improve your organization's quality output. The great thing about most SPC tools is that they're simple to implement (you need only basic graphing and math skills), and, when used in combination, they can tell you most everything you need to know about your production process. Although many of the concepts are based on some pretty deep statistics, you don't need to understand all the mathematical groundwork to use them to improve the quality of your processes. Knowing the statistics can help you understand your processes better (like anything else, the more you know, the better!), but you don't have to be an expert in statistics to use the output of the tools.

The following list presents the tools commonly used in SPC:

✔ **Flowcharts:** Excellent tools for visualizing a process. A good flowchart shows how a process works by documenting the flow of material or information through the process in sequential order. (You can find more info on flowcharts in Chapters 12 and 16.) The best time to use a flowchart is at the beginning of a quality improvement project to ensure that everyone agrees on how the process functions. Technically, flowcharts aren't statistical tools, but they give your organization a great way to start a quality project off on the right foot.

✔ **Histograms:** Great tools for graphically viewing quality data. Histograms are the primary tools used in SPC (see Chapter 8 for more). A histogram can tell you information about the average of quality data, the amount of variation in a data set, and what the pattern of the variation is. It also can illustrate how well the data stays within customer specifications (refer to Figure 10-1).

✔ **Scatter diagrams:** Designed to find a pattern in data or a relationship between two variables (see Chapter 8 for more information).

✔ **Pareto charts:** Great tools for getting the most bang for your buck in quality improvement efforts. Pareto charts show the most frequently occurring factors that cause quality problems, and they give you direction for tackling the most important problems first. (See Chapter 9 for more on Pareto charts.)

✔ **Run charts:** Graphs that show the values of processes over time or in sequence. A run chart can show a single factor in order to spot a trend, or it can show two factors to find out if a relationship exists. Run charts aren't based on statistics, but they're still useful for the aforementioned purposes. A run chart is your main tool for controlling your process on a day-to-day basis.

See Figure 10-3 for a sample run chart that shows the relationship between two values (in this case, temperature in a work area and the diameter of a hole in a part). Notice how two different Y-axes make it easier to see the relationship. The X-axis shows the sequence of the measurements taken. In this example, the lines for temperature and diameter seem to run together, so a relationship between the two attributes probably exists.

✔ **Control charts:** Simple, yet powerful tools for identifying whether an operation or process is in or out of control. Based on the idea of a run chart, a control chart adds the concept of control limits and a mean line that indicates when a process is getting out of control. Control charts are such an important part of SPC that we go into much more detail about them in the later section "Using Control Charts Effectively."

The pros and cons of SPC

Like any other quality control concept, Statistical Process Control has its pluses and its minuses. We cover both in the following sections.

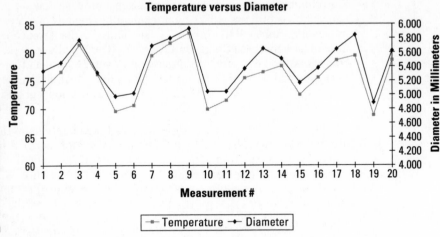

Figure 10-3:
A run chart can show the relationship between two factors.

The pros

Pluses of SPC include the following:

- ✔ Focuses on detecting and monitoring process improvement over time
- ✔ Guides you in taking the appropriate action to improve your production processes
- ✔ Helps you understand your organization's capability of achieving targets (usually based on customer specifications)

We assume that you won't use SPC because of your love for statistics (well, maybe you will; some of us do!). We assume that you'll use SPC for the same reason people do anything in business: to make more money. SPC helps your organization make more money by

- ✔ Improving the quality of your product or service
- ✔ Reducing waste
- ✔ Improving productivity
- ✔ Making your processes more efficient
- ✔ Improving customer service

The cons

Minuses of SPC include the following:

✔ SPC requires some understanding of statistics.

✔ SPC doesn't guarantee that you'll send no bad products to the customer.

✔ SPC is just a tool, and like any other tool, it derives much of its value from the skill of the people using it (see Chapter 5 for ideas on training employees).

Using Control Charts Effectively

What you really want to know through Statistical Process Control is whether your organization's production process is making items correctly based on customer specifications. Control charts are your best tools for tracking your process to detect variation that isn't caused by normal variation in the process, but rather by some fundamental change in the process that needs your attention. The bare-bones procedure for creating and interpreting a control chart is as follows:

1. Sample the process at some regular interval.

2. Plot whatever statistic you're using on a control chart.

3. Look at the chart to see if the process is in control.

4. If the process isn't in control, look for the cause and correct it.

In the following sections, we show you the ideas behind control charts, and we let you know how to use control charts in order to verify that your process actually does what it should be doing.

Detecting different types of variation

All control charts have the same basic purpose: to detect variation in a production process — unnatural variation that isn't a part of the normal process. You deal with two different types of variation in a process:

✔ **Common-cause variation:** The variation inherent in the process. As long as the process doesn't change, the common-cause variation stays the same. Common-cause variation is part of the production process for one or more reasons: because of the nature of the system, the way the process is operated, or the way the process is managed. You can change common-cause variation only by making a change to the process itself. For example, the precision of a machine used in drilling a hole determines how much variation is normal for that machine. If the machine is capable of centering the hole within 0.25 millimeters of the desired location, any variation within 0.25 millimeters of the desired location is the common-cause variation for that machine.

✔ **Special-cause variation:** Occurs when a change takes place in the process. It could be an undesirable change, such as a tool wearing out, or it could a desirable change, such as the implementation of a new machine that has less variation than the previous machine. Special-cause variation is usually due to some kind of exception to the process, and it's often specific to a particular machine, production shift, operator, or batch of raw material.

The main purpose of going through the SPC process is the identification and removal of undesirable special-cause variation. If you can explain the variation and identify it as a good thing (such as a more precise machine), you're okay; if not, you must track down the source of the change and remove it.

One of the keys to properly using SPC is correctly identifying a variation as common-cause or special-cause. It can be difficult to tell the difference, so we give you some tips in the later section "Reading a control chart."

Understanding a control chart's elements

Before we can talk about how to build a control chart, you need to know some terms in order to understand how it works; we cover the lingo you need to know in the following sections.

Population, sample, mean, and range

Four basic, yet important, statistical concepts are population, sample, mean, and range. Everything else you do builds on an understanding of these topics:

✔ *Population:* The entire group of members of whatever it is you're measuring or counting. If you're talking about a production process, the population is all the items that you produce by using that process.

✔ *Sample:* A subset of the population. In most cases, you can't test all the items you produce, so you have to test a representative sample. (Chapters 4 and 9 have the full scoop on the sampling process.)

✔ *Mean:* The arithmetic average of all the values that you measure for a given test. You calculate the mean by adding up all the individual measurements and then dividing by the total number of measurements.

✔ *Range:* From the largest to the smallest. For instance, customer satisfaction scores between 20 and 100 have a range of 80.

Standard deviation

Standard deviation is a measure of the range of a variation around the average of a group of measurements. In other words, it's the average distance that each measurement is from the mean of all the measurements. In Statistical Process

Control, the Greek letter sigma (σ) refers to the standard deviation of an entire population. (You can find out more about the use of sigma in Chapter 17.)

You calculate standard deviation by following these steps (we include a simple example throughout the steps to keep the math easy):

1. **Take the difference between each recorded measurement and the mean to get the deviation for each measurement.**

   Say you have the following five measurements: 6, 8, 7, 9, and 10. Add the measurements for a total of 40. Then divide 40 by 5 for a mean of 8.

   Now take the difference of each of these measurements from the mean:

   $$6 - 8 = -2$$
   $$8 - 8 = 0$$
   $$7 - 8 = -1$$
   $$9 - 8 = 1$$
   $$10 - 8 = 2$$

   So, your differences are –2, 0, –1, 1, and 2.

2. **Square each of these differences that you calculated in Step 1.**

   The squared values are the following:

   $$-2^2 = 4$$
   $$0^2 = 0$$
   $$-1^2 = 1$$
   $$1^2 = 1$$
   $$2^2 = 4$$

3. **Add each of the squared values from Step 2 together.**

   You have $4 + 0 + 1 + 1 + 4 = 10$.

4. **Divide the added value from Step 3 by the number of samples minus 1 (known as the *sample fudge factor*).**

   Subtract 1 from 5 for a total of 4, and then divide 10 by 4 for a total of 2.5.

5. **Take the square root of the value from Step 4.**

   The square root of 2.5 is 1.58, which is your standard deviation.

In the big picture, what the standard deviation tells you is that for most processes, 69 percent of all measurements fall within one deviation on either side of the mean; in the example, you should expect 69 percent of your measurements to be between (8 – 1.58) and (8 + 1.58), or between 6.42 and 9.58. In addition, expect 99.4 percent of all measurements to fall within two standard deviations and 99.9966 percent to fall within three standard deviations.

Control limits

The *control limits* (both an upper limit and a lower limit) are the ranges you use on your SPC control charts. All production processes fluctuate over time, but if the processes are stable, they'll stay with certain limits. Businesses normally set the control limits at three standard deviations (sigma), plus and minus, from the mean or target value (see the previous section for more on calculating sigma). Ideally, your mean is your target value. In the previous section's example, the values normally vary on either side of the mean.

You use control limits to guide your SPC process for two main reasons:

- ✔ You don't want to spend time on each little change in a process that's due to random chance.

- ✔ You don't want an excessive number of false alarms.

Checking out different kinds of control charts

You can use several different types of control charts for Statistical Process Control, with each one using a different statistic. You create different types of charts depending on the type of data you're collecting. The two types of data you focus on for control charts (we cover in detail the types of data in Chapter 4) are

- ✔ **Attribute (or discrete) data:** Data that references whether a certain condition exists, such as a color or a yes/no situation.

- ✔ **Variable (or continuous) data:** Data that you measure on a continuous scale, such as length, diameter, or temperature.

For variable data, here are the most commonly used control charts:

- ✔ **X-bar chart:** Tracks the mean of a set of samples over some period of time. X-bar (usually written as the letter "X" with a line over the top) is a statistical notation for the mean. This chart is probably the most commonly used control chart out there, as you normally want your process mean to equal the customer's specification.

- ✔ **R (Range) chart:** Used to track the range of a set of samples over time. In most cases, a low range is good; it indicates that your process is consistent.

In practice, you look at the X-bar and R charts together. Although range is important, by itself it doesn't tell the whole story. Range tells you how much variation you have in your process, but is no range always good? No! What if your customers want a 3-inch hole in a product and you send them products with 8-inch holes? The X-bar chart shows that you're outside the customer specification, but the R chart says everything is wonderful.

For attribute data, here are the most commonly used control charts:

- **p chart:** The "p" stands for the proportion (or percentage) of the sample that's defective.
- **np chart:** The "np" stands for the number (or count) of defective items in the sample.
- **u chart:** The "u" stands for the number of defects per unit in the sample.
- **c chart:** The "c" stands for the count of the defects from a sample.

Building a control chart

In this section, we walk you through the creation of a control chart with help from what's probably the most commonly used chart, an X-bar chart (see the previous section). We use Microsoft Excel to build the chart because most everyone has access to a copy of Excel.

Follow these steps to create an X-bar chart, using Microsoft Excel:

1. **Collect the sample data (as we explain in Chapter 8) and insert it into Excel.**

   See Figure 10-4 for an example. Each row in the spreadsheet represents a sample of five measurements (the test number is indicated in column A), with the measurements entered into columns B through F. In this case, we've taken 20 different samples of 5 measurements each. The samples could've been taken minutes apart or days apart — it depends on your process.

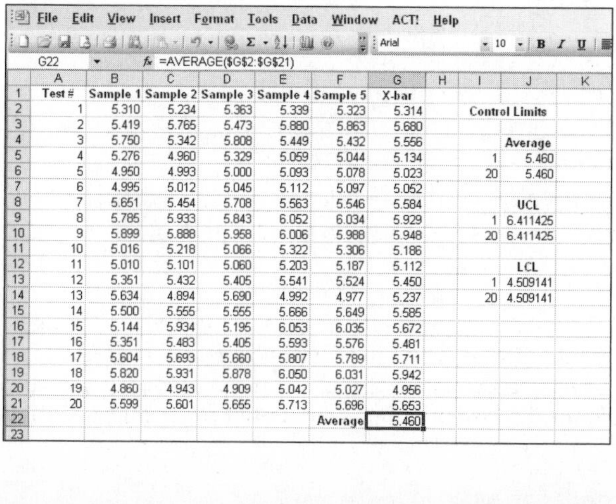

	A	B	C	D	E	F	G	H	I	J	K
1	Test #	Sample 1	Sample 2	Sample 3	Sample 4	Sample 5	X-bar				
2	1	5.310	5.234	5.363	5.339	5.323	5.314		Control Limits		
3	2	5.419	5.765	5.473	5.880	5.863	5.680				
4	3	5.750	5.342	5.808	5.449	5.432	5.556			Average	
5	4	5.276	4.960	5.329	5.059	5.044	5.134		1	5.460	
6	5	4.950	4.993	5.000	5.093	5.078	5.023		20	5.460	
7	6	4.995	5.012	5.045	5.112	5.097	5.052				
8	7	5.651	5.454	5.708	5.563	5.546	5.584			UCL	
9	8	5.785	5.933	5.843	6.052	6.034	5.929		1	6.411425	
10	9	5.899	5.888	5.958	6.006	5.988	5.948		20	6.411425	
11	10	5.016	5.218	5.066	5.322	5.306	5.186				
12	11	5.010	5.101	5.060	5.203	5.187	5.112			LCL	
13	12	5.351	5.432	5.405	5.541	5.524	5.450		1	4.509141	
14	13	5.634	4.894	5.690	4.992	4.977	5.237		20	4.509141	
15	14	5.500	5.555	5.555	5.666	5.649	5.585				
16	15	5.144	5.934	5.195	6.053	6.035	5.672				
17	16	5.351	5.483	5.405	5.593	5.576	5.481				
18	17	5.604	5.693	5.660	5.807	5.789	5.711				
19	18	5.820	5.931	5.878	6.050	6.031	5.942				
20	19	4.860	4.943	4.909	5.042	5.027	4.956				
21	20	5.599	5.601	5.655	5.713	5.696	5.653				
22						Average	5.460				
23											

Figure 10-4: Enter your collected data to start creating an X-bar control chart.

2. **Calculate the statistic for the type of chart you're creating.**

   In this case, you calculate the sample mean. Column G in Figure 10-4 uses the AVERAGE function in Excel to calculate the average for each sample.

3. **Calculate the mean for all the data collected.**

   In Figure 10-4, this value appears in cell G22. You calculate the figure by using the AVERAGE function of all the sample mean data in column G.

4. **Calculate the values for the control limits.**

   In Figure 10-4, the values for the upper and lower control limits (UCL and LCL) appear in columns I and J. The formula for the UCL is

   =$G$22+(3*STDEV($G$2:$G$21))

   You're using three sigma (or standard deviations) from the mean (stored in cell G22) as your control limit. The lower limit is the same formula, except that you subtract rather than add three sigma. The numbers 1 and 20 in column I represent the first and last test numbers to match up with the sample data when you draw your chart.

5. **Highlight the X-bar column from rows 1 through 21 and click the Chart Wizard button (or choose Chart from the Insert menu if you can't find the Chart Wizard button). Select the XY Scatter chart with data points connected, as shown in Figure 10-5.**

   This task creates the run chart on which your control chart will be based.

6. **Create the chart and adjust the chart options to make your chart look similar to the one in Figure 10-6.**

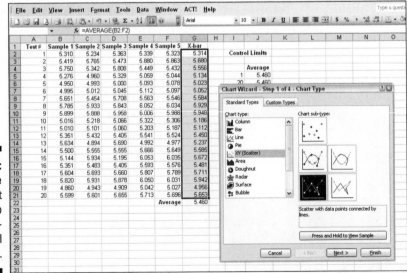

Figure 10-5: Use the Chart Wizard to create an X-bar control chart.

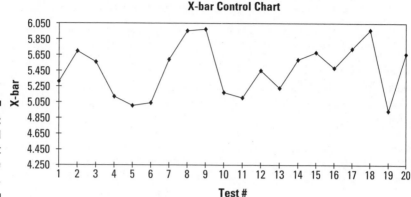

Figure 10-6:
This Excel
X-bar chart
plots the
mean data.

7. **Start adding the control limits with the average line (for this chart, you go with the center line). Highlight the values for the average (cells I5 to J6) and then move your cursor to one of the borders of the highlighted numbers.**

8. **Right-click and drag your cursor to the data area of the chart and release the mouse button. A dialog box will appear, as shown in Figure 10-7. Check the options shown in Figure 10-7, and click OK.**

9. **Repeat Step 8 for the upper and lower control limits.**

Your completed X-bar control chart should look like the one in Figure 10-8.

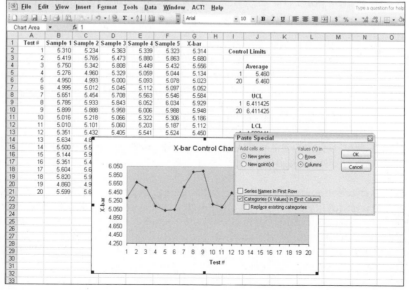

Figure 10-7:
Create the
control
limits in
Excel by
pasting your
average
values.

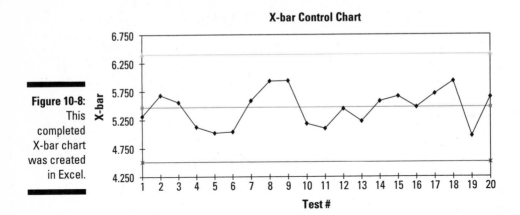

Figure 10-8: This completed X-bar chart was created in Excel.

Now that the X-bar chart is complete, take a look at what we've presented in Figure 10-8:

- ✔ The X-axis represents the sequence of samples that we took.
- ✔ The Y-axis represents the average (X-bar) for each set of samples we took.
- ✔ The center line on the chart represents the average of all the samples, which, if we've set up our process correctly, should be the desired value for each item made.
- ✔ The upper control limit (UCL) and the lower control limit (LCL) are the two other horizontal lines on the chart.
- ✔ The points on the chart are the mean values for the samples we took, each connected by a line.

 To create a different chart, you simply substitute X-bar with the desired statistic and follow the same steps. For example, to create an R chart, you calculate the range of each sample rather than the mean by changing column G to range and using the following Excel formula for each sample to get the range:

=MAX(B2:F2)-MIN(B2:F2)

Fit the range of the values on the X-axis, and you end up with a chart like the one shown in Figure 10-9.

 We recommend easy-to-use software packages over Microsoft Excel for long-term quality control use. Although Excel is capable of creating charts, using it on a production basis is difficult because the values must be updated and the chart redone with each new measurement. Find out what others are using in your industry, or research available packages by using an Internet search engine.

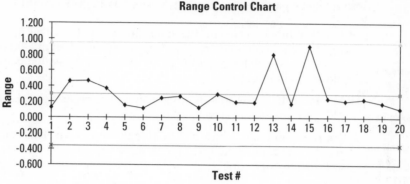

Figure 10-9:
You can
complete an
R chart in
Excel by
using a
unique
formula.

Reading a control chart

After you create one or more control charts, your next step is to evaluate what the charts say about your process. The basic idea is that the process should stay within the control limits; if it does, you conclude that the process is "in control." However, you need to look for other factors besides points outside the control limits that may suggest that your process is guilty of some kind of special-cause variation, which is a potential problem with your process (see "Detecting different types of variation," earlier in this chapter, for details). Check out the following sections for tips on evaluating any control chart.

Here are a couple of important assumptions that control charts make about the data that you plot:

- ✔ **Each data point is independent from every other data point.** This means that you can't predict future values from current values. The data you're measuring isn't affected by any value it held in the past.

- ✔ **The data is normally distributed.** This is statistic speak for "the data will vary around the average, with the most values being closer to the average." As you get farther from the average, the frequency of data decreases. (See "The importance of the normal curve," earlier in this chapter, for more information.)

Looking at both sides of the center line

Many forms of chart evaluation are based on statistical reasoning. For example, you can examine where your data falls relative to the center line of the chart. Because your sample should be clustered around the mean, there's a 50-50 chance (0.5) that any single sample is above or below the center line. Your samples are independent of each other, so the chance that two samples fall on the same side of the center line is 0.5×0.5, or 25 percent. Therefore, it stands to reason that if you get enough samples on the same side of the line in a row, your process may have a problem.

Here are some patterns to look for when evaluating your control chart:

✔ **Seven points in a row on the same side of the line.** This applies only to X-bar charts (see the section "Checking out different kinds of control charts" earlier in this chapter). This occurrence is statistically improbable and should be checked out.

✔ **Six points in a row steadily increasing or decreasing.** This is a good indicator that a tool is wearing out.

✔ **Fourteen points in a row alternating up and down.** This can indicate that two alternating factors are causing results to change, such as alternating operators.

✔ **Any other unusual pattern that you can't readily explain.**

Zooming in on zones

One common evaluation practice is to divide a control chart into three "zones" to look for patterns. You divide the area between the center line and each control limit into three zones, called A, B, and C:

✔ **Zone C** is the area between the center line and one sigma from the center line (see the earlier section "Standard deviation" to figure out a particular sigma).

✔ **Zone B** is the area between one and two sigma from the center line.

✔ **Zone A** is the area between two and three sigma from the center line.

Here are some patterns to look for within the control chart zones:

✔ **Two out of three points in a row in Zone A or beyond.** This pattern could mean that your whole process has shifted; that is, your process has changed in one direction so that now your process mean is different.

✔ **Four out of five points in a row in Zone B or beyond.** Again, this pattern could mean that your whole process has shifted.

✔ **Fifteen points in a row in Zone C.** This pattern could indicate that your process variability has changed. Such change isn't necessarily a bad thing; it could be an opportunity to tighten your control limits (see the later section "Changing your control limits").

Responding to different types of variation

After you detect a variation, what do you do about it? The first step is to determine whether the variation is of the special-cause type (probably bad) or of the common-cause variety (probably okay). Your control charts can alert you that you may have a problem, but by themselves they won't necessarily tell you what's causing the problem. The techniques in the following sections help you find the cause of the problem so you can fix it.

Don't get so wrapped up in statistics that you forget why you're doing all this work: to detect variation in your process as quickly as possible so you have time to get the process back on track before it starts making bad items.

Special-cause variation

If a production process that you examine with a control chart exhibits any of the patterns we describe in the earlier section "Reading a control chart," it may be out of control due to a special-cause variation. If the special cause is harmful (which is true in most cases), you need to eliminate it. If the special cause is beneficial, you should identify it and make it an official part of your process. The chart itself can't tell you whether the special cause is good or bad; you need to find the cause to make that determination.

You need to deal with special causes as quickly as possible while any unusual circumstances that may have created the special causes are fresh in your quality team's minds. Follow these steps when you discover a possible special cause:

1. **Fix any problems or damage immediately.** At this stage, you provide only a short-term fix until you can get to the real cause of the issue. Be careful not to make a long-term fix too quickly. For example, if a tool is wearing out, a short-term fix is to replace the part; a long-term solution may involve changing the process so the part wears out less frequently.

2. **Search for the cause of the variation.** Interview everyone involved in the production process to find out if anything unusual occurred that may explain the variation. Be careful not to blame individuals because you'll want their cooperation in the future. Keep careful records about the process under examination, as this problem or a similar one may occur again in the future.

3. **Develop a long-term solution after you identify the special cause for the variation.** Remove the special cause if it has a negative effect on your process. Make the special cause an official part of your process if it has a positive impact.

Common-cause variation

What if your process doesn't exhibit any of the special-cause variation we discuss in the earlier section "Reading a control chart"? Does that mean you can just kick back and enjoy the view? Of course not! Your process may be consistent and still produce bad products or services. What if we told you that you could reduce even the common-cause variation in your process so that you could increase your quality and lower the cost? Yep, we thought you'd be interested. Although achieving this feat is harder than finding and eliminating special-cause variation, you may just find the process very worthwhile.

Even with processes that are working well, businesses can usually find plenty of good ideas floating around in employees' heads. If only someone would just ask! Here are three commonly used processes for finding and eliminating common-cause variation:

✔ **Stratification** of data is simply the separation of data in categories (Chapter 8 has an overview of stratification). You can use stratification on different categories and levels within categories to search for patterns. Categories can consist of a single variable, such as production by machine, or multiple variables, such as shifts and assembly lines.

Be careful not to read too much into stratification by taking small differences between categories too seriously. Only the larger differences are worthy of your attention. Also, don't assume that any differences you find are automatically the cause of the problem with your process; the categories you identify may not hold the actual problem, only clues to the actual cause.

✔ **Experimentation** is the concept of testing a theory about the cause of a problem, even though you have little or no data to support your theory. In Statistical Process Control, you use the *Plan-Do-Check-Act cycle* (or PDCA cycle), first described by Walter Shewhart and made popular by W. Edwards Deming (a student of Shewhart and a famous quality guru in his own right). The cycle is really nothing more than taking a scientific method that's been around for several centuries and applying it to quality control. The PDCA cycle uses experimentation and observation to discover the root causes of quality problems; Chapter 3 has more details.

You can repeat experimentation over and over to make continuous improvements to your production process. It requires both creative and analytic thinking to move past how your organization handles production today to come up with new and innovative solutions.

✔ **Disaggregation** is the process of breaking down a process into its individual components in order to isolate the cause of a problem. You can use the tactic in tandem with either experimentation or stratification to uncover problems that may not be apparent within your process when examined as a whole. Think of disaggregation as a way to see the forest and the trees at the same time. For example, if you're evaluating the quality of classroom instruction for a particular subject, you may need to break the data down further by teacher to reach the cause of the problem.

You need to make sure that you don't optimize a single part of the process at the expense of the final objective of the process. For example, if you speed up the process of making pizzas for delivery faster than you can deliver the pizzas, you haven't really improved the entire process of making and delivering pizzas to your customers.

Part III

Whipping Quality Control into Shape with Lean Processes

The 5th Wave   By Rich Tennant

"Ted and I spent more than 120 man-hours together evaluating the quality data, and here's what we discovered: Ted borrows pens and never returns them, he intentionally squeaks his chair to annoy me, and, evidently, I talk in my sleep."

In this part . . .

A Lean organization is one that has examined its processes and squeezed all the waste out of them. The company minimizes work-in-process materials and focuses the entire workforce on continuous improvement. Achieving Lean status is a tall order and takes companies many years to accomplish. They constantly dig deeper into why processes are the way they are and work to make them the way they ought to be. In this part, we introduce the general concept of Lean and provide handy tips on implementing specific Lean methods.

The first action of Lean, after implementing Value Stream Mapping for a clear view of your current process, is to clean up the workplace. Some workers never let go of any materials, causing junk to pile high and obscure the work that needs to be done. Using a process called 5S, you can clean out workplaces and organize them for efficient action and quick changeover. If a particularly troublesome area is holding up important work, a Rapid Improvement Event can quickly 5S an area and implement Lean concepts at the same time. This one-week event is fast-paced and requires considerable planning, but we prepare you here.

Last but not least: An area that many companies labor with is minimizing the amount of on-site materials. Kanban is a technique for minimizing work-in-process materials and for rapidly responding to customer requests that always circulate as "hot jobs." We show you the Kanban way here.

Chapter 11

Gathering the Nuts and Bolts of Lean Processes

*P*eople in the business world have tossed around the term "Lean processes" ever since Japanese automakers seized a large share of the North American market by using them. The idea behind going Lean is simple. A non-Lean (fat?) process is bloated with waste. Waste lowers product or service quality and increases cost, much like buying food and drink at a ballgame or concert. A Lean process, therefore, focuses on customer satisfaction and cost reduction by eliminating waste.

In this chapter, you find out about the principles behind Lean processes, different types of waste in organizations, and mapping a process to reveal wasteful tendencies. You also find out about two important tools in Lean processes: Takt Time and the 5 "Why's."

Chapters 13, 14, and 15 go into more detail on several important Lean concepts: 5S, Rapid Improvement Events (RIEs), and Lean Materials and Kanban. You also can check out *Lean For Dummies,* by Bruce Williams and Natalie Sayer (Wiley), for more intensive information.

Boning Up on the Lean Basics

You can't make an omelet without breaking a few eggs. Likewise, changing a company's actions from current practices to Lean processes requires some changes. But before you break any eggs, take a few moments to understand the foundations of Lean and how you may apply the concept to your business. In the following sections, you discover the principles that guide Lean, the major steps for implementing Lean, and the pros and cons of going Lean.

Considering Lean cornerstones

Many companies have embraced the concept of Lean as a reaction to poor customer response or as a preventive measure to always produce high-quality products and satisfy customers. Some choose to implement selected Lean tools in particular segments of their businesses. Others make Lean a cornerstone of their company cultures. Although the Lean approaches and results may differ, all Lean initiatives have a couple of elements in common. A Lean process

- ✔ Continuously focuses on the elimination of waste
- ✔ Always strives to exceed customer expectations

These two fundamentals — waste elimination and exceeding customer expectations — are the keystones within Lean processes.

"Muda," the Japanese word for waste, is most often recognized in the business world as time, effort, material, and information that don't add value for the customer; therefore, they don't add value to the process they're involved with (see Chapter 12 for more about nonvalue additions). You meet and exceed customer expectations when you eliminate waste. To the customer, improvement may be reflected in

- ✔ Improved cycle times (the length of time required from receiving an order to delivering it)
- ✔ Reduced pricing
- ✔ Increased quality levels

Within the organization, you can see the effects of Lean in

- ✔ Reduced inventory levels
- ✔ Cost improvement
- ✔ Reduced space requirements

Other principles support the elimination of waste and the goal of exceeding customer expectations. These principles include careful planning of production schedules, prompt attention to quality problems, and worker involvement (they often have the best ideas).

Taking important steps for getting Lean and mean

The steps in the following sections support your organization's Lean journey. Your organization needs to address all the steps, but the sequence in which you move and the emphasis you place on the different steps depends on your specific situation.

An organization can view processes at the micro level, such as the process of answering a phone, or from a broader perspective, such as the process of taking a customer order. Lean tools, when implemented in an established company, are best applied at the micro level. A company can attempt to tackle higher-level processes after it Leans some of the component processes. As the company Leans its processes, it may evolve into a Lean enterprise. The company shouldn't view the transformation as a one-time initiative; instead, it should adopt a long-term, enterprise-wide view of all processes. Lean operating principles become the overall culture of the organization, with the elimination of waste as the target for improvement based on exceeding customer expectations.

Agree on areas to target

Before you target certain processes for Lean, you should start by addressing the core value stream of the organization. The important thing for Lean is that the top executives agree on the areas to target and involve themselves in the process of the change. This agreement and involvement does two things:

- It demonstrates the commitment of the leaders.
- It allows the leaders to identify waste in the organization's core processes.

All workers involved in the Lean movement should view the changes from the perspective of changing the culture of the organization and demonstrating a "bias for action."

Here's some advice for company leaders: Take the time to do your homework before you jump in. There's plenty more to becoming Lean than just implementing a single tool or changing a single process. People have written books on the process of implementing Lean, and legions of consultants, integrators, and other professionals are ready to help (see Chapter 5 for details on finding these folks). Talk with other companies that are sound examples of Lean enterprises or are solidly on their way; most of these organizations will be willing to share their experiences. Benchmarking is an excellent way to find out about the processes that support Lean organizations.

You shouldn't copy *exactly* what other successful Lean companies have done. No executives or workers want to repeatedly hear that "this is the way Company X does it." Internalize the change, and make it your culture. Your objective is to become a "learning organization." Nurture and develop your leaders from within; you'll need them to grow.

Install Lean leaders

Most successful Lean transitions have the support of a Lean "guru" — someone who serves as a mirror to the actions of the enterprise to make sure changes always move in a Lean direction. The guru may be a top leader; at a minimum, the guru should be a leader recognized for his or her ability to influence others. Many companies bring in an expert from the outside. This expert is considered to be a neutral party and isn't initially associated with any internal faction.

Be careful that outsourcing a guru doesn't send the wrong signal to the current leadership group. If you send a message that the only path to success is to enter from the outside, your company may begin to lose knowledgeable, talented, experienced leaders.

Chapter 5 has more details on selecting a sponsor for quality initiatives.

Implement communication and training

Communicating information about Lean throughout your organization is important. Lean is a change from the traditional manufacturing mindset. It's important that all workers be trained on understanding and applying Lean techniques, that early examples of success be made available to illustrate how Lean works, and that all workers maintain a dialogue so that positive experiences are shared and misunderstandings about Lean are corrected.

Unfortunately, managers often think that informing employees about Lean changes leads directly to action — it seldom does. You need to supplement your communication with training. Your workers need to understand the information you present. Look for commitment. Write down and post agreements. You can train effectively in a chalkboard environment, but nothing beats hands-on learning. Use training sessions as a means of supporting the changes you make in a process. Encourage managers and executives to roll up their sleeves and get involved in implementing or supporting the changes.

Chapter 5 has details on communicating your quality intentions and training employees on quality methods.

Concentrate on value streams

Most organizations are structured along functional lines. However, the products or services created run across various departments, so examining how departments work doesn't help. Examine the key value streams of your enterprise. What's the primary value of your product or service to the customer? If you provide multiple products or services, which ones provide the greatest profit or are the most important to your company?

After you identify the value streams, you can select one to improve. For example, an assembly line operator working on the main value stream must be your primary focus for support. As important as researching new technology may be, it isn't the main value stream in this case. You begin concentrating on Leaning your value stream with the receipt of customer requests and finish with delivery of the product or service.

Strong, seemingly functional departments that have great value to your organization may resist Lean changes. Skillful leadership is required to bring the team together in pursuit of what's best for the overall process.

Select metrics that reflect overall performance to focus on as an organization. Dealing with too many micro metrics will muddle the Lean transition. Keep all eyes on the overall performance measurements.

Develop process maps as a guide

A *process map* is a picture that shows how a product, a piece of information, or a service is transitioned to a finished good. The map begins with a specific event and ends with a specific deliverable. Creating a process map that documents how a process currently operates — a *current state map* — helps to make waste more visible. The current state map also forms the basis for describing where you plan to go — the *future state* — and ultimately describes what would be the ideal state for your process and deliverable product or service.

Making the current state of a process visible with a process map is a great way to identify waste and make immediate change. The current state should show where problems are in terms of defects, wasted time, wasted money, and so on. A visible future state map helps everyone involved in the process understand where your organization plans to go. The future state should depict the solutions in terms of goals for reducing defects, time, and cost. Any changes you make to a process should always move toward the ideal state, or your organization's ultimate goal for improvement.

See the section "Identifying the Seven Wastes That Can Plague a Process," later in this chapter, to find out how to identify waste. Also, Chapter 12 discusses the concept of drawing a picture of your process.

Focus on waste elimination

You can use several Lean tools to focus your organization's attention on waste elimination. You can structure process mapping (see the previous section) and 5S workshops (see Chapter 13), for instance, in a cross-functional Kaizen event. (*Kaizen* is the Japanese word for continuous improvement; see Chapter 14 for more about Kaizen events, also known as Rapid Improvement Events.) Chapter 15 discusses another option: Lean Materials.

Waste elimination is a cornerstone of a Lean enterprise, not a one-time exercise (see the earlier section "Considering Lean cornerstones"). Processes are constantly fine-tuned to optimize performance through worker suggestions for ways to eliminate waste. It never ends.

Follow up to ensure that improvements are sustained

Conducting a successful Lean event, where you eliminate the waste from a process to make a better product or service, is a great first step. However, you shouldn't let the success slip away; not being fully committed to the new process will send the wrong message to your organization and industry. Your leaders must demonstrate commitment at the line level, with managers as the change leaders, and the top leadership group should show its support.

You have several ways to ensure that fixed processes remain fixed, including the following:

- The work team conducts a review one week after the change is made to discuss any new problems that the change may have created. Some companies do this again after four weeks.

- Update all the process work instructions to use the revised process.

- Implement performance metrics based on how well the process performed after the change. Update these measurements weekly, and post the results over time. If performance isn't improving, a supervisor must investigate why.

Successes make good models. Use successes within and outside of your organization as examples your workers can observe to better understand Lean concepts. Interview employees about what they've done to reinforce the lessons learned and to sustain results.

Weighing the pros and cons of Lean

Lean techniques can transform a sluggish company into a more profitable dynamo. However, introducing something new is always disruptive. If the change is poorly done, the disruption can be serious; the entire change (the good with the bad) is discarded, and life returns to the old way. So, you should focus on the good, work toward the good, and avoid the bad. The following sections cover the good and the bad of Lean.

The pros

Lean processes produce four primary types of benefits, the first of which leads to the latter three:

- Elimination of waste
- Improved quality

> ✔ Reduced lead time
>
> ✔ Reduced total costs

These four benefits are the classic goals of many quality initiatives outside of Lean process improvements.

Other advantages of Lean include the following:

> ✔ An organization can apply Lean techniques to all types of processes.
>
> ✔ In most cases, changing to Lean doesn't require an increase in capital costs — it simply calls for the reassignment of people to more productive purposes.
>
> ✔ Lean processes uncover deficiencies in production planning and materials management that were hidden (and unaddressed) in current processes.
>
> ✔ Lean energizes workers as they see how it simplifies their work.

The cons

Transitioning to Lean processes has many benefits, but the road to molding a Lean enterprise can be littered with disadvantages:

> ✔ As with any quality change, a certain level of support is required when implementing Lean initiatives — particularly amongst employees. From the line workers to the executive ranks, everyone should be supportive of the Lean changes, or at least not resistant to them. Recognizing the need for change within a successful organization isn't easy. The classic attitude, "If it's not broken, don't fix it," is prevalent in many successful organizations. (See Chapter 5 for more on getting employee support.)
>
> ✔ Sculpting a well-functioning Lean process, though it may seem quite simple, is complicated. Lean thinking isn't necessarily natural for most businesspeople. An organization that wants to be Lean must become a learning organization, willing to take measured risks and grow. Transitioning to a Lean enterprise requires that all employees are properly trained, educated, and supported. Managers need to be hands-on implementers of Lean initiatives and willing to sustain process improvement. Executives need to adopt long-term strategies that move the entire enterprise to become Lean. All these requirements seem daunting, but they're worth it in the end.
>
> ✔ Lean isn't suitable for processes that require a high degree of craftsmanship. Artisanship takes time; a creative process trades inefficiency for creative results.

If key executives in your company aren't willing or can't make the commitment to Lean processes, consider limiting your Lean transformation to a short-term implementation of Lean tools.

Identifying the Seven Wastes That Can Plague a Process

The elimination of waste is one of the keystones of Lean processes, making it the perfect place to start a Lean transformation. To eliminate waste in your processes, you need to understand how to identify waste. You may think that you know waste when you see it, but you'll have a much smoother transition if you understand a few key issues and agree on types of waste. ***Note:*** Be careful not to label everything that a manager doesn't like about a process as "waste." This type of insincere action undermines the process of change.

The seven types of waste in the following sections serve as the common framework in defining waste. Chapters 12 through 15 include helpful methods you can use to eliminate these wastes.

The seven kinds of waste grew out of the Toyota Production System (TPS). As a result, their descriptions and many of the examples rely on manufacturing processes. With the evolution of Lean and other quality improvement techniques, the business world has transitioned to looking at the overall supply chain, service industries, and other areas for waste. Examining a supply chain simply requires looking outside the four walls of a factory and recognizing the movement from facility to facility, utilizing different forms of transport. When you look at a production facility, the product flows from machine to machine and process to process; the end result is the delivery of a quality product to the customer. The same is true of a service. The product may not be as visible, but the process still involves a flow that ultimately adds value. Waste is still waste, whether it exists inside a small workstation or around the world.

Some experts add an eighth type of waste: the underutilization of skilled employees. Why use the time of a skilled tradesman, manager, or data-processing technician for performing simple clerical work? Every employee must do some portion of simple documentation, but in some cases, paperwork can consume a skilled person's day.

Waste of overproduction

Overproduction occurs any time a process makes more of a product or part than what the next customer in line needs. Overproduction is one of the most prevalent types of waste, but it can be difficult to recognize. This makes it the perfect place to start identifying and eliminating waste. Want another reason to start here? Getting rid of overproduction is likely to yield some of the greatest rewards.

If you're involved in manufacturing, you should look for piles of inventory. If a process creates large batches with the intention of yielding high productivity, the result is a single operation that experiences high productivity while subsequent processes waste time handling products that they don't need. Another common place for waste is in areas where you store stationary supplies. How many places can you find an inventory of lined pads waiting for use? Start with the people who use the pads and work back to the source. You'll probably find many drawers and cabinets devoted to storing this material. What about pens, forms, e-mail, files, and so on?

The rationale for overproducing is often protection and efficiency. No company wants to run out of an item. Executives may believe that processing in large batches is efficient for the overall process. Both of these justifications, however, run counter to even production flow and producing to the cadence of customer demand (see the later section "Moving to the Beat of Takt Time" for more about Lean production rates). In the case of protection, overproduction masks other problems, such as poor supplier quality (internal and external). For more on having too much inventory, see Chapter 15.

Waste of waiting

The *waste of waiting* is pretty self-explanatory. You can easily spot people standing around, not being productive. In fact, most managers have personal experience with this type of waste. Have you ever been the customer waiting in a checkout line, wandering through a store looking for an item, or waiting on the phone for assistance? Quality teams can identify this type of waste in manufacturing, service, administration, and all other environments. Eliminating waiting allows workers to focus on their jobs.

Waiting is a topic that many employees will freely identify and discuss. How many times have they complained about waiting for someone or something to appear? They may be waiting for a PC technician, for parts delivery, or even for a decision from a manager. In some cases, other work can fill the time, but other times, the waiting results in idle workers.

Another sad consequence of the waste of waiting is when employees act busy to avoid the appearance of waiting. By doing other non-value-adding activities (see Chapter 12 for details), employees create another form of less-visible waste. The common executive decree, "Don't just stand there — do something," often compels workers to trade one form of waste for another.

On occasion, waiting can be difficult to avoid — especially in processes that feature a high degree of variation to the inputs. You do, however, have ways to make the best of wasteful situations. One way is to provide secondary work that isn't time-essential. When primary work isn't available, workers begin on secondary efforts, such as assembling small components and resupplying other workers in continuous effort assignments.

Waste of unnecessary transportation

Transportation waste is time (labor), equipment, and floor space spent shuffling material around. Perhaps the best way to analyze transportation waste is to identify the shortest/quickest path when moving from the start of a process to the end. You can identify the following as waste on the journey:

- ✔ Places where workers stack material in one place for a while, move it to where people will eventually use it in the process, and then move it to the point of application. Each of these moves takes time and equipment.

- ✔ Long distances between where the material enters the facility and where workers use it. It's time consuming to truck materials from the rear docks of a two-million-square-foot factory to the front area.

Look for the following clues of unnecessary transportation waste in different workplaces:

- ✔ **Manufacturing:** Wasted transportation may take the form of conveyors that move products long distances, when locating departments closer together would be a better method of operation. Just because an item is on a conveyor doesn't mean that the process isn't wasteful. Machines such as conveyors may eliminate the need for operators to move the material, but they require maintenance and aren't flexible tools.

  Movement of overproduction to holding areas is another common wasteful transportation move in manufacturing. The more overproduction you have, the more space and transportation you require to handle the situation. (I cover the waste of overproduction earlier in this chapter.)

- ✔ **Service, administration, and other soft-product processes:** When an office responsible for handling paper isn't in close proximity to operators who handle products, a form of transportation must move the paper back and forth. This slows the updating of records, which negatively impacts cycle times. All the handoffs in a process — between employees, departments, and organizations — are potential areas for transportation waste.

Eliminating transportation waste provides several financial benefits:

- ✔ It eliminates the steady flow of forklifts from the warehouse to various points on the shop floor. Similarly, it eliminates long conveyors that move material long distances around the facility. Both are expensive to purchase and maintain.

✔ It eliminates the labor spent moving material to an endless string of interim stops.

✔ It provides many benefits under the waste of eliminating excess inventory, which is covered later in this chapter.

Waste from unneeded processing steps

Be careful that a *Kaizen* project (see Chapter 14) you undertake isn't Leaning an unnecessary process step. It isn't uncommon for a business to identify very efficient tasks that don't add value to the overall process. Eliminating process steps is a great area for checking customer expectations. Ever received a report and sent it straight to a file or the trash? Stop producing a report for a while to see if anyone notices. If an action doesn't add value to a product or service in the eyes of the customer, stop doing it!

In manufacturing operations, the flow of material and products is visible. Waste within the process is often visible, too, particularly to outsiders who are likely to ask why something operates the way it does. Identifying waste in information processing is a bit more difficult, although the opportunities are greater. Creating a report that's simple and to the point may be difficult, but creating a complicated report or analysis is not only wasteful for the preparer, but also takes added (wasted) time for the recipient to digest and understand the information. When eliminating waste, look for unnecessary reviews and approvals. One common step to avoid action is to further analyze or question pieces of data. Looking at all the steps in a process and asking "why" is a great way to identify and eliminate waste (find out more about asking "why" later in this chapter).

Eliminating unneeded processing provides immediate benefits:

✔ **Reduced labor costs:** More time is available for productive labor.

✔ **Reduced defects:** Each step in a process is a chance to do something wrong. The fewer steps a process has, the fewer chances workers have to make mistakes.

✔ **Reduced material costs:** This applies if the eliminated steps used materials.

Waste of excess inventory

Excess inventory is material beyond what's needed for the task at hand. In a perfect one-piece flow process, cadenced to customer demand (see the later section "Moving to the Beat of Takt Time" for details), you see no excess inventory; all the inventory is in the process, moving toward the customer. Of course, a perfect state rarely exists, so you must view most of the inventory in your processes as waste that you need to reduce and possibly eliminate.

When walking through your factory, warehouse, office, or other place of business, look around for piles or stashes of inventory. In a factory or warehouse setting, excess inventory may appear as raw material or other process inputs. It also may appear as goods and services that workers are processing or that are finished and awaiting use. Outside the factory or warehouse, check file cabinets for excess supplies, obsolete information, and other forms of waste. And keep in mind that inventory isn't just in the form of physical products. Documents, forms, tools, and other items are inventory.

Eliminating excess inventory provides some benefits:

✔ Excess inventory represents money spent by the company to purchase materials and, if the material is partly finished, the labor to create that component. Less inventory means less money spent.

✔ Excess inventory must be stored and tracked somehow. Less inventory requires less storage and tracking.

Perhaps the most damaging waste associated with excess inventory is that it hides problems. Excess inventory often covers for poor product quality; companies stock more because some of the material is defective. When supply processes aren't dependable (shipments aren't on time, aren't delivered properly, and so on), companies can stock more to cover for this inadequacy. These and other problems remain hidden by excess inventory. As your organization implements Lean processes and reduces inventories, be prepared to address the problems that inevitably surface. (For more on eliminating excess inventory, see Chapter 15 on Lean Materials.)

Waste of unnecessary motion

Unnecessary motion is excess movement by an operator. The waste may be as extreme as requiring an employee to walk a long distance to obtain supplies rather than storing them within easy reach. Or, the waste may be as simple as the operator having to sort through an unorganized or improperly marked file to obtain required information.

You can find wasted motion in manufacturing operations as well as in clerical or administrative tasks. As you walk through a process, ask yourself:

✔ Can you find cluttered work surfaces where tools don't sit in well-marked locations?

✔ Are telephones located in convenient spaces so that employees can easily reach them, or do they have to make uncomfortable movements to answer calls?

✔ Do you have pens and paper on hand for recording required information?

Excess motion not only wastes time, but also presents a safety and ergonomic issue that negatively impacts the health of employees. An electrical extension cord, stretched across the room from an overhead projector to the nearest electrical outlet, requires employees to take extra care to avoid injury. A mistake here may damage the projector or may injure the employee in a fall. Other actions, such as straining to see a computer screen or typing from an improper position, may lead to ergonomic problems.

Tired workers make mistakes. They're grumpy and no fun to work with. Time spent studying worker motions and providing assistance is always appreciated. Most companies have a staff engineer trained in ergonometric studies to identify and resolve problems.

Injured workers also cost companies money. Lifting heavy objects, which leads to twisted backs and sore knees, adds up to worker fatigue and more defects. Happy workers are far more productive than hurting, tired ones.

Waste of defective products

A *defective product* is one that doesn't meet the customer's requirements. Creating a defective product is wasteful enough, but attempting to correct a defect is pure waste. The extra waste begins with the inspection process. The added time taken to inspect may prevent a defective product from reaching the customer, but the effort is still wasteful. After the inspection detects the defect, you must expend extra energy correcting, reworking, and disposing. All this is wasted time and effort to fix a defective product that you should've created correctly in the first place. If the product is made right the first time, you have no need to inspect it (see Chapter 4 for more on inspection).

The worst possible situation occurs when the customer detects the problem. You now must deal with the customer's dissatisfaction. Corrective action is often much more difficult than finding a problem before it reaches the customer. A product return routinely costs four times what the delivery process sets you back. Unless your business has a huge profit margin, return and replacement of a defective product is a sure path to loss. Inspection, though wasteful, is surely a better option until the process can be improved to create defect-free products.

A much Leaner process is one that's "error-proofed." Ever started to complete the assembly-required step after purchasing a product only to find that one of the nuts or bolts is missing from the baggie containing all the parts? Not a pleasant situation. The company could address the problem with packaging that has a specific slot for each item. Perhaps the company doesn't perfectly error-proof the process, but its solution does make a problem more visible.

Having standardized, documented work processes is another tool in preventing quality problems. Good Lean processes often require that you check quality problems against the standardized work process to determine what created an error. Attention to sound process design and adherence to the process are essential if you want to produce a quality product and eliminate waste. (See Chapter 3 for more about quality assurance.)

Everyone can think of products they've found to be defective. Likewise, they can think of products they like and recommend to others as reliable. Benefits of defect-free products include

- ✔ Reduced marketing costs through repeat customers
- ✔ Reduced or eliminated inspection costs (However, don't eliminate inspectors until *after* the process reliably produces defect-free products or services.)
- ✔ Reduced liability because safety is built into every product, every time

Creating defect-free services is an entirely different animal than creating defect-free products. Products can be mass-produced in advance, but service involves an interaction with the customer each time, and each interaction is different.

Moving to the Beat of Takt Time

One of the key elements of a successful Lean process is the consistent flow of work (parts or products) with minimal variation (in other words, minimal waste and costly labor). For most organizations, having successful Lean processes means that they set production to the cadence of customer demand — a concept known as *Takt Time*. In the following sections, you find out how to calculate customer demand to satisfy the army of consumers you serve, set Takt Time for your processes, examine effective process design, and balance the overall flow of your process in order to have successful Lean processes.

Listening to customer demand

Because the goal of Lean processes is to have a consistent process that cadences production to customer demand, you need to understand customer demand. This may sound easy, but it isn't. Many businesses operate in a "Push" environment, where the goal is to keep machines busy churning out the products. These companies rely on sales teams to influence demand and somehow sell what the companies have produced. Other organizations must wait for demand. In the service industry, companies maintain a certain amount of inventory as buffers and then replenish the buffers as customers consume them. The service adds value to the customer by being immediately available. (See Chapter 6 for more on the voice of the customer and Chapter 15 for more on a Push environment.)

You can observe a wide variety of customer-demand requirements in manufacturing and service industries. Different companies take varying approaches to satisfying customer demand. What separates a Lean enterprise is that it focuses first on customer requirements (demand) and then sets up its production processes to satisfy the customer, all without creating waste.

You can estimate customer demand in a variety of ways (all of which are indicators and no guarantee of success):

- ✔ Market projections for total demand, usually published by industry groups
- ✔ Age of existing customer equipment
- ✔ Information from customers (from a vehicle like a survey)

Many enterprises are internally focused. They set production based on a variety of internal metrics (production targets, inventory turnover, budgets, forecasts, and so on). Internal metrics aren't bad things; in fact, they're often key tools within Lean enterprises. However, metrics should be secondary to focusing on customer demand.

Setting the process tempo and considering process design

When you have a grasp on your customers' requirements, you can set the tempo of your processes to satisfy your customers (and avoid waste or leaving your customers without the necessary supply). Companies that fail to do this find themselves with piles of finished goods that their customers don't want. Here's how you can calculate Takt Time to set a process tempo:

Total available work time per shift or per day ÷ Customer demand per shift or per day

For example, say your customers purchase 16,800 units per month, and your process works 20 days per month. You must produce 840 units per day. If your workday has 7 productive hours (or 420 minutes), you must produce one unit every 30 seconds. This is the overall rate of production when all your processes are connected. However, each task doesn't necessarily create a single piece every 30 seconds.

See Figure 11-1 for an example of examining a process design. Within a Takt Time of 30 seconds, you can evaluate different processes to see which ones need adjustments to satisfy customer demand. For this example, all the units of production must first go through Process A, and it takes five minutes to complete this process. Ten workstations perform Process A to produce a unit every 30 seconds. You can follow the chronological thought process that ensues:

1. Following the flow, suppose 50 percent of the output from Process A must go through Processes B and C, and the other 50 percent must go through Process D.

2. If Process B can produce a unit every two minutes, Process C produces a unit every 30 seconds. Four B workstations and one C workstation maintain the one-unit-in-30-seconds Takt Time.

3. However, you can see that Process D produces a unit in 0.4 minutes (or 24 seconds). This rate is faster than the Takt Time and needs to be adjusted.

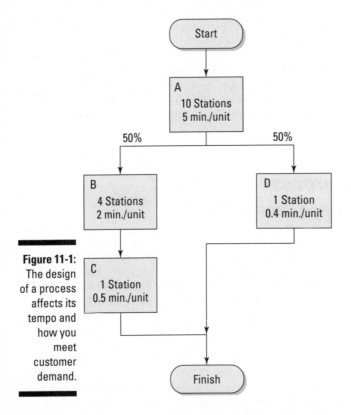

Figure 11-1:
The design of a process affects its tempo and how you meet customer demand.

The tempo of a process's production depends on the design of the process. Some processes take longer than others. For processes that can't be completed faster, parallel workstations must be established to work on more than one item at a time. If a facility has physical limitations on the rate that it can produce an item (such as everything must pass through a single, very unique machine), it can add additional work shifts to maximize this constraint (see Chapter 19 for more about identifying and maximizing constraints).

Balancing for a smooth flow

All processes aren't created equal, even in Lean operations. When you look at your total operation, connecting all the necessary processes, you're likely to find that some of the processes have individual requirements.

Work in a process must be balanced for the smooth flow of products. The key to balancing work is to understand all the work steps at each workstation. Workflow smoothing should first try to eliminate all unnecessary movement. Next, adjacent steps receive actions that they can perform without special tools, in essence moving small slices of the work up- and downstream.

For example, Task 1 finishes work on an item and passes it to Task 2, but Task 1 can deliver items faster than Task 2 can complete them. To rebalance some of the work, Task 1 takes on some of Task 2's work. When Task 1 is finished with an item, it now flips it over and orients it so that Task 2 can go right to work, eliminating the need for Task 2 to do this. It's a small action, but it saves time.

Getting to the Heart of an Issue with the 5 "Why's"

The *5 Why's,* a basic tool within Lean operations, is a problem-solving process that encourages your organization to ask questions to discover the root cause of a problem. The idea behind this tool is a fundamental cultural element of Lean enterprises. Creating and maintaining an environment that truly values asking "Why?" for the sake of continuous improvement is a major shift from traditional business ways. It works to reverse the trend to fix blame on individuals. To use this tool, you don't have to ask five specific questions; the goal is simply to keep asking "Why?" about a problem until you find its cause.

In the following sections, you discover how to unearth the root of a problem, and you go over ways to improve your company's environment so that all employees may feel free to ask questions.

Digging to find the real problem

When people encounter a problem, many immediately jump to a conclusion and think that they have the solution. The first order of business when encountering a problem, however, is to boil down the situation to get a good idea of its basic cause. For instance, if a person finds an open gate that should be closed, he or she may immediately assume that someone was careless. If the person checks a bit further, however, he or she may discover that no instructions are in place that say "close the gate after entering." Or, the gate may have a latch that isn't functioning properly. What this example tells you is that asking "why" about the wrong cause won't get you a good solution.

After you clearly define a problem, you can begin an investigation by asking, "Why did this happen?" You won't find anything magical about the "5" in the 5 Why's. The tool is based on a belief that a single question can't identify an answer that's the root cause of a problem. When you first ask "why," the initial response describes a symptom. Asking another "why," and so on, moves the investigation closer to the root cause. Asking "why" five times is simply a good rule of thumb; you may ask fewer or more times to discover a problem's cause.

Here's an illustration to demonstrate how a company can use the 5 Why's in everyday operations. I (contributor Dennis Dreyer) worked at an automobile manufacturer for over 34 years, always in the operations area of the business. During this time, the company had a good reputation for focusing on safety. It had safety talks on a regular basis, put up signs proclaiming the importance of safety, and enforced all safety regulations. However, despite the company's efforts, employees still got injured, and on rare occasions the injuries were fatal. To the company's credit, its leadership realized that business as usual wasn't good enough.

To change the situation, the company implemented many new processes, and the end result was a significant improvement in safety performance. One of the processes that the company turned to was the use of 5 Why's for injuries. The process required that employees evaluate all injuries against the 5 Why's, at which point a supervisor communicated the results to plant/division leadership, generally within 24 hours. The situation went something like this, from injury to corrective action:

Injury: Employee fell and sprained his right wrist.

Description: John Doe, a second-shift material handler, was walking to a production workstation to deliver parts when he tripped and fell, injuring his wrist. He was taken to a medical station and is expected to return to work in one week. Further investigation revealed that a 16"-x-18"-x-4" box of bearings, weighing 25 pounds, was on the floor, and it caused the employee to trip.

Investigation:

1. Why was the box on the floor?

The maintenance department stores bearings there for rapid repair of conveyors.

2. Why doesn't maintenance store the bearings in a safe location, as designated by the workplace organization drawing?

Other items are overflowing from maintenance's designated staging area into the area designated for bearings.

3. Why are parts overflowing the designated area?

The designated area isn't large enough.

4. Why is the other area not large enough?

Total workplace space limitations prevent maintenance from having adequate storage space and from following the rules.

5. Why didn't maintenance follow the rules?

The workplace isn't well organized and needs to be redesigned.

Corrective action: All parts have been moved to their designated storage spaces and a 5S workshop (see Chapter 13 for details) is scheduled for next week.

Establishing a good environment for asking "why"

"Curiosity killed the cat," as the saying goes. Unfortunately, in many situations, employees think that curiosity will kill their job status and retirement benefits, too. Many employees don't view curiosity as a good thing. Workers may not see how asking questions improves the quality of the overall operation. It may take time for the culture of your company to evolve, but you need to create a positive environment where everyone looks for ways to eliminate waste and satisfy customer requirements. You may just have to remove a few roadblocks before going down this path. Follow these guidelines to start off:

- ✔ Be sensitive that everyone likes to do a good job. Asking "why" may put employees on the defensive. Ensure that they understand that the issue is the process, not them or their work performance.

- ✔ Draw employees into the game. Work together to drive the "why's" into the process and figure out the issues. Jointly draft and sign process improvement recommendations. No secrets!

- ✔ Publicly thank employees for their help.

Dennis Dreyer of Dreyer Solutions, which provides consulting services in supply-chain management and logistics, contributed this chapter.

Chapter 12

Keeping Your Eyes on the Process: Value Stream Mapping

They say that a picture is worth a thousand words. A visual image can convey a complex idea or process much more effectively than words or numbers. In Chapters 9 and 10, you see how graphs and charts can provide useful information about your production process. But in your organization's zeal to improve the production parts of your process, you mustn't forget that what's important is the sum of the parts of the entire process for delivering a product to your customer.

The rub is that your customers' only reason for interest in your company is the product or service that you provide. The customers don't care about how good each step of your production process is or how magnificent your Pareto charts look; they just want a product or service that meets their needs.

No worries: Value Stream Mapping (VSM) is here to bring your picture back into focus. VSM is a process that allows you to see the big picture to make sure that your entire process is focused on producing the best possible product for the customer. VSM's main purpose is to help you identify and eliminate wasted time and effort. In this chapter, we explain the basics of VSM and describe how to create several types of maps.

Sketching the Basics of Value Stream Mapping

All processes that create a product or service for an organization start with inputs to the organization, where some sort of transformation takes place and a finished product or service is delivered to the customer. Both material and information make this transformation possible in most cases. For an organization to achieve a high level of performance, and thus produce a product or service that satisfies customer requirements, the flow of material and information must be as efficient as possible. You should find no barriers or wasteful practices to prevent material and information from moving smoothly as they travel through the organization.

The benefits of having efficient processes include lower inventory levels, reduced lead times (the total time it takes for the customer to receive the product or service after the order is placed), and higher throughput (the number of items made per unit of time).

Value Stream Mapping helps you analyze your processes to improve the flow of material and information through your organization. VSM is basically a set of tools you use to document your overall processes in a visual form that makes it easy to see where barriers to flow clog up your processes. With the information garnered from VSM, you can redesign your processes to eliminate the clogs and wasteful practices.

In the following sections, we further define and describe VSM. We also go over the steps of creating a map, and we present VSM's pros and cons.

Breaking down the definition of VSM

So, what exactly is Value Stream Mapping? Take a look at the term one word at a time:

- ✔ *Value* is what the customer is buying from you. Your product or service must provide something of worth to the customer. You may need to think beyond your immediate customer base to see the value you add.

- ✔ *Stream* is the process flow through your organization that turns inputs into a product or service of value for the customer.

- ✔ *Mapping* is the action of documenting the value stream so that you can analyze it to find areas to improve.

VSM is simply a set of tools that allow you to analyze your process flow by presenting it in a visual form. The form enables you to look for ways to redesign the process to eliminate barriers to the flow or identify waste in the process — steps that don't add value. Why go through all the hassle, your superiors ask? Because you can reduce labor time, costs, loops, and so on.

Examining important VSM attributes

VSM is similar to other process-charting techniques, such as flowcharting (see Chapters 16 and 17), but it's different in several important ways:

- ✔ A Value Stream Map contains data boxes for the inclusion of process-flow metrics such as cycle time, changeover time (the time it takes to alter a machine or workstation from making one product to another), batch size, error rates, processing time, demand rate, percent complete, work in progress (WIP), costs, inventory, and so on. A typical process flowchart doesn't include this specific metric information.

- ✔ Flowcharting typically focuses on employee processes, such as the steps required to make an item or provide a service, whereas VSM focuses on material and information flow in the manufacturing of products and on delivery for services.

- ✔ A flowchart often has a box for every action, whereas VSM combines all steps where the material is continuously flowing.

- ✔ You can create a Value Stream Map, usually by hand, much quicker than a typical process flowchart.

- ✔ A Value Stream Map looks across all processes, departments, and functions. A flowchart is a detailed look at a single process.

- ✔ Flowcharts are used to document current processes; VSM requires that you document both current and future state flows (see the section "To the Drawing Board: Creating a Current State Map" for more on the current state).

- ✔ VSM uses different icons to signify when the organization pushes along material or services instead of the customer pulling. A flowchart typically uses a standard icon for all processes. (See the later section "Eyeing icons" for more.)

Walking through the basic steps to create a Value Stream Map

The overall process for creating a Value Stream Map consists of five steps:

1. **Build a cross-functional team to create the map.**

   To make sure that you cover everything that goes into the process, you need to involve people from different parts of your business. This allows issues to receive input from different viewpoints, and it facilitates company-wide acceptance when the time comes to implement solutions.

2. **Determine what process or value stream you want to map.**

    Don't try to map every product and process flow right off the bat; that just makes it harder for your team to get started. You want to map the part of the process causing the greatest pain. You can, however, group several related products or services that follow similar process flows. (See the later section "Grouping products and services into families to simplify mapping" for details.)

3. **Create a *current state map* that shows the current flow of material and information, through your chosen process or value stream, required to make your product or provide your service.**

    Make sure you have the perspective of the customer when doing this step; you're more likely to see issues that have an impact on the customer. (See the later section "To the Drawing Board: Creating a Current State Map" for more details on this step.)

4. **Develop a *future state map* that shows the improved process or value stream created by identifying waste, resolving problems, and proposing changes.**

    This step is where you can design ways to eliminate problems from the process by smoothing out the flow of material and information. The future state map allows you to predict what your lead times should be and how much inventory or service capability you need to have on hand. The future state also shows the reduced steps and records the difference from the current state so that management can see the value. (See "Do It Over: Building a Future State Map" for details.)

5. **Implement the proposed changes and measure the resulting improvement.**

    The gap between the current state (Step 3) and the future state (Step 4) is your roadmap for making changes. (See the later section "Taking action after finishing your future map" for more information.)

Value Stream Mapping shouldn't be a one-time event. You really won't know your process until you've gone through VSM several times. Successful organizations continually review process flows and make continuous improvements in their processes — a practice that keeps their customers continually satisfied with the end products and services.

Checking out the advantages of VSM

Value Stream Mapping is a great place to start to examine your production or service-delivery process in a holistic manner to see if it's in prime condition to deliver customer satisfaction. The benefits of VSM include the following:

✔ Allows you to visualize how all operations fit together instead of viewing only individual processes

✔ Provides a common language for everyone involved in analyzing the production process

✔ Shows how material and information flows are linked together

✔ Makes process-flow problems easy to spot, which allows you to discuss alternatives

✔ Helps you avoid optimizing one part of your process at the expense of the entire process

✔ Documents where you want your organization to be and provides a roadmap for getting there

✔ Proves more useful than quantitative tools for identifying steps that don't add value in the process (we discuss non-value-adding steps later in this chapter)

✔ Helps you identify wasteful points in the process and the sources of the waste during each of the following phases:

- Designing the product or service, from the initial concept to customer approval

- Building the product or service, from customer order to delivery

- Servicing the product or providing additional services during customer use

To the Drawing Board: Creating a Current State Map

Before you can make improvements in the process of delivering your product or service, you have to thoroughly understand your current process. A current state Value Stream Map gives you a starting point for looking for improvements. In the following sections, we describe the icons that go into maps, show you how to build a current map, and explain the convenience of mapping product families.

Although a Value Stream Map is more than a simple flowchart (see the section "Examining important VSM attributes"), anyone with basic flowcharting skills can create it. You *can* buy software to help create the map, but most users are better off just drawing the map by hand. If you're truly not confident in your drawing abilities, check out your favorite Internet search engine to find available software.

Eyeing icons

Like with other flowcharting processes, you use icons when creating a current state Value Stream Map — icons that have specific meanings and standardize how you communicate with this tool. Although it's no "official" standard for current state VSM icons, Figure 12-1 contains the most commonly used icons and their meanings.

No "rule" prohibits you from making up your own icons to better describe some unique situations in your production or service-delivery process. You may have symbols or icons that have specific meaning to your organization or industry that make more sense to you. Just keep them simple and make sure that everyone agrees on a clear definition. The key is to be able to create a map that your cross-functional team can agree on and understand.

Mapping the flow of materials and information

Using the VSM icons from the previous section, you can begin creating your current state map. You start by doing an initial walkthrough of the process to get a basic understanding of the flow of the map.

You may find it useful to go through the process backward — from the customer to the input of raw materials or the first step in providing a service. With this strategy, you start from your customers' perspective and work your way to the beginning with a more customer-centered viewpoint.

After your mapping team walks through the process, build your current state map by using the following steps (Figure 12-2 shows the finished map):

1. **Draw a basic high-level map of the flow of material or activities.**

   Using your VSM icons, map the major activities that occur to deliver the product or service.

2. **Collect detailed information about each step in the process and add this to the map.**

   The information you take down can include things such as cycle time (the time between when a new item is started and when the next one begins), batch size, uptime percentage (the percentage of time that the step is functioning — in other words, "up"), inventory levels, or scrap rate (the amount of scrap generated over a unit of time).

Icon	Meaning
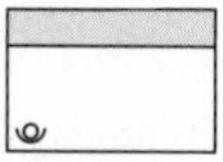 Process	A process, machine, department, or operation. The number stands for the number of machines, departments, and so on.
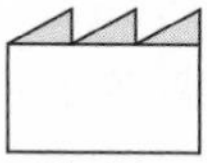 Outside Sources	Typically used at the start of the process to represent a supplier and at the end of a process to represent the customer.
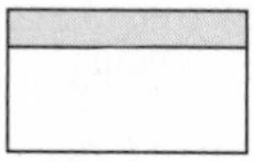 Production Control	A central production control operation or department.
 Data Box	Denotes significant information required about another icon.
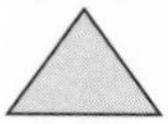 Inventory	Inventory stored between two processes.
 Push Arrow	The pushing of material from one process to another.
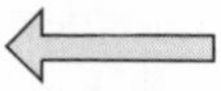 Shipments	Raw materials that come from a supplier or the movement of finished goods to the customer.
 External Shipment	Shipments from suppliers or to customers using external transport, such as a truck.
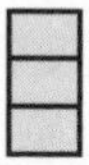 Buffer (Safety) Stock	Inventory kept in case of problems, such as downtime or sudden fluctuations in production demand.
Operator	An operator with the number required for the process.
 Manual Information Flow	The general flow of information from manual sources, such as memos or reports.
 Electronic Information Flow	The flow of information by electronic means, such as electronic data interchange (EDI) or the Internet.

Figure 12-1:
Value Stream Mapping icons standardize communication about processes.

 **Schedule/Timeline**	Shows the times when the process adds value to the product and times waiting.
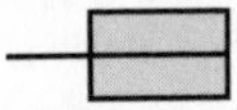 **Timeline Total**	Shows the total time when the process adds value to the product and total times waiting.
OXOX **Load Leveling**	Used to batch Kanbans so that you level the production volume and mix over time.
Withdrawal Kanban	A card or other device that signals to a material handler to transfer material to the receiving process.
 **Production Kanban**	A card or other device that informs a process how many of what item to produce.
 **Signal Kanban**	Shows when a batch of material is needed.
 **Kanban Post**	A location used to store Kanban cards or other devices.
 **Physical Pull**	Material pulled by a process.
—FIFO→ **FIFO Flow**	Material pulled by using a first in–first out process.
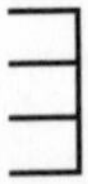 **Supermarket**	A controlled inventory of materials.
 **Quality Problem (Kaizen Starburst)**	Identifies improvement needs.
Sequenced Pull	A pull system that gives instruction to subassembly processes to produce a predetermined type and quantity of product.

Figure 12-1: (continued) Value Stream Mapping icons standardize communication about processes.

3. **Add both manual and electronic information flows to the map.**

   Use arrows to show the sequence and direction of the flow of information. This includes things such as schedules, orders or product specifications, and so on.

4. **Create a timeline at the bottom of the map.**

   You record the times for value-added steps at the lower part of the timeline, and you record the times for non-value-adding steps at the upper part. At the end of the timeline, record the lead time, which is the total of all the time from when the order is received until the customer receives the item (both the upper and lower parts of the timeline), and the value-added time, which represents only those times on the lower part of the timeline where value is being added to the product. (We cover value-added and non-value-added steps later in this chapter.)

Check out Figure 12-2 for an example of a completed current state Value Stream Map. The figure illustrates the overall process of creating direct-mail pieces. You can glean the following information by looking at the figure:

✔ We receive shipments from our supplier twice a week.

✔ We store work-in-process in inventory stashes between each of our major processes, which adds significantly to the time it takes to complete an item.

✔ We record the cycle time (C/T), the changeover time (C/O), and the uptime percentage for each process.

✔ We indicate at the bottom of the timeline the time the product sits idle in inventory (non-value-added time) and the actual time spent working on each item (value-added time).

Grouping products and services into families to simplify mapping

For many organizations that produce only a few items, selecting the processes for which to draw current state Value Stream Maps is simple. If you have hundreds of products that you produce, however, you can't produce a map for every single process. One way to simplify your situation is to group your products into a small number of product families. You can then draw a map for each product family rather than for each product.

To create your product families, follow these simple steps:

1. **Create a list of the final products that you deliver to your customers.**

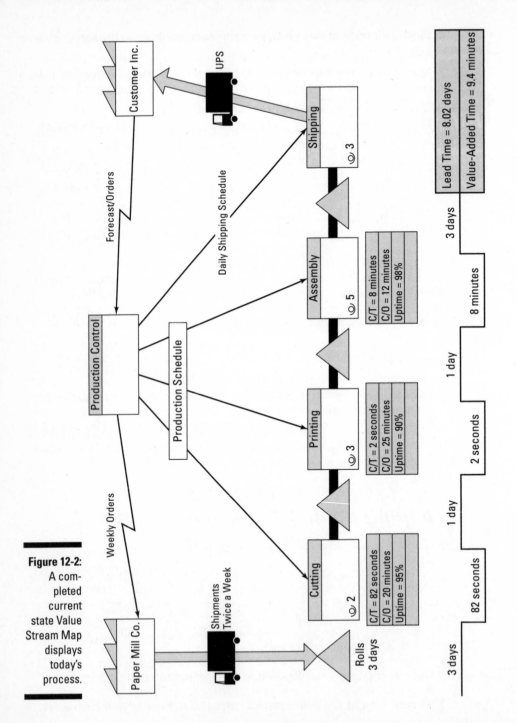

Figure 12-2:
A completed
current
state Value
Stream Map
displays
today's
process.

2. **For each product, list the major processes that it goes through during production.**

   You begin to see that many products go through several identical steps; this occurs most frequently in the early stages of production. Most differences occur in steps near the end of the process.

3. **Group the products that go through several identical steps into families for VSM purposes.**

You'll most likely find that products and services that aren't related from a customer point of view go through several of the same steps during production. The trick is to focus on processes that many products share. Also, don't get stuck trying to match up products perfectly; creating the perfect Value Stream Map has no value to your customer. Focus on the purpose of VSM: to help you identify waste in your processes, which in turn allows you to produce better products or deliver better services.

Do It Over: Building a Future State Map

After you map your current process flow (see the previous sections), you can begin looking for ways to improve your process. You create a *future state* Value Stream Map based on the current map to document the improvements you make. This is where you smooth the flow of material and information to eliminate problems. In the following sections, we explain how to analyze the value of steps in your process and how to use that analysis to build and act on your future map.

Evaluating value-added steps and non-value-added steps

The most important part of analyzing a Value Stream Map is understanding the difference between process steps that add value to your product or service and steps that don't add value. Here are some definitions:

- *Value-added steps* add value to the product or service. Simple enough! These steps typically transform the product or service in a way that's important to the customer. This may include a task such as assembly.

- *Non-value-added steps* don't add something to the product or service that the customer would pay for. This may include moving products from one area to another or storing products in inventory.

As you analyze the steps you identified in your current state map, you can begin to build your future state map. Here are some questions to answer:

- How long is your lead time?
- What percentage of your total time do you spend on value-added steps?
- How much inventory do you have on hand at any one time?
- Can you identify any communications problems?
- Can you combine any processes to eliminate inventory?
- Do you have any obvious bottlenecks?

Most organizations are surprised to find out that much of the time that goes toward making their products is spent on non-value-added steps. Most find that 80 percent or more of the total production lead time is non-value-added. By doing what you can to eliminate the non-value-added steps, with the help of your future state Value Stream Map, you can drastically reduce your lead time and make your overall process more efficient.

Sometimes, you can't eliminate non-value-added steps. Examples include steps necessary to remain in legal compliance. Consider these steps the cost of doing business. It isn't in your company's best interest to cut corners that may place it in legal jeopardy. Other examples include the following:

- Gathering data for reports on the amount of air pollution emitted
- Taking actions to prevent insider trading before stock offerings or prior to reporting quarterly earnings
- Collecting and paying taxes on materials, payroll, and so on
- Collecting asset information for claims in case of a loss

Constructing a future state map with your newfound knowledge

A future state map is designed to reduce or remove time, effort, and dollars from the entire production or service-delivery process. Every situation is unique, but most processes are guilty of having waste in areas such as product handling, inventory sitting around between steps, communications between internal and external processes, and changeover time for workstations.

Take a look at Figure 12-3 to see a possible future state map for the information we collected in the current state map in Figure 12-2. Notice the following improvements planned through the future state map:

- ✔ We've improved our handling of the product to reduce the amount of time it sits around by implementing a "supermarket" inventory system to better control inventory (see Chapter 15 for details on implementing a Kanban system).

- ✔ We've combined a couple of processes (printing and assembly) into one work center to eliminate inventory between the two processes.

- ✔ All together, we've reduced the lead time for filling an order from just over eight days to a little over four.

- ✔ We've noted that we think we can make further improvements by reducing the changeover time on the cutting machine.

Taking action after finishing your future state map

Upon completion of your organization's future state Value Stream Map, you should prepare an action plan to make the future map — and the improvements outlined within — a reality. The gap between where you are today — the current state map — and where you want to be — the future state map — may seem enormous, but you may be able to break it down into a number of small improvements that your organization can easily make.

Factors to look for when implementing your future state map include the following:

- ✔ Have you eliminated all bottlenecks in your process?

- ✔ Is information available when needed for each process?

- ✔ Are you keeping inventory to a minimum?

- ✔ Are you creating several small batches of products or a few large ones?

- ✔ Is the demand for your product Pulled by the customer, or do you Push material through the system as it becomes available (see Chapter 15 for more on Push versus Pull)?

You can't look at each of these things alone; a reduction in inventory in one area may create a bottleneck in another. Ask these questions over and over as you move toward your future state.

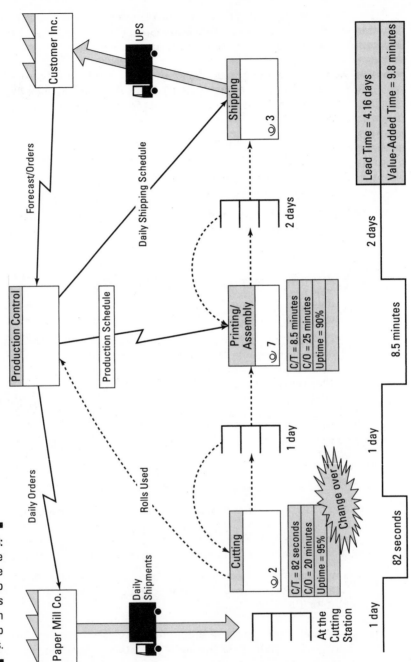

Figure 12-3: A future state Value Stream Map provides guidance on cleaning up processes.

Customer Inc.

UPS

Shipping
◎ 3

Forecast/Orders

Daily Shipping Schedule

Production Control

Production Schedule

Printing/
Assembly
◎ 7

C/T = 8.5 minutes
C/O = 25 minutes
Uptime = 90%

2 days

Cutting
◎ 2

C/T = 82 seconds
C/O = 20 minutes
Uptime = 95%

Change over

1 day

Daily Orders

Rolls Used

Paper Mill Co.

Daily Shipments

At the
Cutting
Station

Lead Time = 4.16 days
Value-Added Time = 9.8 minutes

2 days

8.5 minutes

1 day

82 seconds

1 day

Chapter 13

Focusing on the 5S Method

- -

In This Chapter

▶ Recognizing the advantages and disadvantages of 5S

▶ Rolling out a 5S program in your workplace

▶ Implementing the five phases successfully

- -

*P*erhaps your company's work areas are cluttered — not just the desktops but under the desks, on the shelves, in the drawers. The work areas are dusty, smelly, and, well, dirty. In some places, everything in sight is nice and neat, but all the closets contain piles of rubbish. No one wants to work in filth (with the exception of third graders, of course). A bright, clean work area is a pleasant place (as for the actual work, that may be another story).

The 5S method is the Japanese concept of housekeeping. 5S is a methodical approach to eliminating waste in time and materials. Its philosophy is that a simplified work area operates more efficiently, cheaply, and safely. The belief is that a sloppy workspace is, by its nature, filled with waste: wasted time looking for items, wasted costs in excess materials and tools, wasted space, and so on. The five *S's,* loosely translated into English, are Sort *(Seiri),* Straighten *(Seiton),* Shine *(Seiso),* Standardize *(Seiketsu),* and Sustain *(Shitsuke).* 5S's mantra is "only what is needed, in its proper place, clean and ready for use."

The words all begin with an *S* in Japanese, but their real translations into English begin with different letters. For example, *Standardize* should be *Organize.* Just to remove the clutter of non-S's, someone dug up comparable English words that begin with an "S."

In this chapter, we show you the pros and cons of using 5S in your workplace. We also explain how to introduce 5S to your employees and successfully move through the five phases.

Understanding the Pros and Cons of 5S

Using the 5S method in your company has a variety of benefits, but you also need to be aware of some disadvantages before you decide to move forward. We cover the pros and cons of 5S in the following sections.

The pros

Simple processes are the easiest to complete with the fewest errors. Cleaning and organizing a work area with 5S simplifies activities because you have fewer chances for errors. Here are a few more benefits of using 5S:

- ✔ Cost savings through
  - • Reduced materials inventory
  - • Fewer tools used more often
  - • Faster office processes with fewer approvals
- ✔ Improved morale through a cleaner workplace

  Who enjoys working in a dump? Well, perhaps landfill managers, but at least they work with *organized* filth.
- ✔ Increased safety through reduced clutter
- ✔ Swifter changes from doing one process to another
- ✔ Ease of moving workers around because each area uses similar processes

So, how can 5S improve quality for your company? Let us count the ways:

- ✔ **5S simplifies processes.** By examining workflows in a department, removing the need to work around clutter, and making needed material easy to find, you greatly simplify processes.
- ✔ **5S increases materials visibility.** The same material is now always located in the same marked places. The materials stockman can see when materials are running low and address the situation before you run out.
- ✔ **5S reenergizes the workforce.** 5S is an employee-driven program. They organize the work areas, and they decide what stays and goes; the result is cleaner, more efficient workspaces.
- ✔ **5S improves quality of management.** The work in progress is more visually obvious now that the clutter is gone. Incoming materials are always in the same places, and you can tell when they're running short.

> Finished goods are always in the same places, and you can tell if they're on schedule.
>
> ✔ **5S improves the quality of changing over to occasional production runs.** You plan the locations of processes and materials and mark their locations on the floor, which reduces confusion and improves product quality.

The cons

The 5S process can flop if your company lacks the courage to promptly resolve questions. Additional disadvantages of introducing 5S to your company include the following:

✔ People develop a comfort level for the way things are today, whether the methods are efficient or wasteful. Radically changing practices can be unsettling to people who live their lives within daily routines. People may resist giving up their secret stashes of parts and tools.

✔ Cleaning up a mess that took years to create takes time. Your organization needs to clean up the entire facility.

✔ The results of 5S fade away without management support to maintain the initiative.

Rolling Out 5S with Communications Boards

5S is an easy concept to understand. Most work areas (including offices) can benefit from a thorough cleaning and reorganization. However, 5S is more than a one-time event. 5S is a way to approach all manner of work: everything in its place, no clutter, and so on.

People are funny creatures. Some "forget" to clean up after themselves, and some packrat everything away just in case. Over time, the buildup of clutter can be overwhelming. After a taste of what 5S can do to improve their work situations, few people want to go back to the old ways.

As with all quality programs, you must introduce 5S to employees and train them on its steps; we provide general information about these tasks in Chapter 5. In the following sections, we discuss a special element of rolling out 5S to your company: the use of different communications boards.

Kick off a 5S program during the company's slow season. Some companies find slowing down individual departments one at a time to implement 5S too disruptive. Instead, they make 5S a single, facility-wide event. This technique minimizes the overall disruption to production. An alternate strategy is to implement 5S in one or a few teams at a time. Over time, the local 5S program learns more, and each subsequent event is smoother than the last.

Establishing a facility communications board

Critical communications tools both for the Rollout and for the Sustain phases (which we cover later in this chapter) are the 5S communications boards. One board is set up for the status of each 5S team (see the next section for details). A facility-wide 5S communications board tallies overall facility information. The facility board contains

- ✔ A formal statement of executive support — usually the 5S announcement letter
- ✔ A picture of the facility's 5S leader, along with a statement of the program's goals
- ✔ A schedule showing which departments have completed 5S and when the rest of them plan on finishing
- ✔ A department-by-department listing of floor space freed by 5S
- ✔ A listing of the materials and tools returned to the warehouse for reissue
- ✔ The dollar value of the returned materials (in LARGE type)
- ✔ Before and after pictures of some of the "worst" cases

Always communicate with the workforce. To keep 5S alive, employees must believe that it makes their jobs easier and more pleasant. They must see how valued their ideas are for continuously improving the work areas. In short, involving employees in 5S decision making from the beginning provides them with pride of ownership. Management recognition of a good job also helps.

Starting a status board for each department

The first thing to do after you schedule a department for 5S is to establish a large signboard for the department. Most signs are 4'-x-6' sheets of plywood painted with light colors. The signboard is a central source for a department's 5S journey.

The left side of the board features the "before" information, and the right side features the "after":

✔ On the "before" side of the board, post pictures taken from multiple angles to show how the work area looks before cleanup. Take plenty of pictures to include the overall layout, a typical workbench, materials storage areas, incoming materials, and finished goods. Office pictures may show materials stuffed into cabinets where the doors barely close, boxes of records that no one ever looks at, cubicles with unused monitors and keyboards, and overflowing trashcans and ashtrays outside the company entrance.

✔ The "after" side consists of pictures taken after the cleanup, an issues log, cleaning assignments, and floor plans showing the reorganized department (we cover all these items later in this chapter).

In the following sections, we show you two important documents to post on a status board before you start the 5S phases: a "before" floor plan and a "before" spaghetti chart.

The "before" floor plan

Create a sketch of the department's "before" floor plan as it exists today. This image doesn't need to be of drafting quality; it just needs to be understandable. Marking major work and storage areas is essential for any type of facility. The key is to identify normal processes and track their flow across whatever floor plan you use. For example, the key elements to indicate in a factory department are

✔ Workbenches

✔ Tool locations

✔ Materials storage

✔ Incoming materials

✔ Finished materials collections/departure points

✔ Large machines (difficult to move)

Office floor plans should indicate any common areas — such as a room full of printers shared by all workers — document storage areas, and even restrooms.

Figure 13-1 shows a sample "before" floor plan in a manufacturing facility. In this example, the workbenches are more or less in the upper- to middle-left of the room. Materials are along the opposite wall, with forklifts roaring through the gangway to make a walking worker's trip for parts similar to crossing a highway. Piles of incoming material are splayed out along the top wall, with finished goods collected in the lower right of the room. Spare tools are located near the finished goods.

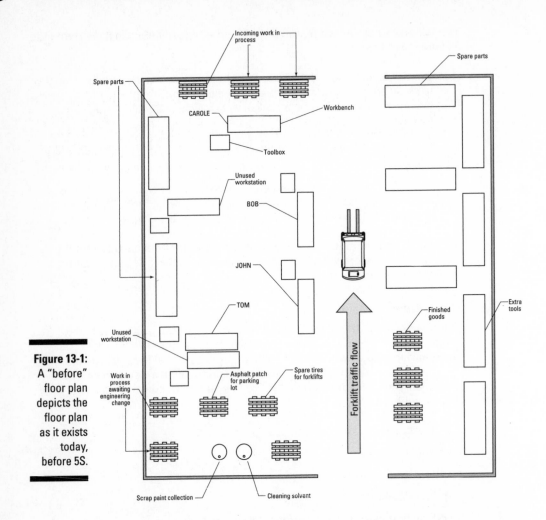

Figure 13-1:
A "before"
floor plan
depicts the
floor plan
as it exists
today,
before 5S.

When you evaluate a floor plan, approach it as something that has evolved over time rather than a well-considered layout. Identify the primary functions for the work area and how the work must flow from desk to desk (or station to station). In Figure 13-1, the empty space in this area seems to have attracted excess material from other departments. The room includes construction materials (an asphalt patch), a barrel of cleaning solvent, and a barrel for collecting paint (potentially hazardous materials).

Other departments aren't the only ones to blame for the excess. The workspace has three places for accumulating finished goods (which workers should send straight to shipping), as well as shelves and cabinets of extra tools and spare parts. Far more work-in-process material is on hand than is necessary for the next two days.

Like many places, this work area reflects personal preferences; it doesn't optimize workflow.

The "before" spaghetti chart

Most people don't realize the amount of productive time wasted walking here and there to collect the materials, information, and tools necessary to complete an assignment. A spaghetti chart, such as the one in Figure 13-2, is a tool you can use to identify the amount of travel time in a process. Setting up and using the chart is easy:

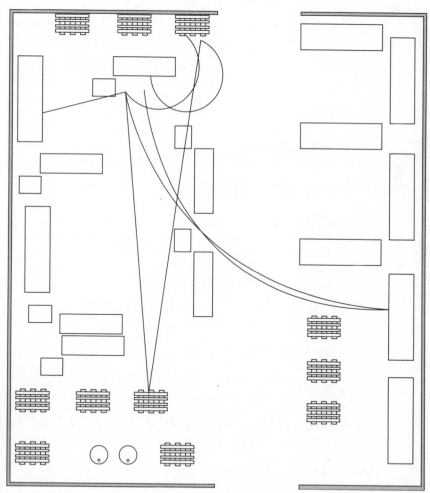

Figure 13-2:
A "before" spaghetti chart logs the travel time of workers.

1. **Use a sketch of the existing floor plan (see the preceding section) to track the movement of workers.**

2. **Follow a worker around for about two hours (after warning the worker that you're going to do this).**

   Every time she leaves her workbench, follow her. On the chart, mark a line that shows where she started and her destination, such as from the workbench to the spare-parts shelves. The lines on the chart can become hard to count, so make a notation of where the worker walked.

3. **When you complete the chart for that worker, measure the distances between all the points where she walked.**

4. **Calculate the distance walked during the two-hour period, and multiply that figure by four to estimate the distance walked per shift.**

Repeat the spaghetti chart process for each worker. Individuals usually have different duties with different walking paths. Tally the walk distance for the entire team. When you convert to miles per week, the number is always impressive!

The Sort Phase: Separating the Gravel from the Gems

Many managers have a justified packrat mentality. Obtaining funding for additional tools, materials, and so on can be difficult. As a hedge against a future requirement, a manager may have stuffed away

- ✔ Anything left over from previous assignments
- ✔ Scrapped items with "still useful" parts attached
- ✔ Anything scrounged from other departments
- ✔ Goods returned by customers

Occasionally, jobs are halted in mid-stride for potential completion at a future date. Instead of returning material to the warehouse, people let it linger in the departments in case the order comes to finish the job. Unfortunately, all this hoarding ties up a considerable amount of company funds in material that sits idle for a very long time.

The *Sort* phase of 5S clears out all the clutter. The goal is to identify the materials needed to perform work over the next two days and keep it on hand. Everything else has to go. The local supervisor can share the production schedule for the next week with the team so workers know what the upcoming requirements may be.

In the following sections, we explain how to prepare for the Sort phase and how to separate the good stuff from the unnecessary.

Preparing to sort

Careful planning is the key to success! Follow these steps to make your sort easier:

1. **Sketch a floor plan of where everything is now.**

   This plan indicates the original location for everything (see "The 'before' floor plan" earlier in this chapter for more details). Everything must have been in its place for a reason, so when changing things around, think about how each item was used in various processes.

2. **Identify a nearby area where you can store occasionally used material.**

   Often, a work area supports low-volume or rarely scheduled processes. The department should store the material and special tooling for those processes somewhere nearby, but out of the way of day-to-day efforts. The key is to make all occasionally used materials as portable as possible. Place large containers of material on wheeled platforms, create carts of tools and small hardware, and so on. Roll these tools and materials in and out as needed.

3. **Obtain green and red tags — twice as many as you think you'll need.**

   A green tag means you want to keep that item where it is; a red tag indicates that you want to move that item out to the disposal site.

4. **Decide where to send material for disposal.**

   Often, this location is a warehouse where your workers can drop off materials. Another popular material drop-off point is the loading dock next to the dumpster. At this point, someone examines everything and determines where it should go.

   When you dispose of office documents, it may be faster and safer to shred them rather than separate private information from public.

5. **Decide how to handle items identified for disposal.**

   Typically, a materials-management clerk and someone from the accounting department jointly decide what to do with each item. Your disposal options include the following:

   • **Return to vendor:** Where possible, recapture value by returning the material to the vendor for a credit. Track the amount of money received from returned or scrapped materials. You may save by collecting excess tools for redistribution.

- **Return to warehouse:** To avoid shuffling piles of materials around the facility, return all unneeded material to the warehouse. (Office employees may return material to the stationary office where they go for office supplies.) Don't allow other departments to scavenge from the pile. If they need something, they must request it through the normal channels.

- **Throw away or sell:** Dispose of an item in the trash (have plenty of trash containers on hand), sell it for its value, or sell it for scrap (such as metal parts).

- **Donate:** Give items to charity.

- **Send to the landfill:** After checking with the local environmental experts, send materials directly to the landfill. *Note:* Always dispose of hazardous materials properly.

Sorting everything with ease

Sorting eliminates much of the clutter in a work area. This step improves safety by removing the amount of junk workers can fall over. It also simplifies the cleaning process. Everyone can see where everything is.

Follow these steps to sort all materials with ease:

1. **Tag all materials to stay (a green tag) or to go (a red tag; see the list in the previous section).** Anything overlooked is missing a tag. (Please don't put a red tag on a lazy manager or a sleeping worker!) Don't tag small items individually; instead, let one tag mark everything within a container.

2. **Open, inspect, and tag every drawer, cabinet, shelf, toolbox, and container in the work area.** Seek out broken or obsolete material and dispose of it. Often, a quick payback for this step is the uncovering of material, tools, and so on that someone stashed away for years just in case of need.

3. **When the 5S team members think the job is done, they should verify that they've tagged everything.** They can start in one corner of the room and methodically work their way across to ensure that they haven't overlooked anything. You also can ensure that everything is tagged when sifting the good from the departing items.

Open areas attract other departments' clutter. Reconfigure the work area to return that unused space to the facility. Don't let any other department shovel its clutter into the newly freed space.

Recognize that for some people, red-tagging their favorite tools, machinery, or secret stashes of parts is an emotional moment. They may grasp at excuses to keep certain items without valid business reasons. They also may hide their clutter in nearby departments to avoid the cleaning. A supervisor must seek out and send this material for disposal.

The Straighten Phase: A Place for Everything and Everything in Its Place

After you finish sorting, the time comes to Straighten. *Straightening* means deciding where to place tools and materials based on the workers' locations. Everything workers need should be within easy reach. Organize the work area so that all materials are easy to find. Assign a dedicated space for each item so only one item goes in that spot. Place tools and materials to minimize worker travel time, not for appearance or optimal storage. We show you how to do all this and more in the following sections.

 Companies occasionally execute the Straighten and Shine phases together, because Shine requires moving items to clean up, and Straighten places them in the proper spot; see "The Shine Phase: Polishing It All Up!" later in this chapter for more details.

Tidying tools and materials

A *tool* can be anything someone uses over and over to hold or shape something; tools include items from a bar-code scanner, to a particular printer, to a special medical machine. Office tools include expensive (nonstandard) telephones, old computer keyboards and monitors scattered about and in closets, excess fax machines, time clocks, and copiers. Workers use some tools only in certain situations, but this equipment saves a lot of time. One thing most tools have in common is that they're expensive and need to be managed.

Materials are the work products — the things being shaped or assembled. For example, a material may be a customer purchase request, where one department checks the customer's credit, another fills the order, and then a third ships it, each adding to the document as it passes through the process.

In any given workplace, people need to straighten both tools and materials. How? Just follow these tips:

- ✔ **Store shared tools on shadow boards.** Tools like wrenches and hammers are inexpensive, so everyone may have one. However, not everyone needs a personal copy of the more expensive and less-used tools. Place shared tools on *shadow boards* (boards that label tool locations with pictures of the tools' outlines). A shadow board ensures that special tools are always in the same place when needed. At the end of the shift, the entire board needs only a glance. If something is missing, the team can see that it's gone. (In an office, shared areas from the coffee room to the printer room should have a proper place for everything identified.)

✔ **Combine toolboxes.** Many departments are plagued with an overgrowth of toolboxes. Each box takes up valuable floor or counter space. If the operation covers two shifts, the space requirement doubles. A common solution is to move to company-owned, shared toolboxes. Organize the shared toolboxes with every tool in its assigned place. Mark tool drawers with what they contain.

✔ **Paint marks on floors to indicate drop points and storage areas for large items.** Big factory items should have a designated floor space. Mark the spot by painting a box around it. Also, do this step for drop points for large containers of incoming material and outgoing finished goods.

An office can clearly mark all file cabinets by using a standard identification system. Employees also can hang signs from the ceiling to identify each department or work team.

✔ **Use shelving to take advantage of vertical space.** Cabinets often hide items, so you can use shelving instead or remove the doors on the cabinets. The goal is to be able to easily locate items with minimal searching. If theft is an issue, you can use doors of wire mesh.

✔ **Store items based on their frequency of use.** Store commonly used items at eye level. Place lightly used items high and low.

✔ **Manage the flow of materials.** Drop large containers of incoming materials in their designated floor areas. Replenish smaller materials by using the Kanban method we describe in Chapter 15. Flow racks, where workers load the material containers from the rear, can keep components in a first-in, first-out sequence.

Identify the amount of each type of material that the department should keep on hand and the best way to maintain that level. Keep only the quantities of material needed for the next 48 hours, and store excess in the warehouse or other storage area. To maintain tidiness, the materials team may have to make more frequent deliveries of smaller quantities of material.

Putting away personal items

Don't permit personal items, such as coats and lunchboxes, to litter the work area. Place them in a dedicated area, such as an employee locker room or a department coat rack. When selecting a storage area, keep in mind that personal items may include muddy boots and wet raincoats. The goal is to minimize messes.

Of course, workers can still hang up personal pictures, comical calendars, and so on. (These items help to soften the sharp edges of an office.) We simply advise that you keep bulky and potentially wet items like coats, umbrellas, and boots away from work areas. Large lunchboxes need to fit under the desks. Also, large plants may be pretty, but they use up scarce workspace; limit them to cabinet tops.

Labeling items

Label all shelves, containers, cabinets, drawers, and so on with their contents. This way, everyone knows what to store in each place, and by implication, everything else needs to go elsewhere. Because everyone knows or can find out the proper place for items, this step eliminates having duplicate stacks of materials around the work area.

Create standardized labels for use across the facility. At a minimum, the label should provide the part number and the name of the item. An even better solution is to include a picture of the item on the label. With inexpensive inkjet printers and digital cameras, you can easily add images. See "The Standardize Phase: Using the Best Practices Everywhere," later in this chapter, for more about standardization in your workplace.

Another variation of labeling is to color-code parts and tools that support a specific process. For example, all the parts and special tools identified with green labels can support Process #1, and yellow labels can indicate Process #2. Common parts and tools may have plain white labels.

Drawing up "after" floor plans and charts

After you organize and label your tools and materials, draw a floor plan for how you want to organize the entire work area. The drawing is essential so that the maintenance team can plan the movement of electrical, data, and telephone services to the relocated workbenches in factories, cubicles in offices, and the like. The 5S team should do as much as it can on its own, but be aware of safety issues for tasks such as moving heavy objects. The team may need outside help.

Here are a few major considerations for when you draw up a new floor plan, no matter what type of workplace you have:

- ✔ When setting up workbenches, keep parts in the sequence in which workers use them. If five parts fit together into something, place them in a rack from left to right or top to bottom.

- ✔ Set up the workbenches and desks so that work flows across them — incoming work on one side (like a big *in* box) and finished products on the other side (the famous desktop *out* box).

✔ Position materials and tools to minimize the time workers spend walking around.

✔ Place desks close together for workers who constantly share information; for instance, put a manager who must approve special deals in a sales-call center.

Look at the example "after" floor plan in Figure 13-3. The two extra workbenches are off to disposal, and only the four active stations remain. To the right of each workbench is a location for a container of incoming material. The product being assembled moves from the incoming material on the right toward the left, across the workbench to a gravity-fed conveyor along the left wall. Finished material rolls down to the last workbench, where the worker has the additional duty of loading finished goods into a single container.

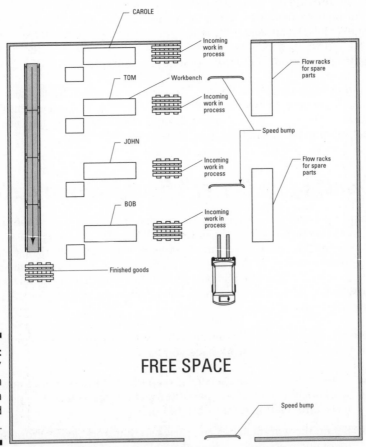

Figure 13-3:
An "after"
floor plan
shows a
revised
work area.

To slow down the forklift jockeys, the maintenance team has installed three speed bumps on the floor. This change keeps the gangway accessible but discourages lift drivers from cutting through the department.

Excess parts are off to the warehouse, and excess cabinets are in the disposal pile. In their place are two sets of flow racks. The racks face the gangway to save walk time. With the speed bumps in place, parts pickers no longer fear becoming smears on a forklift's windshield.

Using the process we describe in "The 'before' spaghetti chart" earlier in this chapter, draw a spaghetti chart for the remodeled work area, as shown in Figure 13-4. Measure the worker walk distance required to complete the same work. Be sure to add this savings of walk time to the 5S status board! (See "Starting a status board for each department" earlier in this chapter for more information.)

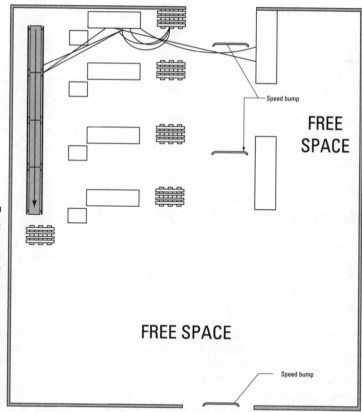

Figure 13-4: An "after" spaghetti chart depicts where workers walk after the department's reorganization.

The Shine Phase: Polishing It All Up!

The third S is to *Shine!* The 5S team cleans work areas and keeps them that way. Sad to say, in many companies, the first business function considered unnecessary is the cleaning staff. Although cutting the cleaning staff saves money in the short run, it costs more over the long term. Excess dirt wears down carpet and tile faster, trash slowly builds, and so on. A clean working area creates a positive and uplifting environment, just as a dirty, cluttered one is rather depressing.

A factory can't afford to be as clean as a hospital's operating room. However, a factory floor can be as clean as an office floor, and most offices can be even cleaner. How clean is clean enough? When in doubt, view the facility through the eyes of a customer. Would your housekeeping inspire confidence that orders will be on time, or does the place look chaotic?

Working conditions also have an impact on workers' attitudes. A clean workstation provides a mentally positive situation for improved productivity. Without a thorough cleaning, all the sorting and straightening up to this point can soon revert to the old dirty ways.

Therefore, cleaning is a logical extension of the Straightening phase (see the previous section). Cleaning has to cover areas from the top to the bottom (ceiling to floor). Leave no area untouched, including hard-to-see places. In the following sections, we discuss gathering needed equipment, handling common areas, cleaning up messes immediately, and paying close attention to maintenance.

Gathering the necessary equipment

Cleaning is a production process just like any other. It keeps the workspace ready to use. This stage includes the cleaning of workbenches, the floor, storage areas, and tools. Cleaning requires proper tools, supplies, and, in some cases, written processes. Begin by making a list of what to clean, along with the tools and materials needed to do so:

- ✔ **Tools:** Think about all the things that you need cleaned, and ensure that adequate tools are available to complete the tasks in the time allotted. Beyond a few brooms and mops (or vacuum cleaners for an office), your organization needs equipment to reach high to clean dusty places. Sometimes, this gear includes stepladders, dust brushes on long poles, and so on. Look for equipment in the work area that may need special items, such as lint-free cloths to clean computer displays or alcohol to clean moisture-intolerant electronics.

✔ **Materials:** Consider the cleaning materials that go along with the cleaning tools, like soap and dusting spray. Your organization must store and replenish cleaning materials in line with the 5S standards like any other production item.

✔ **Processes:** Although some of the workers' spouses may disagree, instructions for sweeping and mopping the floor are likely unnecessary. However, make sure you clearly document the cleaning of any special items or electronic equipment in the work area to prevent damage from improper cleaning.

Even companies that use off-hours cleaning workers for most housekeeping duties provide cleaning materials for use during the day. This step places the responsibility for maintaining a clean work area squarely on the team.

Recognizing that common areas belong to everyone

In addition to cleaning their individual work areas, employees should band together to take care of common areas. Common areas include passageways, locker rooms, break and kitchen areas, and restrooms. 5S says that even if someone else cleans these areas, workers still need to clean up after themselves. Every inch of the facility must be covered and cleaned.

The 5S leader should assign someone to address areas outside the building. After 5S on the inside is complete, someone has to sort through the scrap and other clutter that has accumulated on the outside. Eliminating this material shines the outside of the facility and improves a customer's first impression.

Cleaning as you go

A basic rule of the Shine phase is that all team members clean as they go, now and forever. Workers immediately contain and clean up spills. People gather and take away unneeded packing material. They promptly empty overflowing trash bins.

Peer pressure quickly steps in. Some people are accustomed to leaving their messes for others to deal with. Not anymore! Instead of their mothers telling them to pick up after themselves, their co-workers tell them — likely with more emphasis.

Another component of the Shine phase is to post cleaning assignments for all team members on the team's 5S board (see "Starting a status board for each department," earlier in this chapter, for details). This posting sets expectations concerning who needs to do what and lets everyone know about the responsibilities of the workers. (Step back and watch the peer pressure on the slackers!) Spread the responsibility to clean specific parts of the work area among the team. If an area's housekeeping is below standard, you can see who isn't performing his or her job.

Addressing maintenance issues and fixing problems at the source

Shine means more than cleaning; it also means identifying the root causes of messes and eliminating them. In an office, this step may mean installing (or at least changing) the dust filters in the air-handling equipment. In a factory, preventing messes may mean putting splash shields around cutting tools, placing drums of liquids on spill-containment pallets (which absorb leaks), or installing vacuum dust collectors around processes that create dust.

Cleaning up a work area often highlights maintenance issues within the facility. Maintenance issues have a major impact on how clean a work area can become. In addition to those we previously mentioned, common issues include the following:

- Leaky pipes, leaky windows, broken shelves, and the like
- Poor lighting
- A short supply of electrical outlets and/or unlabeled switches

Make sure that someone documents all these maintenance problems on the issues log on the "after" side of the team status board. This list holds all the open requests to other departments, pending decisions from executives, and known problems. The team's supervisor updates each item at least weekly. Post the list prominently on the board so everyone can see the open issues and the progress made toward resolving them.

Turn over all facilities issues to the maintenance department for prompt action. Management needs to ensure that all issues are resolved; in the empowered workplace, any issues that the team can safely resolve are its responsibility.

Shine phase housekeeping isn't a substitute for prompt maintenance. Instead of tending to an ongoing leak, you should promptly repair the leak. Quickly driving to the root cause of an issue is important. The goal is to spend little time addressing the problem rather than a lot of unproductive time treating the symptom.

The Standardize Phase: Using the Best Practices Everywhere

The *Standardize* phase gathers the results of the first three phases and spreads the best practices across the facility. Even though various teams have determined the best places to store tools and materials, the goal is to standardize practices across the facility.

Standardized processes are important aspects of the 5S concept. The workplace allows room for individuality. However, personal styles add complexity when applied to tools or processes shared with others. Standard processes shorten the time required to cross-train workers, bring in substitutes, or expand the work teams. After the best practices become standards, everyone knows the best ways to address certain situations. A visitor should be able to understand where item is within 60 seconds.

Find the right balance between standardization and unique workstation requirements. Simple processes are the easiest for people to accept. To standardize practices in any type of facility, try the following:

- ✔ **Define facility-wide cleanliness standards.** Organizations often document standards with a picture book showing clean areas with notations of the areas to remember to hit.

- ✔ **Gather the best practices from each 5S team, and appoint representatives from the various teams to select practices for use across the facility.** Take plenty of pictures and post them on or next to the facility's 5S communications board (which we cover earlier in this chapter).

- ✔ **Standardize 5S status board formats.** No matter which department is visited, the same information should always be in the same place on the board.

- ✔ **Standardize labels and signage.** Visual controls remind employees of the proper places to store items, as well as where to find things. Wherever people need reminding for safety or process reasons, include a visual control.

  Visual controls take advantage of shape, color, brightness, and location. Color should be high contrast. Most workers are already comfortable with the traffic-light approach of red for *danger* and green for *okay*. When making signs, pick colors that make the messages jump out from the background colors instead of blending into them.

- ✔ **Include a standard to label every work cell and every person's workstation.** Functions and departments sometimes move around, so labeling the work cells makes finding things easier. Placing workers' names on workstations builds personal pride in the 5S condition of the workstations.

✓ **Schedule a facility-wide time for daily cleaning and for weekly 5S team meetings.** Cleaning usually occurs at the end of the workday. The meetings take place just after lunchtime before work restarts.

✓ **Standardize the process for auditing the 5S status of work areas (see "Auditing the ongoing results," later in this chapter, for details).** An audit is a check sheet you can use to verify that all the work areas and assigned common areas are properly cleaned and organized. Over time, this sheet should indicate a team's ever-higher quality of 5S performance.

A final note about standards: Over time, workers may suggest exceptions to published standards. If these exceptions become part of the unofficial way of doing business, you may need to update the old guidelines. A standard that you don't enforce is merely a piece of advice, so to keep processes universal, you have to take note of when the published standards are no longer suitable.

The Sustain Phase: Upholding the Gains

The ultimate goal of the *Sustain* phase is to ingrain 5S in the work habits of all employees so that they follow the habits without reminders from others. The Sustain phase merges the 5S program into the basic company processes. Many companies find this to be the most difficult challenge, because old habits slowly begin to reemerge. The Sustain phase requires that the company recognize the 5S areas as the official standards that all employees will follow.

In the following sections, we explain the importance of clarifying that 5S is here to stay in your workplace and keeping up with responsibilities. We also show you how to perform a daily checkup and audit 5S results on an ongoing basis.

Stressing that 5S is permanent

Up to this point, employees who have been watching all the 5S bustle from the sidelines have either bought into the idea or figured that this program is just another of management's flavor-of-the-day initiatives. These workers just smile and stay out of the way, waiting for the fad to blow over and for everything to be as it was before.

During the Sustain phase, the 5S leader has to shatter employee dreams of ever turning back the clock. The leader attempts to ingrain 5S principles into the company's work ethic for now and evermore. How does the leader do that? Try the following:

✔ **Integrate 5S results into managers' performance evaluations.** Recognition of a well-maintained work area never ends. 5S needs to become the standard for doing business rather than a temporary success.

✔ **Turn the department 5S status board into the 5S Sustain board.** The before and after images are still useful, but the board needs updates. The issues log never goes away, because the team is constantly looking for ways to improve. During walkthroughs, management should focus on the department 5S Sustain board. Doing so demonstrates that management reads the board and that it must remain current.

✔ **Schedule peer inspections, in which one team inspects another team's 5S status.** This evaluation keeps 5S awareness high and helps teams share their best practices.

Continuous improvement is an idea in which no matter what people do on a job, they're always looking for ways to do things better, faster, and cheaper. 5S is no exception. Each work team should identify actions for improving what they do, the way they do it, and when they do it.

Keeping up with responsibilities

During the Sustain phase, the team members have to maintain the current gains and constantly improve them. Here are some guidelines:

✔ Ensure that every person stays responsible for sorting and cleaning as they work rather than leaving it for later.

✔ Schedule periodic cleaning — list the activities on the department's status board, including who and when.

✔ Review best practices that other teams identify for potential inclusion in another team's program.

✔ Discuss upcoming workflow changes and design the best ways to address them.

✔ Discuss issues and identify their root causes.

✔ Meet for 15 minutes weekly to discuss 5S issues.

Treat housekeeping and process layout as ongoing process improvements and include them in new process designs.

Doing a daily checkup

Create a 5S daily inspection sheet with an attached pen. Hang it next to the department 5S Sustain communications board. Every day, the supervisor conducts a one-minute inspection of the area to ensure it meets all standards. If the inspection takes longer than one minute, better visual controls (see "The Standardize Phase: Using the Best Practices Everywhere" earlier in this chapter) may be necessary. Note any issues uncovered on the issues log sheet.

Supervisors need the self-discipline to do the checkups properly every day. They're responsible for driving issues to completion. The facility's 5S leader has to inspect the issues sheet weekly.

Auditing the ongoing results

As team members become proficient with 5S over time, they may become complacent and start the slow slide back to the way things were before. A valuable tool for continued enforcement of 5S practices is the work area audit. Every week, workers from other parts of the facility select approximately 10 percent of work areas for an audit. This maintains peer pressure toward compliance and maintains pride of ownership of the program. The in-house 5S leader chooses workers for the audit team.

During the audit, the team spot-checks various parts of the work area for adherence to the current published standards. Team members also talk to others about their ideas for improving the 5S program.

Executives need to understand the 5S process well enough to notice something out of place when they visit a workstation. Whenever they visit a workstation, they can make snap audits of the work area to verify that it meets standards. These snap reviews are important because they reinforce ongoing management support for the program.

Chapter 14

Empowering Workers to Make Changes with Rapid Improvement

The work of a company all begins with a process — a series of steps performed by workers to create or add to a product or service. Workers may join to assemble a car door, create a payroll check, or prepare a patient for an examination. Any action or series of actions that a company performs repeatedly is a process. And like anything involving people, some processes work and some don't. Your job, as a quality control team, is to monitor the processes that work and improve the ones that don't.

A *Rapid Improvement Event* (RIE) is a short, intense effort carried out by a team of workers to improve a failing process; an event is typically three to five days long. The workers who support the process should design the improvements and set them in place. These workers should be trained to pull apart the process and rebuild it to run more efficiently.

In this chapter, we explain the advantages and disadvantages of RIEs. We explain how you can staff a team, choose the proper process to improve, and document your current process. Don't worry, we also get into the good stuff: how to complete an RIE in five days.

Companies measure RIE improvements in thousands of dollars per year, not millions. Still, it isn't often that the workers of a company can honestly say that they've personally improved their company's financial situation. Simpler, more efficient processes provide higher quality through fewer chances for error. Some benefits, such as improved quality, won't be immediately apparent, but they do shine through eventually.

Another name for a Rapid Improvement Event is a *Kaizen event.* Kaizen is a Japanese word meaning "continuous improvement." Many managers in the United States can't force themselves to wait for the end benefits brought on by many small changes, so they use a Kaizen "blitz" as a short, intensive effort to force Lean principles into an existing process. (See Chapter 11 for a quick introduction to Lean.)

Considering the Pros and Cons of Rapid Improvement Events

All business processes start out operating perfectly (that's the plan, anyway). Over time, however, things change. Gradually, a simple process becomes more complex, and this complexity can breed inefficiency. Rapid Improvement Events aim to identify and remove the "extra" from processes and return them to efficiency. The events

- ✔ Train workers how to use tools and techniques to identify waste in a process and eliminate it.
- ✔ Set new expectations for process performance.
- ✔ Educate the workforce to "think Lean." Over time, employees become intolerant of poor quality, poor communication, and poor process performance.

Rapid Improvement Events can provide immediate benefits to a company, but an organization also has to keep an eye on the potential disadvantages, too. In the following sections, we cover both the pros and cons of using RIEs.

The pluses of RIEs

You can point to several obvious advantages of Rapid Improvement Events when considering them for your quality process. With careful planning, all these benefits can be yours!

- ✔ **Cost savings:** Your company will save money through
  - • Faster, streamlined process performance
  - • Reduced labor costs

- Improved quality through fewer errors

- Less cash tied up in partially finished goods

✔ **Energized workforce:** Workers organize the work area, analyze the process, identify waste, and eliminate it. Employees' ideas solve the problem, so they "own" the solution.

✔ **Immediate payback for improvements:** This payback is often the result of streamlining labor and returning excess material for use elsewhere.

✔ **Relatively inexpensive to conduct:** An RIE has minimal paperwork and overhead.

The minuses of RIEs

Before your organization embarks on a program of Rapid Improvement Events, you need to consider these possible problem areas:

✔ **Improvements are isolated to one area.** To gain full benefit from Rapid Improvement Events, an organization must undertake a company-wide conversion to Lean processes.

✔ **The process you seek to improve must be out of service for about a week.** Consider working ahead to stockpile material to use during the event.

✔ **RIEs may raise unmanageable worker expectations.** Carefully set team member expectations so they'll know what to expect, and count on them to spread those expectations to others in the organization. Process changes focus on what's possible within the event's duration.

✔ **RIEs make a process run faster and more error-free; however, if the process was making poorly designed parts to start with, it will now make them faster.** RIEs are based on the premise that the product or service created is the optimal product desired by the customer. If the process output specifications are for poorly designed parts or services, then the team will create the poor design faster and more efficiently. However, it won't improve customer satisfaction.

Seek and Improve: Selecting a Process Victim

Careful selection of a process to undergo a Rapid Improvement Event is important. Everyone will closely watch the first RIE. The person sponsoring the RIE at your company must look for the worst-case process — a place where savings are easiest to see — and to concentrate on the most troublesome aspects of the process. (See Chapter 5 for more about quality sponsors.) Choose a process and steps of the process where employees will be able to *see* the difference after the RIE. It helps if the process's workers are in favor of participating. In the following sections, we explain how to select a process victim and target certain steps of that process for improvement.

Identifying a problematic process

When selecting a problematic process within your company, look first to the following:

- A bottleneck process that delays other work
- A process that creates poor results, causing scrap or rework
- A critical process that's in disarray

After looking at the major factors in the previous list, you can intensify your search to select a process that you could easily measure in terms of its benefits. Signs of a good target for improvement may include the following:

- A process that's too expensive or takes too much time
- A process that workers complain is awkward
- Work is late, which requires express (read: expensive) shipments to customers
- A high scrap rate, which requires express shipments of incoming material
- Areas cluttered with material to rework
- Regularly expedited orders with "hot order" tags
- Production of items that don't meet customer expectations (see Chapter 6)

For the first RIE, "pick the low hanging fruit." In other words, select the one place that is visible to everyone and provides the greatest financial payback. Both of these factors are important for breaking down internal barriers against future RIEs.

Concentrating on tasks within the process

In a big-picture sense, a production process extends from the point that a customer order enters the building to when the final product leaves. The entire process is too much for an RIE to tackle at once. Instead, your quality team should focus on the worst-performing steps in the process.

Here are methods you can use to spot the process steps to pick on:

✔ Examine existing quality inspection data to determine the point in the process where defects begin to show up. Backtrack through the process from there to determine the guilty process step. (See Chapters 7, 8, and 9 for details on data.)

✔ Ask the workers on the line. They are a wealth of information about the process they work with every day.

✔ Walk through the process step by step and note the points of greatest chaos.

Finding a Few Good Workers: Staffing an Improvement Team

A Rapid Improvement Event team is much like any sports team or even any military outfit: It requires excited workers, an experienced leader, and support from management. This is a truth you must handle to enjoy RIE success!

A typical RIE team is made up of six to eight people. More than this, and chaos reigns! Half of the people should come from the process step being attacked. Add one representative from the preceding step in the process and one from the next step in the process to ensure that the process results pass smoothly. As the RIE progresses, "part-time" team members may be called on to advise the team through some part of the effort, such as engineering, facilities management, human resources, and so on.

In the following sections, we discuss the important folks who should be part of any RIE team.

Workers are the heart of the team

The core of your RIE team needs to consist of the workers who normally perform the steps of the process under examination, along with some of the people who support them. No one knows a task like the people who do it day in and day out, often for years at a time. They know what should be done in a particular situation and why, and they know what has worked in the past and what hasn't.

Most process steps have four or fewer workers. If there are more workers than that, then the supervisor of that step should select four workers to assist with the RIE and reassign the remainder to other tasks for that week. Don't pick the passive ones! Select the most knowledgeable worker, the best worker, the biggest complainer — those folks who dive into the task and don't sit back, hoping that someone else will tell them what to do.

If the process step runs on other shifts, try to include all shifts equally. The team may be a bit larger than optimal, but the different insights will be valuable.

The workers you choose must be free to work on the RIE. Therefore, you need to "turn off" their work area during the RIE. Schedule the event for a time when work is slow so everyone can pay attention to the improvement program. This also allows your team the freedom to move things around without disrupting work.

Include representatives from your company's maintenance and IT staffs. When the RIE team is ready to test the improved process layout, the members from the maintenance crew can rearrange the target work area — often after hours. This task takes more than scooting around a few desks; the crewmembers must move telephone and data communication wires, provide additional electrical service, and so on.

An experienced leader is essential

Having an experienced event leader as part of the RIE team saves time and provides many other tangible and intangible benefits, including the following:

- ✔ An RIE leader knows how to tune the RIE method to meet a company's unique challenges.

- ✔ The leader's expertise is valuable when selecting the first target operations.

- ✔ A leader can interview the team supporting the process to be sure that they agree with what the team will be trying to accomplish.

- ✔ RIE leaders present classes and moderate team discussions as they rebuild the problematic processes.

- ✔ During the event, the leader can meet daily with workers involved with the process who aren't on the team to explain the day's results and ask for advice. The goal is to maintain support by keeping them informed.

Most companies use experienced leaders from the outside as "honest brokers" who don't have ties to internal politics. Look for a consultant with "Kaizen event" or "Kaizen blitz" experience. See Chapter 5 for details on seeking outside experts.

Managers also have a role to play

Process managers have a role to play during a Rapid Improvement Event. They must

- ✔ Implement changes recommended by the team.

- ✔ Break down internal barriers to freethinking and change. Some suggestions for improvement may not be practical, but the most common answer should be, "YES!"

- ✔ Ensure that the improvements made are permanent after the RIE work fades into distant memory.

Before the Fun Really Starts: Documenting the Current Process

Before the Rapid Improvement Event begins, the RIE leader gathers information on the existing process you choose for improvement (see the earlier section "Seek and Improve: Selecting a Process Victim"). The information should provide a performance snapshot that the team can use before it swings into action. The info needs to include important measurements of the following:

- ✔ How quickly an item passes through the process

- ✔ Any partially finished items sitting between process stages

- ✔ The distance workers travel to complete the process

In the following sections, we cover these issues and other notes you should make as you document the current flow of a problematic process.

Drawing a map of the process flow

The RIE leader and the supervisor of the process under scrutiny start preparing for the RIE by drawing a Value Stream Map to illustrate the flow of products through the process. (We cover Value Stream Mapping in detail in Chapter 12.) Each box on the map should represent a workstation that adds value to the product. With the map in hand, the leader and the supervisor can perform the following functions:

- ✔ **Visit the departments that feed material into the target process and that accept its output.** Note what the departments do with the materials. The RIE's process improvements mustn't disrupt these processes. After all, the goal is to make the entire process work better, not to improve one part that disrupts everything else.

✔ **Note any piles of material in the target process area:**

- Do you see material stacked and awaiting entry into the process?

- Do you see material piled between the workstations?

- Do you see any containers of scrap material?

- Do you see heaps of materials in the area that aren't a part of this process?

- Are there a large number of customer calls sitting in queues?

- Are there stacks of service requests waiting to be processed?

✔ **Collect some "before" data to compare with the "after" data of the improved process:**

- Count the piles of material to determine the cost of semifinished goods sitting and waiting.

- Make copies of the process's quality inspection sheets. What sort of issues do the sheets indicate? Ask the production manager about problems in the target area.

On the Value Stream Map, note measurements that illustrate the problem. For instance, if time is the problem in a step, you should note process time and cycle time above each step. If cost is the problem, then you should note the cost for each process task. If defects are the problem, you should count and note them above each step. These notes may make obvious the area for greatest improvement.

Discovering what the work instructions say

An RIE leader can find interesting information when comparing a target process's design with the way it actually runs. Work instructions describe what workers should be doing at each step of the process. Instructions list the tools and materials required and describe the proper way to complete each task and what to do in special situations.

Make sure the leader compares the process's work instructions to the Value Stream Map to see how they match up. On occasion, workers not following the correct procedure (and the supervisor permitting this) cause the process problem.

In most cases, though, the instructions are simply out of date. Approved changes occur frequently as the mix of work changes. Unapproved changes, however, may be made for a particular worker's convenience to the detriment of the process.

Following a worker through the process

If a worker spends a considerable amount of time at a worktable, create a spaghetti chart to track the worker's motions at that desk. (In fact, you can create a spaghetti chart showing the position of all the workstations and necessary tools and materials; see Chapter 13 for details on spaghetti charts.)

Be sure to note any wasteful steps taken to ensure success in the process, including some of the following, when observing the worker through the process:

 ✔ Where does the worker reach for something?

 ✔ How many parts does the worker take?

 ✔ Where are the tools and fixtures located?

 ✔ Are the worker's movements contorted?

 ✔ Must the worker wrestle air hoses to position tools properly?

 ✔ Are machines shared?

 ✔ Do the machine tools function properly?

 ✔ Are torque wrenches used?

The answers to these questions may point to steps that should be candidates for improvement.

Baselining the process performance

A *baseline* describes the "before" of a before and after comparison of a Rapid Improvement Event.

Before attacking the process, measure its current performance with an RIE scorecard. This measurement is often in terms of time, the number of units produced, and the defect rate of the finished product. Your RIE team uses these three elements to calculate the cost of the process.

One major cost in any process is labor. An RIE calculates labor as the number of minutes required to complete a task within a process or to complete the entire process. The event uses this measurement as a gauge of process improvement, because the removal of waste and an improved workstation layout should save worker time, which reduces the amount of labor (and cost) required to build the part.

Observe the target process in action before the RIE and record these factors of the process:

✓ How long it takes a part to pass through the process from end to end.

✓ Amount of time spent adding value to a part. This can be attaching a bolt, approving an order, or chopping lettuce for a salad; they all add *something* to the item that makes it closer to being finished.

✓ Amount of time the part sits idle.

✓ Number of work-in-process parts. This number represents a company investment in labor and materials, yet the objects haven't reached final form, and they can't be sold. Until it reaches its final form, the in-process material has little value. Examples of work-in-process material are a customer service complaint that no one has addressed and a half-finished truck hood.

✓ Distance traveled by each process worker in a day. This number is usually measured over a two-hour period and multiplied by 4.

During the 5S portion of the RIE on the second day (which we cover later in this chapter), additional data is added to the scorecard to show how much the 5S process improved the work area.

Figure 14-1 is an RIE scorecard featuring the previously noted categories. You can use this form to organize your process-performance information before you conduct the RIE.

RIE Scorecard

	Baseline	After the RIE	One Week Later	Gain/Loss
Time spent adding value	12 minutes			
Time spent idle	90 minutes			
Process end-to-end time	102 minutes			
Units completed	100			
Quantity of work-in-process	225			
Travel distance	960 ft.			
Defect rate	2%			
5S floor space recovery	1,725 sq. ft.			
5S cost recovery — materials				
5S cost recovery — tools				

Figure 14-1: A baseline RIE scorecard keeps track of current process performance.

Set improvement goals, such as a 40 percent reduction of work-in-process materials, a 20 percent reduction in labor, or a 50 percent reduction in floor space. Don't set the goals too low, or the event won't reach its full potential!

After your team completes the RIE, you rate performance again to show the benefit (or lack of benefit) of all the work of the RIE. The summary report determines future management support for RIEs. (See the section "The Fifth Day: Finalize Changes and Report to Management," later in this chapter.) To be credible, the RIE scorecard must measure improvements over time. After the dust settles and all the executive attention is turned elsewhere, the long-term improvement must be verified as real. The last two columns of the scorecard in Figure 14-1 provide a place to revisit the process one week later.

The First Day of the Event: Train the Team

Training your Rapid Improvement Event team is important. Individual workers may know a lot about their process areas and the company as a whole, but little about process engineering, for example. RIE tools and techniques are easy to grasp, so a little bit of training goes a long way. You count on the RIE leader and the company's quality control manager to provide the training on the first day.

Start the RIE on the first workday of the week. This allows time at the end of the week in case the event runs longer than anticipated. The weekend before the RIE provides a nice mental separation from the last workday, and the team members will be fresher.

Workers involved with the RIE must appreciate that they're the bosses, the designers, and the troubleshooters (at least for the length of the event). Team training must empower them to speak up, to challenge conventional wisdom, and to offer suggestions for improving the process.

In the following sections, we go through the different types of training presentations and discuss the types of lists and maps to create and update for the event.

Kick off the RIE training with a short pep talk by the highest company executives available. Attendance by executives demonstrates the company's commitment and interest in the success of a program mostly run by individual workers. RIEs are designed to generate a lot of employee enthusiasm, and the presence of company leaders and their encouraging words help focus this energy on the problems at hand.

Surveying important presentations

Each team member has knowledge of the specific job he or she holds, but members lack expertise in other areas of the company frequented by other team members. The first six hours of the first day is for training provided by the RIE leader. Presentations center on the following topics:

- ✔ Team building
- ✔ Value Stream Mapping (see Chapter 12)
- ✔ 5S (see Chapter 13)
- ✔ Waste identification (see Chapter 11 for details on eliminating seven types of waste)
- ✔ Takt Time (see Chapter 11)
- ✔ Mistake proofing
- ✔ Spaghetti charts (see Chapter 13)
- ✔ Information security

We cover a few of these subjects in the following sections; you can check out the previously noted chapters for full details on other presentation topics.

The RIE leader needs to set the team's expectation of what's possible within the event. RIEs quickly (or rapidly, we suppose) generate short-term changes, such as cleaning and rearranging a work area. Long-term changes, such as the purchase of capital equipment, are beyond the limits of the event. The RIE team documents the need for long-term improvements and passes the documentation on to the RIE sponsor for consideration.

Team building

An RIE requires a new view of the workplace from its team members. People work within an established pecking order. A few are outspoken, some are obnoxious, and others will never work well together. Teamwork training aims to break this mold and motivate employees to speak up and share their ideas. It emphasizes examining ideas based on facts and not on personalities. The success of the planned RIE rests on how well the RIE leader handles the people issues (see "An experienced leader is essential," earlier in this chapter, for more about selecting a team leader).

Teamwork training discusses the various ways that people interact, and it typically involves role-playing, a bit of lecture, and a lot of discussion. Training emphasizes "knowing yourself" and recognizing the best ways to communicate with others. Topics may include the following:

- ✔ Simple tests to help people identify their own personality traits
- ✔ Identifying and addressing interpersonal conflicts

✔ Appreciating the value of different points of view

✔ Active listening

✔ Respect for others

The RIE leader must focus the training energy on the problem and prevent team members from drifting astray, but he or she also must ensure that the team receives full credit for their innovations. If your company fails to use worker suggestions, the fostered enthusiasm will wither away, and future RIEs will provide limited or no benefit.

Mistake proofing

People don't intentionally make mistakes. Most often, the problem is poor process design. Workers may perform the same tasks over and over all day long. A worker isn't a machine that can do everything the same way, every time, all day long. Even a momentary distraction can cause an error.

Mistakes are expensive. Potential costs come in the following forms:

✔ Labor and materials to create a product that customers can't use

✔ Labor for inspection because the process isn't reliable

✔ Reworking, if possible

✔ Scrapping

✔ Delays in later processes that won't receive enough material

The answer isn't more inspection; it's fixing the problem at the source. *Mistake proofing* aims to develop tools, techniques, and processes to reduce the chance of making mistakes. The objective is to prevent, or at least detect and weed out, defects as early as possible in the process.

Mistake-proofing techniques fall into two primary categories, which the RIE leader presents during the team training on the first day:

✔ *Control,* which eliminates the possibility of an error

✔ *Warning,* which detects that an error has occurred or may occur

The basic methods of mistake proofing are

✔ **Elimination:** Redesign the process to eliminate a problematic task or part from the process. No task, no mistake! In a buffet, for example, if customers select their own dishes, then the waitress can't make mistakes with their orders.

✔ **Replacement:** Use a more reliable process in place of the faulty one. For example, a technologically advanced company could use robots rather than people who get tired and make mistakes.

✔ **Prevention:** Redesign the components of a process to fit together the only correct way. For example, software may require completing specific fields on a screen before accepting what's been entered.

Prevention is always preferred over detection. It's better to prevent the damage than to rework it after the error has already been made.

✔ **Facilitation:** Use visual controls to detect an error. One facilitation method is to color-code components (connecting red to red, blue to blue, and so on) so that it becomes obvious when an incorrect connection is made.

✔ **Detection:** Identifying an error before it leaves the workstation. One possible method is to provide a kit of parts to an assembler. If any parts remain in the kit upon completion, the worker knows he or she omitted something in the process.

✔ **Mitigation:** Designing products to include extra margins to guarantee some aspect of performance, such as extra-strong components and thicker walls than the minimum requirements to absorb machining stresses.

Information security

Some processes use sensitive data. During team training, the RIE leader should address that target process changes must ensure the continuing security of customer information. You need to protect personal information about employees, customers, and patients from casual view; these aren't only good business practices, but also legally mandated.

Creating and updating lists and maps

As the discussions progress during the training session, the team should start several process-improvement lists. You can tape the lists to the wall to share knowledge among the team. Team members can walk up and add to the lists at any time. For example, you may write down ideas for the following areas:

✔ Known process problems

✔ Critical-to-customer quality characteristics (focusing on product or service performance, timely delivery, and cost; see Chapter 6 for details)

✔ Process wastes

✔ Possible areas for mistake proofing

Team members also discuss and update the Value Stream Map of the process (see the section "Drawing a map of the process flow," earlier in this chapter). The map shows the difference between how the supervisor said the process worked and how it really performs. Add the map to the wall.

Team members should keep pads of stick-on notes handy. Expect to hear all the process's horror stories and special exceptions. Use the stick-on notes to attach possible changes.

For the last part of the first day, the team should visit the work area and simulate the movement of the product through the target process. At each step, the person(s) who works there can explain what's done and why. Bring the Value Stream Map and lists, and update them as needed. Team members can point out areas for possible housekeeping, opportunities for mistake proofing, and points of waste.

The Second Day: Review the Training and Clean the Work Area

During the second day of the Rapid Improvement Event, you should briefly review the first day's training and the lists and maps on the wall. Add to and update the lists you created on the first day:

- ✔ **Value Stream Map:** List any updates

- ✔ **Known process problems:** Bring up during the day's discussions

- ✔ **Critical-to-customer quality characteristics:** Should be about final by now

- ✔ **Process wastes:** The less obvious wastes should appear

- ✔ **Possible areas for mistake proofing:** More ideas from the discussions

By now, the team sees the process from a new perspective, and you can identify areas for gathering further information. Examples include

- ✔ Quality reports on defects (see Chapter 4 for more about defects)

- ✔ Materials reports for components in and finished goods out

- ✔ Management reports on hours charged

- ✔ Measuring reports for the walk time for the process

Assign a team member to track down the desired information.

The RIE leader should release the team to apply 5S for the rest of the day (see Chapter 13 for 5S details). Here are some tips for applying 5S during an RIE:

- ✔ Measure the amount of floor space used before and after the 5S event.

- ✔ Use the necessary cleaning supplies, provided by the RIE leader.

> ✔ Schedule facility maintenance support to move heavy items.
>
> ✔ Record every piece of material you send to the warehouse as savings, including tools, assembly materials, common parts, shelves, and so on.

The Third Day: Draft the Improvement Plan

First thing in the morning on the third day of the RIE, the team should wrap up any unfinished 5S activities from the second day. If the activities are finished, update the Value Stream Map and the process-improvement lists you created on the first day.

At that point, you can stop dwelling in the past and start creating the future! The RIE leader should moderate a discussion for each item on the lists:

✔ **Known process problems:** Figure out what the team can do to eliminate each problem.

✔ **Critical-to-customer quality characteristics:** How can the team protect or enhance these characteristics?

✔ **Process wastes:** Determine what the team can do to eliminate each waste.

✔ **Possible areas for mistake proofing:** How can the team modify the process or work product to reduce the potential for errors?

Based on the suggestions you come up with, the team creates a future vision for the process as a *to be* Value Stream Map. The new process should minimize worker movement, simplify workflow, and reduce work-in-process materials. The new process must balance the work among the workstations to provide a smooth flow and to eliminate bottlenecks. Changes to the work area should be focused on achieving something specific (waste reduction, less walk time, logical positioning of tools and materials, and so on). The RIE leader should make sure the new objectives are clear to everyone on the team.

Hah! Service companies aren't off the hook on this task. You can easily apply a *to be* Value Stream Map to any work situations from firehouses (to sequence equipment for fast grab-and-go when firefighters are dispatched) to the ways that retail stores rearrange their clothes racks after hours.

If team members come up with contending ideas about the best way to rebuild the process, set up experiments and try each of them out.

After this brainstorming meeting, the RIE team should meet with the maintenance team to rearrange the process work area. If changes require new fixtures, include the tool room in the meeting. Both teams may work into the evening to prepare the work area for the next day.

The Fourth Day: Test Changes and Document the Results

You spend the fourth day of the RIE finding out how well the redesigned process works and then documenting the results for future reference.

Taking the revised process for some test drives

Every diamond has its flaws. Before rearranging everything to use the team's solution, take some time and run some tests. Briefly do things the new way to shake out unforeseen problems. This is also a great time to fine-tune the new process. Installing a new or modified process is an unnecessary risk because it may do more harm than good.

Here are the steps for testing the improved process:

1. **Complete the setup begun on day three, if necessary, and run the revised process for a short time.**

   You usually run the process for 15 minutes.

2. **Meet as a team and identify possible adjustments to improve the process.**

   Record all changes and reasons for the changes before you make them.

3. **Run the process again for a longer time.**

   This time, go for about a half hour.

4. **Meet as a team and identify possible adjustments to improve the process.**

5. **Repeat this back and forth as many times as it takes until the team believes the process is as efficient as it can be.**

6. **Call the organization's safety and information security managers over to examine the process and approve the final design.**

   The new process must not violate any company guidelines for safety or information security.

7. **When the team believes it has improved the process as far as possible, run the process one more time and fill in the "After the RIE" column on the RIE scorecard (see Figure 14-2).**

8. **Calculate the gain or loss for each row of the card. Skip over the column for "One Week Later" because those boxes are for use one week later!**

RIE Scorecard

	Baseline	After the RIE	One Week Later	Gain/Loss
Time spent adding value	12 minutes	10 minutes		-2 minutes
Time spent idle	90 minutes	5 minutes		-85 minutes
Process end-to-end time	102 minutes	15 minutes		-87 minutes
Units completed	100	110		10
Quantity of work-in-process	225	25		-200
Travel distance	960 ft.	400 ft.		-560 ft.
Defect rate	2%	2%		0%
5S floor space recovery	1,725 sq. ft.	1,313 sq. ft		-24%
5S cost recovery — materials		$5,250		$5,250
5S cost recovery — tools		$1,775		$1,775

Figure 14-2: A completed RIE scorecard shows the improvements made.

By the end of the fourth day, the process must be ready for use the following Monday. Any changes that the team can't complete by the end of the fourth day go onto an "Open Issues" list.

Documenting your tests and research

The RIE team needs to document and standardize the new and improved process. Part of this task is updating the work instructions for each process station, with the applicable process supervisors reviewing and approving the changes (see the earlier section "Discovering what the work instructions say"). At that point, it becomes each supervisor's responsibility to ensure that workers follow the work instructions (no going back to the old way!). This supervision makes the changes a permanent part of the process.

During the fourth day, update the lists with the latest information. Bullet points should be clarified in sufficient detail.

The Fifth Day: Finalize Changes and Report to Management

And on the fifth day, your RIE team shall not rest! Your team has the following three things to do on the last day:

✔ Complete the "after" documentation

✔ Prepare a presentation to management

✔ Make the presentation

The team needs to make sure that all the paperwork for the final process design is updated and ready for review, including the new Value Stream Map, a spaghetti chart for process flow, and work instructions approved by the process supervisors.

Some process and company-wide changes just take a long time. To accommodate these changes, create a list of recommended actions that your team can't complete during the current RIE. The list may include capital improvements, tools that you can't create on short notice, and so on.

The RIE team then drafts and presents a one-hour management report on the completed RIE. The team members, especially the ones who will use the new process, should make the greater part of the presentation. This reinforces their commitment to embracing the "new way." The audience should include, at a minimum, the executive sponsor and as many managers in the chain of leadership over the process. The report should include

✔ The former state of the process. Include the Value Stream Map, known problems, critical-to-customer quality characteristics, rates, Takt Time, quality issues, and any other pertinent information.

✔ The journey to your recommended solution. Include training discussions, mistake-proofing suggestions and actions, waste discussions, proposal tests, and 5S activities.

✔ The format of the new process.

✔ The RIE scorecard for before and after (refer to Figures 14-1 and 14-2).

✔ Open issues and recommendations for future capital improvements.

Companies have limited supplies of money, so RIEs need to demonstrate their savings. A bit of public relations with the bosses ensures that they understand the improvements made by the RIEs.

RIE improvements are measured in thousands of dollars per year, not millions. Still, it isn't often that the workers can honestly say that they have personally improved the company's financial situation. Simpler processes provide higher quality through fewer chances to mess up. Some benefits such as improved quality won't be immediately apparent.

When the RIE is declared complete, the RIE leader collects the lists and other documents created during the event. They're used to improve the company-wide RIE process training and progress evaluation.

One Week Later: Did the RIE Make a Difference?

People are creatures of habit and will drift back to the old and comfortable ways of doing things. The real test of an RIE is to come back a week later and reevaluate the new process. Sometimes, after running for a week, the learning curve kicks in. People learn the new process and invent ways to improve it. In most cases, all factors improve slightly. In some instances, what seemed to be a great idea needs adjustment to accommodate unforeseen situations.

The RIE scorecard (refer to Figure 14-2) includes a column for taking measurements one more time after the revised process has been running for a week or so (each site selects what it thinks is a reasonable time to check back). Recalculate the "Gain/Loss" column to record the process's long-term score (really, the only one that counts).

Chapter 15

Looking at Lean Materials and Kanban

*O*verstock sale! Some companies never seem to accurately predict their materials requirements. They constantly buy more than they need, so they must sell the excess at "giveaway" prices (or so they claim). Other companies run ads with great deals on their products, but the items never seem to be in stock. These companies deal with constant shortages, expedited shipments, or piles of the wrong materials on hand. Over time, many companies accumulate odds and ends that suck up space but add little profit.

For this chapter, we focus on companies that must deal with excess (or incorrect) inventory. Companies often overstock to avoid problems. When a business experiences a materials shortage, its workers have nothing to do, but the company still has to pay them. To overcome this, managers purchase more material than needed, just to have a cushion. Unfortunately, these cushions of material build up; some can be used later, but some one-time materials may never be needed again.

Excess materials cause big problems and drive up costs. Your organization must move extra materials and store them somewhere. In some cases, you may have to protect materials from moisture, heat, and a wide range of other factors that cause products to decay, corrode, or shrink. And we haven't even mentioned possible theft and the loss of value while material sits and sits. So, who needs the excess? Not you!

You want your organization to become as lean as possible, and a great way to accomplish this is with a Lean system. A *Lean Materials system* is an important component of Lean Processes (see Chapter 11). Companies apply it according to their production volumes and unpredictability. Managers must select the degrees of Lean Materials that fit their organizations' situations. Along with Lean Materials, you see other complementary techniques, such as Kanban and Just In Time. Companies may use all three techniques in parts of the same facility. As always, you should apply the tool that fits the problem at hand.

In this chapter, we explain the concept of Lean Materials and Kanban, and we describe the pros and cons of the processes. We briefly touch on the Just In Time approach so you can decide if it might work for you. We also show you how to implement a successful Lean Materials process and work with suppliers to keep everything on track.

Getting the Gist of Lean Materials and Kanban

Lean Materials is a technique for freeing up large quantities of company funds currently tied up in materials that sit here and there around your facility. The technique is most useful for materials-intensive operations, such as sites retailing capital goods, food service companies, or factories. However, Lean Materials can still save money for even the smallest business.

It takes a lot of money to make something. The cost of labor, tools, and materials used to create a product or service determines a *unit cost of manufacture* (what it costs to make the product or service). The tool costs (buildings, conveyors, forklifts, and so on) are constant, whether the process is running or sitting idle. The same goes for the labor; the cost of idleness is reflected in the per-unit cost.

To minimize unit cost, manufacturers push to keep workers and expensive machines fully occupied. To ensure that workers are busy and to lower acquisition costs, many companies order a lot of material and place it around their facilities. The companies purchase excess materials *just in case* they need them. Sounds like hardware scattered around a messy garage!

Compounding this mess is a company's desire to build up piles of finished goods — the stuff it ships out the door to customers. It may be nice to have items ready-made to ring up quick sales, but often this material sits around, and the costs keep adding up.

Together, these situations create some problems:

✔ Excess material in a facility takes up time when you move it to storage, causes delays, and inhabits valuable floor space. Your organization has to pay someone to track where it is, to periodically count it, and to issue it when needed. If excess material goes bad in storage, you may have to scramble to get a replacement load to keep the line running.

Think excess material is easy to manage? How many times has a product sat in your pantry or refrigerator until after its expiration and after you've purchased a duplicate product?

✔ If some portion of an assembly line stops, all the other workstations keep going and piling up work-in-process goods until they run out of material. Each "island" works as far ahead as it can, sometimes storing semi-finished materials in a warehouse as it continues to make even more goods that the next process step can't handle!

This is where a Lean Materials process (including Kanban signals) comes in to tackle problems. In the following sections, we describe the concepts of Lean Materials and Kanban and explain how they make up a "Pull" production method that's better than a "Push" method.

Contemplating the concept of Lean Materials

Lean Materials removes most of the material in a facility, prompting a company to

✔ Order only the amount it needs

✔ Deliver the material to the workstations that need it

✔ Order and deliver materials only at the times it needs them

The only material that should sit in a work area is what the workers immediately need for use. (As Lean Materials managers say, "It's a factory floor, not a warehouse.") This may be a scary idea for companies that always keep plenty of material around to avoid running out. These packrats focus on pumping out the most work from their processes and avoiding idle workers or machines. The funny thing is, even though they tie up piles of money in materials, these companies still run out.

Businesses build small stockpiles of material called *buffers* to cushion their processes from variations in work speed and equipment reliability. Lean

Materials works to minimize buffers, but they never go away. Your organization should set buffer size by examining the risk that your workers may run out of material.

Big buffers hide problems that an organization ignores but should address. Converting to Lean Materials reveals many of the sloppy scheduling and materials issues hidden by excess inventories. Be ready to address these issues as they emerge.

Supplementing a process with Kanban

A *Kanban* is an indicator, or a signal, that workers need more material in a production process. The material may come from sub-assemblers within a facility or from outside suppliers. In a Lean Materials context, Kanban is one way you can manage the flow of Lean Materials throughout your facility. You can implement basic Kanban where you provide material for empty containers, or you can use Kanban to its fullest to control the rate of production, as well as the flow of materials. Most facilities use their own version of Kanban based on their unique situations (and willingness to change).

How you use signals in a Kanban system is limited only by your creativity. Each company establishes what works best for its processes. Some companies may trigger a signal when clerks scan the bar codes on empty containers. Other companies may use colored lights, turned on by workers and off by supply clerks who bring in material. Some organizations even use Web cameras that focus on work areas to see what's needed from a distance. For the most part, however, simple approaches cause the least confusion!

Another common Kanban signal is a card. Examples of information that you can put on a Kanban card include the following:

- **Contract numbers:** An identifier of who supplied this material. You can use the number to trace suppliers that send you junk to work with.

- **Line location:** The workstation that requests the container of parts.

- **Lot number:** Used by the supplier to identify the point in time that its process created the pieces in a container. The number helps suppliers pinpoint problems within their processes. Also, if a company or the supplier detects a bad lot, all the containers from that lot can be returned.

- **Part number:** A unique identifier for the component needed (all the different screw sizes look the same to a near-sighted materials clerk). A readable description makes the container easier to identify (as a result, fewer people call requesting cases of size 5 blue "thingies").

✔ **Quantities in a batch:** The number of units in a container.

✔ **Shelf location:** Lets the delivery person know where to put a container within the requesting workstation. (You'll have a mess if the delivery person drops all the boxes at once and walks away.)

✔ **Supplier name:** The name of your supplier and a telephone number for contacting the company with problems.

✔ **Unit of issue in readable form:** For example, you may identify 12-ounce tubes of frequency grease. You should put a different part number on 6-ounce tubes so this unit-size description further describes the part number.

The Kanban card in Figure 15-1 is for a container from an external supplier. Both bar-coded (for reading into a machine) and readable information (for anyone who wants to know the information) are available. A Kanban for an internal order would be similar. In both cases, a company develops a format that works best for its processes.

Figure 15-1:
A Kanban card contains helpful production information.

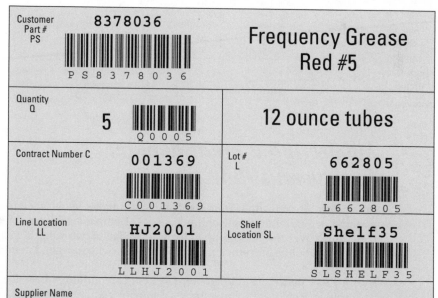

Figure 15-2 illustrates how the basic Kanban approach works. Each process within the process is loaded and ready to work. When the last process on the right (the one closest to the customer, #3) passes its finished item to the customer, this leaves a gap in front of the worker at that station. The worker reaches to the left and takes the output of the previous process (#2) and begins to work on it. Now that worker has a gap, so he reaches to his left and takes the output of the first process. The first process relies on the materials supplier to fill his gap.

The gaps (or Kanban cards) signal the processes to begin making more items for the process chain. In an ideal continuous process, this give and take occurs at an even rate. However, when no customer is present to take away the finished item, the entire process stops.

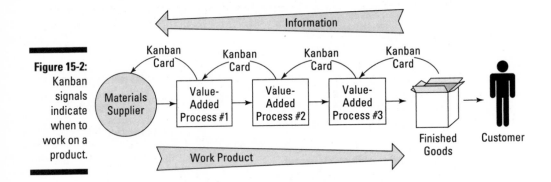

Figure 15-2: Kanban signals indicate when to work on a product.

Monitoring a great debate: Push versus Pull

How does a worker within your company or a supplier know when to send more material to a point in the assembly process? Companies have refined various techniques over the years, but all techniques fall in two general categories: "Push" (predictive line stocking) or "Pull" ("I'll tell you when I need it").

- ✔ A *Push* **materials management system is technology based.** Computer software defines the inventory a company requires based on its projected build rate.

- ✔ A *Pull* **system is market oriented.** The customer defines the production rate. A company creates products to replace what it sells.

In the following sections, we explain the differences between Push and Pull, and we explain why the Lean Materials method opts for the Pull system.

Food for thought: Kanban in everyday life

Many people like to describe the Kanban system of materials management by using an analogy to a grocery store. In this analogy, multiple items sit in their designated shelf locations. A customer takes an item, and this action sends an electronic signal to the warehouse that describes what the store has sold and where the manufacturer needs to restock. The warehouse prepares a replacement for the exact item and quantity sold. In modern supermarkets, Kanban signals come from checkout scanners, and the signals travel electronically to the warehouse.

Another Kanban variation is the potato chip truck. The truck drives from store to store, where it examines the stock to see what products need refilling. Where a potato-chip rack has a gap, the driver replenishes it from the supply in the truck.

Pushing materials out

In traditional manufacturing, a company's decision makers decide what it needs to build, which translates into a bill of materials multiplied by the number of units. (Every item built in a factory has an illustration that communicates the designer's intent to the worker who has to build the item; the drawing has a list of all the parts, called a *bill of materials*.) The company's supplier "rounds up" the needed parts to the next full container size it offers. Often, the company orders its entire materials requirement at once to ensure that everything is on site. As soon as all the materials are on hand, the company schedules the products to be built.

This *Push system* predicts what the company needs and automatically issues material to the assembly line based on manufacturing forecasts. Often, this strategy clogs the assembly areas with leftover parts not needed for immediate tasks. The parts remain to save the labor of sending them back and then having to reorder them.

How about an everyday example of the Push system? In many countries, homeowners keep small refrigerators and pantries. They purchase food almost every day to ensure freshness. In the United States, however, consumers purchase food in bulk from warehouse clubs and store the food at home. This strategy requires space in the home; buyers have to keep track of inventory; and inhabitants have to throw away expired food (which happens all too often).

Predictions can also come up short, which presents other problems. Say, for example, that the first 90 percent of the units built in a process had sufficient material, but at that point shortages of this part or that one start to appear.

By the time the end of the manufacturing run nears, the company has to order many small quantities of parts by express delivery.

It all comes back to costs. Management will have cost problems if it express-orders small shipments or orders piles of materials to avoid shortages. If you order high-quality materials delivered in the proper manner, your cost problems wouldn't exist! That's where the Pull system comes into play.

Pulling materials as needed

A *Pull* material management system resolves many of the problems created by the Push system (see the previous section). After a company provides its assembly line with its initial stock, it sends nothing else until workers request it. This method ties material movement to actual production movement. You can use Kanban signals to request the additional material (see "Supplementing a process with Kanban" earlier in this chapter for details on these signals).

Pull-line stocking works best with continuous processes where the workstations essentially perform the same tasks all the time. One example is a company that assembles personal computers. You see variation in the different components, such as more memory in this unit or a second hard drive in that one, but the work is essentially the same. Another example is a company that assembles trucks, furniture, or washing machines. The method can handle variations among the product, but it requires close managing if your organization changes production frequently.

So, how do you know which materials are best for the Pull system? Materials management can be as simple as ABC! *ABC analysis* ranks parts based on their value, focusing management efforts on the components that have the biggest financial impact on your organization:

- ✓ **"A" parts:** The most expensive or most critical to a process. "A" parts are probably only 15 percent of the items you require, but they represent 80 percent of your total inventory value. You need to closely manage these parts, which are candidates for Just In Time delivery.

  A *Just In Time item* has little stock in the facility. Throughout the day, a supplier delivers small quantities of the material. Typically, the supplier delivers the material to a receiving dock very close to where it's needed. For example, a supplier may deliver driver's seats every two hours, with the seats already sequenced in the same order as they'll appear on the assembly line. Another example is a restaurant that has fish delivered fresh every day from fishermen.

  By receiving material in small batches, you use less floor space and require less handling. Also, if you find a problem with the material, you have fewer items to repair.

✔ **"B" parts:** The next 35 percent of the components you require, which represent 15 percent of your inventory value. Together with "A" parts, these parts work well for Pull-line stocking. In the restaurant, if the fish are the "A" items (the most expensive and important), the B items could include lettuce, an inexpensive material used to complement the fish.

✔ **"C" parts:** The last 50 percent of the pieces that go into your processes, representing about 5 percent of your inventory value. "C" parts are usually common hardware like nuts, bolts, nails, and so on. You can get by with keeping a small supply of these on hand. In the restaurant, "C" parts may include napkins, bags of flour, salt, and so on. These items may be bulky, but they're inexpensive to buy in large quantities; however, you shouldn't let them overwhelm your facility's floor space.

Reviewing the Pros and Cons of Lean Materials

At first glance, Leaning your facility's materials seems like a lot of work and a lot of stress from the possibility of running out of materials. And it is a good amount of work. In reality, though, switching to Lean Materials isn't much more work than what your company does today. You can enjoy some great benefits if you can deal with the challenges that Lean Materials poses. In the following sections, we present the pros and cons of this technique.

The pros

Lean Materials has great advantages if your organization properly implements it (see "Going with the Flow of Lean Materials" later in this chapter for details on implementation). Pluses of Lean Materials include the following:

✔ Cost savings through

- Reduced taxes on stored materials
- Less inventory shrinkage (*shrinkage* is anything that reduces the quantity or quality of goods)
- Reduced floor space taken up by materials
- Reduced administrative paperwork
- Reduced labor (you don't need workers to count materials, verify what's in stock, and track where items are)

✔ Reduced handling and disposal of packing material

✔ Fewer problems from material lost in the facility

✔ Higher quality products

"Fresher" materials produce better products. Whether you work with food for a kitchen (potential for rot) or metal items for a factory (potential for corrosion), storing materials for later use can lower quality.

✔ Faster problem identification and resolution.

Excess materials can hide problems. If some of the material is defective, workers will toss it aside and use the extra. Sidestepping of this nature does nothing to recapture the value of the scrap or to fix the problem.

The cons

A poorly planned implementation of Lean Materials can bring a business to its knees. The cons of Lean Materials include the following:

✔ Receiving docks must be available around your facility, because having smaller quantities of materials on hand means requiring more frequent deliveries. If you receive material through a single dock, Lean Materials will greatly increase your delivery vehicle traffic.

✔ Increased labor from

- The handling and shipping of reusable containers.

- The constant communications to suppliers about line stoppages.

- More frequent deliveries into your facility and movement to the work areas.

- The potential redesigning of incoming parts packaging.

✔ Increased supplier costs (passed on in their prices), which your organization must negotiate. Consider these factors:

- Having fewer vendors to simplify your supply management reduces flexibility and competition and raises prices.

- Supplier negotiations must include ways your organization can reduce the cost of more frequent deliveries to your facility.

- Suppliers must reduce the size of their shipping containers and packing material to minimize the amount of trash created from their containers (see the section "Packing materials in the best containers").

- Small suppliers may find multiple daily deliveries too expensive.

Check out the following section for advice on how to work to solve these potential disadvantages.

Going with the Flow of Lean Materials

A change to Lean Materials requires two things: faith and trust. Faith that materials will be available when needed. Your faith will be well founded if you plan work far enough in the future to obtain the materials when workers call for them. Trust because it makes people very uneasy to lose their buffers of materials.

In reality, most companies already operate with Lean Materials. They may have plenty of "stuff" sitting around, but the only materials that count are the ones needed. Often, companies must order materials on short notice to meet a specific task anyway.

Companies often ease into Lean Materials slowly. One wrong move and the entire facility will be sitting idle, waiting for a box of bolts.

To begin the Lean Materials journey, follow these steps:

1. **Select the products to start with.**

   You have a couple of options:

   - Start with an item that's very expensive and hard to move. A truck-assembly facility builds a bus or truck every three minutes. That's a lot of engines! Rather than build an inventory of large, expensive, hard-to-move items, the company can schedule truckloads of engines to arrive at the facility two hours before workers need them. The result is a buffer (or store of materials) large enough to guard against traffic delays but small enough to manage. (This is an example of a Just In Time delivery of "A" parts, or expensive items; see the section "Pulling materials as needed.")

   - A different starting point is selecting an item that's too expensive to sit around for long. For example, a PC manufacturer that has to buy Operating System licenses represented as stickers attached to each unit may select the stickers. Each sticker costs $70, and 10,000 snuggly fit inside a shoebox. Not the sort of item to order by the truckload due to cost, yet the stickers are too valuable to mix with other boxes in a truck!

2. **Determine how many of the item you need in one day, one week, and one month, adjusting for seasonal variables.**

   Under the Lean Materials technique, you pay attention to floor space. The only material that should be on site is what you plan to use in the near future (each company must determine what "near future" means). Consider a medium/heavy-duty truck assembler in Ohio. Each vehicle requires a standard-model steering wheel. Steering wheels are bulky and made at a facility about 20 miles away.

3. **Calculate how long it would take for a shipment of the minimum amount to arrive from the supplier you work with.**

   This depends on how reliable your supplier is and how much lead time it requires to create what you need. A dependable supplier works closely with its customers and welcomes their forecasts of requirements (because forecasts help the supplier to Lean out *its* materials). The farther away the supplier, the longer it takes to react to a supply interruption. For example, if the delivery truck has an accident, you must have enough material on site to carry on until you can receive an emergency shipment.

   In the case of the truck company, it takes 40 minutes for a shipment to move from the supplier's shipping dock to the buyer's unloading area. Therefore, the truck company should have enough steering wheels on site to continue building trucks for the 40-minute travel time and for a "safety time" of another 40 minutes.

4. **Select the required containers and the number of units per container for your item; this is the basic size for shipping.**

   The supplier must provide material in containers that are easy to move to the assembly line. Container size is also dictated by the amount of line-side space available for the item. In the case of the steering wheels, each container holds enough material for two hours. The containers are bulky, and the company has room for only two at a time. (See the following section for more information on this topic.)

5. **Specify the number of containers you want to begin with.**

   You determine this number by accounting for two items in the assembly station rack, plus one ready to ship by the supplier, plus however many you need in transit to ensure the production line doesn't run out.

   In the case of the steering wheels, the shipping containers rest on the floor and not on a rack. However, the wheels come in special containers that minimize bending and make it easy for workers to pick parts up.

6. **Select a way to signal for another shipment (see the section "Supplementing a process with Kanban" earlier in this chapter).**

7. **Fine-tune the number of containers you order by reducing the number one at a time until you have the least amount of containers circulating possible.**

   A well-tuned system should always be on the edge of running out. Excess signals and materials encourage sloppy scheduling and a careless attitude toward materials.

The frequent shipment of expensive parts ("A" and "B" parts; see the earlier section "Pulling materials as needed") may make sense, but what about the small, inexpensive items you use in multiple places — like nuts and bolts? Well, you can store these items in *supermarkets* as close to your production areas as you can. At the supermarket, materials come in containers suitable for workers to carry, or they sit on wheeled carts. The key is that you're able to move the containers of materials without the use of forklifts. (For more on supermarkets, see the later section "Setting up 'supermarkets.'")

In the following sections, we provide additional information on implementing Lean Materials in your company. We explain how to choose the best containers for your needs, set up supermarkets, and arrange for easy deliveries to keep your process on track. For more details on dealing with suppliers, see the section "Working with Suppliers to Keep Lean Materials on Track" later in this chapter.

What can you do if you have so much inventory that you need to get rid of some before you start to implement Lean Materials? You should have enough to fulfill project requirements for the next two weeks; anything more is a candidate for disposal. It isn't unusual for companies to have enough parts to fulfill requirements for several years. To get rid of inventory, just follow these steps:

1. **Implement 5S style "housekeeping," which we describe in Chapter 13.** This cleaning removes excess inventory from the workplace and returns materials to the warehouse for reissue. 5S organizes work areas for better flow of material in and out.

2. **Begin draining the warehouse of excess stocks.** Often, this action uncovers material your organization purchased for long-gone projects.

Packing materials in the best containers

A goal of Lean Materials is to receive only the parts and materials that you need to reduce unneeded inventory. A big part of this reduction is receiving containers that contain the right amount of parts and that don't require heavy machinery to maneuver. You can further Lean your processes by providing reusable containers, which cut down on trash and labor. We cover these topics in the sections that follow.

Size matters: Selecting a container

An important part of Lean Materials is the delivery of small quantities of components. To deliver materials, a supplier loads parts into containers of specific sizes — usually provided by the buyer. Parts come in various sizes, so containers must also. An ideal container is small enough for a typical worker to carry, yet large enough to hold the amount of material that meets requirements.

Typically, a container should hold enough components to feed a process for an hour (based on the production rate). However, the containers for common hardware items, such as nuts and bolts, may hold enough for several days due to their small size and minimal cost. For example, in a truck assembly plant, containers of headlights may hold enough material for one hour's usage, but containers holding the small screws for installing the lights may hold enough material for a week.

Lean recycling: Opting for reusable containers

Lean companies can provide local suppliers with reusable containers of the correct size (see the previous section) and require them to fill the containers with the correct number of pieces. This approach is practical for suppliers who do a lot of business with a company. A benefit of these containers is that you no longer collect, compact, and pay to landfill the trash. They also make line-side work areas much less cluttered. And, because you provide the reusable containers, the seller should reduce its prices because the company no longer provides the shipping containers.

A common problem with receiving parts in disposable containers comes in the form of the material that suppliers pack it in (wooden pallets, cardboard boxes, plastic bubble wrap, staples, tape, and so on). You pile up mounds of trash with each shipment, which clutters the assembly areas. Workers have to struggle to shove trash aside to pick out desired pieces.

But, disposable containers and packing materials are cheap. Suppliers use them to minimize the costs of protecting materials in transit. Why not order the goods without the packing? You can order material without it, but then who's responsible if the material arrives damaged? The middle ground for Lean Materials is to use reusable containers, which you can provide to minimize the worry from your suppliers.

Collecting reusable containers and issuing them to suppliers does create additional work. Typically, after a delivery truck drops off its load, it picks up the same number of empty containers to take for refilling. So, on one hand, you have to account for the additional handling of the containers, but this work is offset by the many benefits of using reusable containers.

Companies that supply a small amount of parts may find it expensive to change to standard containers and shipment sizes. For these companies, you can arrange for a *materials aggregator* (a third-party warehouse that receives materials and sorts them) to receive materials and load them into the containers. This step increases the amount of material in process, which provides another argument in favor of having fewer suppliers.

Setting up "supermarkets"

Lean Materials calls for the exchange of a large warehouse in favor of local supermarkets. A *supermarket* is like a miniature warehouse in that materials come from suppliers and are stored in this area. Each supermarket should support one area of your facility; every part workers use in an area should have another container sitting in a dedicated spot ready for use.

When an assembly line signals for more material, the refill can come from a supermarket. A worker takes the material to the line, which leaves a gap on the supermarket's "shelf." The gap signals the supplier to fill another container with that part and send it over. (See the section "Supplementing a process with Kanban" for more on signals.)

The following factors determine the amount of material you should store in a supermarket:

- ✓ **How close your supplier is.** Japanese automakers keep their suppliers within a one-hour radius of their factories, which helps to keep their supermarkets small. If the only supplier for a part is located offshore, you require a much larger safety stock.

- ✓ **Speed of use.** If you need a lot of parts, you should keep a lot of parts in the supermarket. Some companies keep two hours worth of material on the assembly line, with another two hours of material in a supermarket.

- ✓ **Value of the component.** Expensive materials should be delivered Just In Time (see the earlier section "Pulling materials as needed"). Often, the supplier delivers some to the supermarket, which holds a small buffer of material, and then delivers to the nearby assembly area.

Arranging for smooth deliveries and working environments

You have two types of deliveries to consider in the Lean Materials process:

- ✓ **Deliveries from the supplier.** Suppliers make these deliveries several times per day in Lean Materials, based on the items ordered. When the materials arrive, the supplier delivers them directly to an assembly area or to the various supermarkets (see the previous section).

- ✓ **Deliveries from inside your facility.** The ideal situation is having a series of receiving docks near the assembly areas. As material arrives, workers can remove it and reload the vehicles with empty containers, which eliminates the need for forklifts and the like. Unfortunately, few structures have multiple docks near multiple assembly areas, so the only way to make this ideal a reality is to erect a new building.

More commonly, companies have material arrive at the docks of the supermarkets. Workers separate material according to a delivery route (like the postal service does with mail). Carts make scheduled runs from the supermarkets to the work areas on prearranged routes. During the routes, workers drop off material and collect empty containers.

 Tight quantities — a staple of Lean Materials — means that materials can't have defects. Workers and their managers must have direct contact with suppliers to resolve quality problems as they arise. Traditional companies pass information through engineers, which slows down response time.

The purpose of material delivery is for a worker to use it. Your delivery workers can drop shipments onto the floor and require workers to bend over, or management can provide platforms at a more comfortable height. Raised materials platforms aren't a luxury; tired workers make mistakes. It all goes into how you present parts to the worker for use.

Proper presentation makes parts easy to pick up and provides the shortest path to application. Store parts in a logical order (perhaps from left to right), and the presentation shouldn't require the worker to contort his or her body to maneuver the parts. You also should deliver containers with the minimum amount of packing materials required to save time and energy on disposal (see the section "Packing materials in the best containers" earlier in this chapter).

Working with Suppliers to Keep Lean Materials on Track

A funny thing about today's business climate is that buyers and sellers fight over nickels. The bigger picture is that both need each other. It's expensive to find good customers *and* to locate reliable suppliers. Instead of fighting, the business-supplier relationship should be one of cooperation. We give you some tips for working with suppliers in the following sections.

 A *supplier certification program* is a useful tool. It ensures that a supplier provides high quality, trustworthy material, which eliminates the need for incoming inspection. Certification also verifies that the supplier uses approved packaging and delivers materials on time. For more details about making sure that you work with quality suppliers, head to Chapter 3.

Encouraging supplier involvement to control costs

Converting to Lean Materials saves you some expense, but it also creates expense for the supplier. After all, one reason companies have bloated inventories is because taking on excess materials makes it easier on suppliers to schedule shipments and ship in bulk — or so they think. If Lean Materials can save you money, why can't it save a supplier money as well? That depends on the supplier's supplier changing to Lean Materials. Here's the point: If a vendor doesn't convert to Lean Materials, the movement of goods between the facilities will be a constant struggle.

To control costs, many Lean Materials managers work with their suppliers as partners to improve the process of moving goods between the companies. The supplier can share its challenges in improving packaging and explain the tradeoffs between alternatives. The key is in making Lean Materials easy for the supplier to support and to fairly share the savings to cover their costs.

An important tool in supporting Lean suppliers is to provide them with timely and accurate materials requirements. Timely information allows a supplier to use Lean to schedule its own work. If a buyer makes "panic" calls demanding substantial shipments on short notice, it motivates the supplier to hold inventories to meet demand, driving up cost.

Most suppliers maintain stockpiles of finished goods ready for shipment. A small amount gives the company a safety stock, but more than that means the supplier is absorbing the cost of the buyer's Lean efforts without realizing the benefits (in fact, the supplier now needs Lean Materials!). Cost of capital, warehouse space, shrinkage, the risk of items becoming obsolete, insurance handling, and taxes can easily add 20 percent to the costs.

To further control costs, Lean facilities include their suppliers very early in the new-product-design process. Together, a company and its supplier can develop parts and processes that help both companies stay Lean and profitable. This partnership avoids process waste.

As we're sure you know in the business world, a good idea can begin to fall apart when too many cooks enter the kitchen. Partnering with a supplier means investing time to discover its processes and to break down communications and technology barriers between the companies. Every time a purchasing team brings in another vendor that's a few cents cheaper, the coordination effort must begin anew.

Convincing suppliers to ship in smaller lots

When a company receives materials in large containers, workers must unpack it for use. If a worker uses only 10 of an item in a day, why would you move 100 items to the assembly areas? If you're dealing with a small, low-cost item such as nuts or bolts, having excess isn't an issue. However, if the item in question is bulky, it will occupy valuable floor space on the line.

One reason that companies store items in large numbers along their lines is that it's time consuming to make multiple deliveries. This maximizes a delivery person's time to the detriment of the worker on the line. Lean Materials reverses this approach to minimize material on the line.

You should keep only the material you need on site, which means convincing your suppliers to ship in smaller lots more frequently. Understandably, suppliers need time to adjust to making smaller shipments. Often, this means purchasing smaller delivery vehicles or hiring qualified workers. At some point, though, the supplier either supports your purchase requirements or doesn't. You should replace suppliers that can't ship the correct high-quality material on time. If you don't, your factory must maintain high safety stocks, and you won't realize all the possible savings from Lean Materials.

The fastest way to get a supplier's attention is to promptly pay for the goods received. The buyer establishes a process for rapidly accepting receipt of incoming materials. The company can tie the electronic receipt to prompt paperwork processing and payment. Typically, a Lean Materials operation pays its vendors within 15 days, because it's wasteful to hold payment until the last minute (you waste time tracking, storing, monitoring, reporting, and so on).

Part IV
Surveying Other Quality Control Techniques

The 5th Wave   By Rich Tennant

"I understand you've found a system to reduce the number of complaints we receive by 50 percent."

In this part . . .

This part looks at some of the better-known quality improvement methodologies that have recently been in fashion outside the realm of Lean. Each technique has its own advantages and must be applied according to circumstances. For example, Total Quality Management (TQM) uses a Plan-Do-Check-Act loop as an easy way to illustrate how quality improvement is continuous and something everyone can do.

Six Sigma is a statistics-driven approach for finding the deeply buried root cause of a stubborn problem. The process methodically examines, samples, and analyzes a process to find out why a part of it does what no one wants it to do.

Quality Function Deployment (QFD) links a process's specifications to customer desires; so, if a customer wants more of a product feature, you can quickly identify the processes that create that feature.

The last approach in this part is the Theory of Constraints, which says that companies create their own constraints to high quality. The approach demonstrates how to look at quality as a company-wide issue, where problems are often caused by misguided policies and narrowly focused measurements.

Chapter 16

Combining the Best of All Worlds in Total Quality Management

In This Chapter

▶ Understanding the basics of Total Quality Management

▶ Scoping out Total Quality Management techniques and tools

▶ Recognizing who does what in Total Quality Management

▶ Staying on top of continuous improvements

Total Quality Management (TQM) may seem like something out of the '80s — sort of like "your father's QC program." In truth, most components of TQM are still in use (for example, many people refer to Six Sigma, which we cover in Chapter 17, as "TQM on stats"). TQM included mistake proofing, cycle time reduction, and employee-led improvement teams long before these concepts merged into the Lean approach (see Part III for details on Lean processes).

TQM is more than a few data-analysis tools; it's a cultural attitude toward everything "quality." It provides customers (internal and external) with the products and services that best satisfy their needs. TQM is a combination of

✔ **Quality culture:** This concept is a company-wide value system in which workers focus on improving the quality of everything they do. Workers discuss possible improvements at every meeting and in every report.

✔ **Quality strategy:** Strategy involves a published plan with specific techniques and measurable goals for sustainable quality improvement.

✔ **Process improvement tools:** Employees use these tools to support the program.

✔ **Continuous quality improvement:** This concept means that every worker in the company feels empowered to improve his or her individual processes and is encouraged to recommend changes to larger processes. Each person takes ownership in order to make products right the first time and to stop bad products from reaching the end of the line.

In this chapter, we cover the basic principles and steps of Total Quality Management and the techniques and tools your company needs to get started.

We also introduce the roles of different folks in TQM and show you how to keep the quality process working continuously.

Total Quality Management in a Nutshell

Total Quality Management (TQM) is a company-wide, proactive effort to improve quality. *Total* means that all business functions (engineering, production, marketing, and so on) focus on defining and fulfilling (the ever-shifting) customer needs. Each company tailors TQM to fit its circumstances. The unifying theme is to "do the right things, the right way, the first time."

TQM is a result of earlier quality innovations from such eminent experts as W. Edwards Deming, Joseph Juran, Philip B. Crosby, and Kaoru Ishikawa. Like all great ideas, it combines the best techniques of each innovator into a "total" program. TQM was the first quality system that taught businesspeople to look to the process steps in order to improve. One of its greatest improvements was the realization that quality had to be moved out of the back office and into everything an organization does.

In the following sections, we explain TQM's principles, steps, pros, and cons.

The guiding principles

Total Quality Management requires your company executives' ongoing commitment to change. Rather than being the duty of a "quality department" in some distant, dark back room, quality improvement becomes everyone's business. To be considered *total,* quality has to permeate all levels of the organization. Here are the TQM principles:

- **Management commitment:** Quality improvement must be a daily topic. Meetings have to include time for asking, "How can we improve this process?"

- **Employee empowerment:** Resolving something on the spot is much faster than going through the tedious steps of getting endless approvals. Empower employees to immediately address problems they can resolve, and reward them for passing issues beyond their control up the leadership chain.

- **Fast action:** Management should quickly review suggestions for quality improvements. Every day an idea sits in the in-box leads to another day's worth of defects.

- **Fact-based decision making:** You base decisions about changing workflow on data collected at critical points in the process. Data should be the basis for decisions; you shouldn't rely on whims of the moment.

✔ **Customer focus:** Keep the products in sync with ever-shifting customer demands. Yesterday's optional feature is today's requirement. A customer can be either the person purchasing the final product or the next person working in a process. (See Chapter 6 for information on listening to the customer.)

✔ **Continuous improvement:** Processes and products are never good enough. You can always make improvements — to make the product better, reduce its cost, or improve a process's efficiency.

The major steps

Applying TQM to a quality problem is easy. Any worker in your organization can apply TQM by following these steps:

1. **Think of a quality problem in a process that you use every day.**

   Choose something that takes too long, occasionally fails, or delivers faulty products.

2. **Write a statement or brief explanation of what this process does.**

   For example, you could say, "Customers drop off the Web site and give up trying to place orders because the page takes too long to load."

3. **Create a flowchart of the process.**

   Usually this flowchart follows the Value Stream Mapping process (see Chapter 12). Sometimes, just a picture of the process suggests ways for improving it. The process flowchart should use one "box" for each significant step in the process; this setup alone may point out possible bottlenecks.

4. **Write down the problems with the process, both large and small.**

   State each problem and its undesirable result. For example, the biggest problem is a slow Web page (the problem) that causes customers to give up (the undesirable result).

   You may find many problems within the big problem. For example:

   • The Web server is slow due to too many programs running at the same time.

   • The disks are slow.

   • The disks need to be compacted for better performance.

5. **Investigate the potential causes of the problems.**

   Use a fishbone diagram (flip to Chapter 17) to identify the various inputs to the process. Identify several likely causes you can investigate further. The example chart for the Web page would place "slow Web page" at the head and each "fish bone" would identify the various parts of the process.

This chart ensures that you consider every aspect of the process. The problem may lie in a place where no one ever normally looks!

6. **Gather data on the defects, as we describe in Chapter 8.**

   Often, the defect reports are what start the review process. Display the defect data on a Pareto chart (see Chapters 8 and 9 for more about this chart) to identify the most frequently occurring problems — or the most expensive defects. Focus on the significant few defects that cause the most problems. Set the others aside for now.

   For our example, you concentrate on gathering data on the problem Web page's performance. Get the numbers! At the same time, collect performance data from the most likely problem areas, such as the Web server CPU usage, disk utilization, and network speed.

7. **Review past data on the process's performance.**

   Display the quality results on a run chart, which indicates the number of defects over time (see Chapter 10 for more about run charts). This chart outlines whether the problems occur at some specific point in time or with regular frequency. If you find historical data for any of the targeted defect areas, compare it to the present to see if something has deteriorated over time.

8. **After targeting the causes of the problems, apply a fishbone diagram to identify all the sources of variation that go into the process.**

   You apply a fishbone to zero in on each potential problem area to see what goes into it. With this information, you can point out where to try a fix. Collecting a ton of data is time consuming; your goal is to zero in on the most promising areas and minimize your efforts. The first fishbone you created was for a general look; this one should be very specific.

9. **Apply a control chart (see Chapter 10) to the identified problem area(s) to determine the amount of variation that results and how well the process meets the desired performance.**

   With the Web page, visually check the chart. When the page loads fast or slow, what are the critical inputs doing? Often, you can see one of them increasing or decreasing, likely causing the problem.

10. **Identify the input variation with the greatest negative impact on the product, and eliminate or adjust it.**

    Create a test where the suspected problem is varied up and down while you monitor the Web page's performance. If this seems to control the situation, you've likely found the problem.

11. **Start all over again, driving out the next most frequent or most expensive process defect.**

The pros and cons

Total Quality Management helps a company increase employee morale and job satisfaction, as well as product quality. Other advantages of TQM include

- ✔ Increasing supplier, employee, and consumer satisfaction by identifying and fulfilling customer requirements.

- ✔ Saving money by improving processes and reducing defects.

- ✔ Increasing productivity through less time lost to scrap, rework, or inefficient processes.

- ✔ Constantly improving the quality of products and services.

TQM, however, isn't a cure-all quality technique. Cons include the following:

- ✔ Small continuous improvements take too long to show significant results. In contrast, Six Sigma, which we cover in Chapter 17, strives for breakthrough (major) process improvements.

- ✔ Company executives call for "total" quality management, but other management ranks may not be interested in the idea. TQM requires top management to consistently break down internal barriers of communication and control to address problems.

- ✔ Empowering employees to change their own processes may result in sub-optimizing the overall process as each worker strives to do as little as possible. This situation leads to an endless dispute over which workstation should do what task.

- ✔ Many TQM installations are inflexible, with only one way to do things. This lack of flexibility means that tools may be forced on situations for which they're not suited. Your workers may say, "If all I have is a hammer, every problem must be a nail." What works best in the kitchen may not work well in the accounting office.

Shedding Light on TQM Techniques and Tools

Total Quality Management doesn't happen by itself, and it doesn't magically appear overnight. It requires executive support if you want to implement it and keep it going. TQM, in this respect, is a lot like a fire. Someone must prepare the fuel and light it. But with every success, the TQM flame feeds itself.

The more successful improvements your company makes, the more your employees will support your efforts. Gradually, quality takes on a life of its own as employees recognize it as the right thing to do.

And just like starting a fire, you need techniques for starting TQM and keeping it going, and you need the proper tools. We introduce these techniques and tools in the following sections.

Beginning with basic techniques

TQM achieves continuous improvement through the following techniques:

- ✔ **Commitment of senior management and employees at all levels:** At every opportunity, the organization needs to emphasize and reinforce that TQM is the responsibility of every employee. At every planning meeting, ask the question, "How will that impact our quality?" In every edition of the company newsletter, provide examples of how TQM has improved some aspect of the company.

- ✔ **Dedication to meeting customer requirements:** Implement a process for gathering and analyzing customer requirements and desires. (See Chapter 6 for details.) Customer complaints and product returns send powerful messages; they're full of information about things the company can change. Feed this information to the people who can use it! Time is essential. The sooner the problem is reported, the faster you can repair it.

- ✔ **Improvement teams:** Form groups of employees to address quality problems as they're uncovered. Big problems call for special, inter-departmental teams. (See "Building improvement teams," later in this chapter, for more information.) TQM believes that employees know the most about their daily activities and that they have high personal standards of performance. TQM empowers all employees to solve problems with their processes. (See "The importance of empowered workers" later in this chapter.)

- ✔ **Reducing product and service costs:** TQM reduces the chance of creating defective parts or building on defective parts. See the next section for more about TQM's emphasis on eliminating defects.

- ✔ **Using challenging goals and benchmarking:** A company needs to set goals for everyone to work toward. You may set goals to reduce customer complaints, have faster delivery times, or reduce reworked goods. Here are some traits of goals and tips for using them:

  - Choose goals the organization can easily measure, and make sure managers regularly give employees feedback on their progress.

  - Visit companies that are the "best in class" to see what they've done to improve product quality — a technique known as *benchmarking*.

How does a top-rated restaurant provide top-notch service? How does a five-star hotel handle its reservations? How does an overnight express-delivery company keep its aircraft in the air at all hours? With benchmarking, you learn from others so one day you'll be good enough for others to come visit you!

- Select goals that are challenging enough to encourage improvement, though not so lofty that workers become discouraged. TQM can't fix a company overnight.

- Compare goals and results to both previous work done by the company and to work done by other companies.

✔ **Recognition and celebration:** When employees do a good job, let everyone know. Share the success of the company with them (by giving paid vacations, bonuses, promotions, and so on). This gives workers an incentive to try harder in the future.

Emphasizing the deletion of defects

After you determine that a process creates bad results, try mistake proofing it to fix the problem. Here are some good tips for doing so:

✔ **Use techniques that limit errors.** Many defects are preventable through mistake proofing (see Chapter 14 for details on this process). Mistake proofing uses tools such as connectors that can attach only one way or pre-made kits with no extra parts (having pieces left over means something was left out). Web pages use drop-down boxes with the names of states to prevent mistakes. Surgeons use checklists to ensure that every instrument is accounted for before they sew up patients.

✔ **Have a good system in place for detecting errors and fix them immediately.** Your organization can find errors through detection methods such as inspection, automatic weighing, clearance arms to ensure proper orientation, and so on.

As soon as you detect a defect, stop the process and investigate the source of the error. Make repairs to prevent the same mistake.

✔ **If you can't eliminate the chance of a defect, inspect the product immediately after a problematic process step so defective parts don't continue down the line.** When your workers find defective equipment upfront, the company saves money on components and time later on. (We cover inspection in Chapter 4.) Here are some examples of this action:

- If a circuit board doesn't print properly, don't add new components to it; the final product won't work later.

- If a loan application is unreadable, passing it on for a credit check is useless.

Taking prompt action on data

Data is all around. Collecting quality data on processes and products is time consuming. It takes time to take measurements. It takes time to review customer complaints. All this time goes to waste if a process to turn this data into prompt action isn't in place.

Fast action on customer issues requires an internal process that can quickly move the data to where someone can address it. Like fish, quality data and customer feedback are most valuable when fresh.

TQM requires that companies create processes that promptly translate data into action. These processes review the data, assign responsibility to a team for action, and expect a prompt report. Whether the result is a simple adjustment or a new quality improvement project, the speed of the company's response is a true reflection of how seriously it has embraced TQM.

Data collection is a straightforward process. If you plan it well, you have to do it only once. If you plan it poorly, you have to do it over again, change a part of the process, do it over again, and so on. For full details on data collection, see Chapter 8.

Surveying the tools of TQM

Looking at the following list of TQM tools, it's easy to say, "Dude, you've been ripped off!" Many of the tools in TQM are now part of "newer" quality processes, but borrowing is the nature of quality systems. They take the best of the past and let the process evolve to meet current requirements. In fairness, TQM lifted most of the tools it uses from other quality programs:

- ✔ **Brainstorming:** A small team focuses on a quality problem, tossing out whatever information about the issue comes to mind. One team member then groups the notes, and the team uses the ideas as the basis of further action. Brainstorming is most useful when a problem area or a course of action isn't obvious.

- ✔ **Pareto chart:** This chart is based on the 80/20 rule, which says that 20 percent of the issues cause 80 percent of the defects. This chart is a version of a histogram with the highest (most significant) values on the left. With TQM, you should focus efforts on the significant few. See Chapters 8 and 9 for more about histograms and Pareto charts.

- ✔ **Scatter plots:** These graphs are plots of dots where the X-axis represents the characteristics tagged as the *causes,* and the Y-axis monitors *effects.* This tool illustrates positive and negative relationships and indicates trends and the dispersion of values. If the dots aren't clustered around a desired value, something must change! See Chapters 8 and 9 for details.

✓ **Run chart:** This chart shows the values for a characteristic over time; it may identify points where external influences disrupt a process's output. Run charts can illustrate a process's performance over time, and they often highlight differences between shifts, operators, or even between days of the week. See Chapter 10 for more on run charts.

✓ **Control charts:** This chart (based on a run chart) adds control limits and a mean line that show when a process is getting out of control. Control charts, which we discuss in Chapter 10, are valuable for plotting trends.

✓ **Process flowcharts:** A *flowchart* is a visual tool that shows the flow of work through a process. Often, this tool is enough to identify where a problem may be. See Chapter 12 for more about these charts.

✓ **Fishbone diagrams:** Also known as a cause-and-effect or Ishikawa diagram (see Chapter 17), a *fishbone diagram* is a tool that lists, on one sheet of paper, all the things that go into completing a task. The primary bones are material, men, money, methods, machinery, and environment.

✓ **Check sheets:** A *check sheet* lists all the actions that must take place to complete a task. As you complete a step, you check it off! Use these tools to ensure that all important steps have been taken to fix a problem. Check sheets are often used in data collection (see Chapters 7 and 8).

It Takes a Village: The Main TQM Players

A cornerstone of Total Quality Management is understanding your customers' requirements and ensuring that your product fulfills them. Customers exist both inside and outside of your company. The *internal customers* are the workers who support the next step in a process. Increasing internal customer satisfaction is the best way to increase external customer satisfaction. Each position in the management chain works on improving internal customer satisfaction. In the following sections, we cover who does what in TQM.

The role of executives

Executives play a crucial role in TQM because quality improvements take time to analyze and install. The people at the top need to maintain a company-wide focus on quality issues. An executive's job is to support quality initiatives and break down internal barriers to change. Ways to shatter internal barriers ("ordering it" never works) include the following:

✓ Participate on process-improvement teams

✓ Create several teams (with members from each department) to tackle company-wide problems

✔ Publicly promote success stories of process improvements made by company teams

✔ Require all improvement teams to include at least one department that supplies their input and one department that uses their output

Addressing quality issues takes executive attention away from other activities, but management needs to stay focused on the program. A truism is that subordinates follow management's example. If executives take quality improvement to heart and act on it every day, so will their subordinates. If they defer action and don't apply it to the processes in the executive suite, they send the clear message that TQM doesn't matter.

The duties of middle managers

Middle managers have a critical role. They must set the example for applying TQM in all their own processes while pressing their subordinates to do the same. In short, if they believe in TQM and practice it daily, so will others.

In most companies, convincing middle managers to lead the TQM bandwagon isn't hard. They use it both as competition with other departments and to create successes that they hope will lead to recognition and their own career advancement.

Some companies create quality steering committees to oversee their TQM processes. This decision assumes that someone outside the executive suite has more time to address the issues, with a clear channel to executive row for quick decisions. The *quality steering committee* provides constant oversight of the TQM program and quick access to executive decisions when needed.

The importance of empowered workers

Just as TQM requires listening to the voice of the final customer, it requires listening to the voice of the internal customer — the workers. To be successful, TQM needs to become part of the company's culture — a part of daily life for all workers. Line workers (and office clerks, nurses, technicians, and so on) are the ones who touch the products or perform the services daily. They see when things are running well and can tell when something isn't right. In the following sections, we explain methods companies can use to involve their employees in TQM.

Training workers on TQM

An important part of a TQM rollout is to train all workers on the program's principles and tools (see the earlier sections "The guiding principles" and "Shedding Light on TQM Techniques and Tools"). This training ensures consistent application of TQM. TQM training typically emphasizes

✔ **Decision-making techniques:** Rational ways to choose the best course of action

✔ **Interpersonal skills:** Treating co-workers with respect, working in teams, resolving conflict, and so on

✔ **Solving quality problems:** With the TQM toolset, walking each employee through solving problems from his or her workplace

Most companies find it easier to hire instructors from consulting companies to train and mentor employees. Executives and managers already have their hands full keeping their regular jobs going and don't have the time to create training programs. Also, bringing in outsiders adds fresh insights into process improvements. (See Chapter 5 for full details on employee training.)

You need to verify that the training is helpful and relevant. Keeping in touch with employee needs and perceptions ensures that the final product has the desired effect. Some companies use an end-of-course test to gauge how well employees received the materials. However, the best way to evaluate the training is to conclude the process with a mentored exercise where the class works on real problems in their own work areas.

Implementing a suggestion program

An employee suggestion program is the cheapest, easiest, and most effective quality improvement program. Human nature is to gloss over problems in case someone views them as a failure of management. Employees who suggest changes to their team leaders may have their ideas ignored. A suggestion program bypasses these information filters; the new ideas go straight to the top for consideration.

A suggestion program hinges on the fact that management considers every idea, treats them with respect, and promptly investigates them. If management ignores or insults ideas, employees may quickly stop submitting suggestions. A management truism is that you get what you reward.

Speaking of rewards, companies have found that financial incentives keep the suggestions flowing. If a worker's idea saves the company thousands of dollars in eliminated defects, why shouldn't the company share some of these benefits with the person who made them possible?

As the suggestion program piles on the savings, take time to tell everyone about the program's success. Publicly recognize the employees helping the company. This attention confirms to the workers that management hears and appreciates their voice, encouraging further participation.

Building improvement teams

The TQM techniques we cover earlier in this chapter are designed for groups. Most work groups consist of the people who normally work together on a task. Other times, a team includes representatives from many departments trying to pinpoint a cause. Teams provide each member with an opportunity and responsibility to contribute, a chance to lead, and an environment in which to easily and quickly give and receive constructive criticism. In these small groups, peers trade experiences, and informal training is possible.

TQM teams are empowered to make changes. If the change is large, risky, or expensive, they assemble a business case for the change. Workers aren't expected to sit and wait.

The value of external customers and suppliers

External customers are critical to company success. Even if a company has an immaculate staff of well-trained, hard-working, enthusiastic workers and a managerial staff chock-full of devoted leaders, it can't make a dime if it has no customers. If customers become unsatisfied with a product and better alternatives are available, they'll look elsewhere.

TQM thinks of processes as chains of customers. The output of one customer is the input to the next. Understanding and fulfilling the next customer's requirements is important. Additionally, each worker in a company must focus on the ultimate customer who purchases the finished item or service.

A company not only has customers, but also is one. Companies buy from suppliers before they produce products for their customers. As such, companies must ensure that suppliers hear their voices — the voice of the customer. Otherwise, how do suppliers know which features of their products or services to improve?

Customer satisfaction is one of the chief measures of success for a company. Companies implementing TQM track the number of complaints per so many parts sold or per customer. Each complaint provides another opportunity to improve a product and make it more attractive to more customers. See Chapter 3 for additional information on developing trusted suppliers.

Perpetual Motion: How to Enjoy Continuous Improvement

Quality doesn't just improve for a short while and then stop. Products always have room for improvement. Your company can make them more durable, provide more features, lower cost, and so on. When the innovation and improvement process stagnates, so does the company.

Continuous improvement starts at the individual level and leads to bigger things. As a worker solves the problems within his or her control, management should gradually point that employee toward bigger company issues. Consistently supporting continuous improvement efforts is essential.

In the following sections, we give you the basics on the Plan-Do-Check-Act cycle and explain how small improvements make a big difference in the long run. We also show you how to overcome hurdles to continuous improvement.

Keeping TQM moving forward with the Plan-Do-Check-Act cycle

TQM is a never-ending process. You can see this feature in the Plan-Do-Check-Act (PDCA) loop, which we cover in more detail in Chapter 3:

- ✔ **Plan:** Careful planning keeps the improvement team focused on the central issue it's working on.

- ✔ **Do:** Change the process to eliminate the defect. Be sure to have a back-out plan in case the change does more harm than good.

- ✔ **Check:** Monitor the changed process by using the same types of measurements that you used to identify the problem. Measurable quality improvement objectives make demonstrating process improvement easy.

- ✔ **Act:** Ensure the change is firmly entrenched into the process and that the problem is fixed for good. Go back to the problem statement and confirm that the change eliminated the problem. In many cases, the fix eliminates some but not all the defects. Start all over again!

Watching small improvements add up

Some people feel that a true quality improvement effort must be expensive and disruptive. Not true. Companies can reap the benefits of many small changes for increased product flow, better quality, and happier customers if the execs just permit the people doing the jobs to make the changes. These changes should be discussed within the work team to ensure that they're reasonable (and to avoid having employees shove all their work on other people). In most cases, the team approves the changes promptly, which keeps the improvements clipping right along.

When workers can no longer make small, individual improvements, it's time to step back and evaluate the entire process for improvement. You can begin to look at big picture changes. For example, you could move all the desks around for better paper flow; you could change how you refill your patients' records; or you could address the brightness of the work area lights.

Overcoming obstacles

Continuous improvement sounds so simple on the surface. After all, why wouldn't someone leap at the chance to improve a process? But obstacles do exist. The following list presents a few obstacles and tips for handling them:

- ✔ **Resistance to change:** Some people may not be happy with the current situation, but they think that any disruption to the process is just as likely to make the problem worse as it is to make it better. Your best bet is to address any of their concerns before making a change. In some cases, any change is considered bad, so a push from the local manager may be necessary to put an improvement in service.

- ✔ **Challenges of making continuous improvement a daily activity:** An occasional problem-solving meeting is one thing, but to practice improvements daily on all tasks large and small involves a significant workplace change. To gain the continuous improvement "habit," supervisors should hold 15-minute monthly meetings to highlight successes and discuss ways to identify what to improve.

- ✔ **Watching the program grind to a halt after all the easy and obvious problems are fixed:** To keep TQM moving at this point, you can point the individual workers toward specific strategic goals and look for ways they can improve their processes in support of these companywide issues. Examples of goals include reducing the number of late deliveries, cutting down on the number of dropped calls at the help desk, reducing the time required to process a loan application, and so on.

Chapter 17

Fixing Tough Problems with Six Sigma

Everyone has had a job where some part of it has never worked right — a persistent problem that annoys everyone but doesn't seem to have an obvious cause. From time to time, someone tests a solution, but nothing seems to work. If a company has a stubborn problem — something that employees have to work around — then Six Sigma may be the answer to their prayers.

Six Sigma is a collection of quality improvement techniques that identify the root causes of problems in production or service-delivery processes. It uses quality-analysis techniques and a broad application of statistics to pinpoint the process inputs that cause the undesired outputs. The techniques work to minimize the variation of inputs and produce more consistent products.

Some quality improvement techniques, such as the Total Quality Management (TQM) method that we describe in Chapter 16, seek to make small improvements that add up over time to a big improvement. Six Sigma, however, focuses on breakthrough improvements. It's the best tool for fixing those stubborn, they've-always-been-this-way problems.

In this chapter, we cover the basic principles of Six Sigma, walk you through the main steps, and give you a few important formulas (including what the "sigma" actually means). We also explain how your organization can use a few analysis tools and introduce you to some advanced variations of Six Sigma. For more information on the Six Sigma method, check out *Six Sigma For Dummies,* by Craig Gygi, Neil DeCarlo, and Bruce Williams (Wiley).

A *sigma* (σ) is a statistical indication of variation. Statistics is a technique used to make a judgment about an entire group of people or items based on only a few. The study of statistics isn't for everyone; however, just as an understanding of electronics isn't necessary to use a PC, an understanding of statistics isn't necessary to grasp how Six Sigma works its magic within your company. If you're curious about the role of statistics in quality, though, check out Chapter 9 for the basics.

Surveying the Basics of the Six Sigma Way

The Six Sigma process is a collection of tools. The key is to find out enough about each tool so that you apply the right one to the right situation. After all, someone may be able to drive a screw with a hammer but won't be able to loosen a nail with a wrench. In the following sections, we introduce the important components of Six Sigma, such as the use of statistics, the goal of breakthrough results, and the importance of experts. We also list the pros and cons of the Six Sigma way.

Injecting statistics into tried-and-true methods: The foundation

Six Sigma has a quirky label (as if Six Sigma isn't catchy enough): "TQM on Stats." The concept is nothing radically new. It borrows heavily from Total Quality Management (TQM) process analyses (see Chapter 16), Lean Techniques (see the chapters of Part III), and about any other quality improvement method that works. What Six Sigma does differently is to bind these techniques tightly by using statistics to create data-driven decisions.

Cynics say that "figures lie and liars figure," but when you walk company executives or other employees through a Six Sigma report, you'll be able to see the lights come on as the statistics you gather methodically sample inputs into a process and pinpoint the cause of why the output sometimes isn't right. And after you butter up the onlookers, you can go for the kill by showing them an experiment where your QC team varies the problem input in a controlled environment to make the problem appear and disappear at will.

Driving for breakthrough results: The goal

Some improvement techniques shoot for small, constant improvements that usually require no permission to install and come with little cost. Over time, the accumulation of small improvements pays off, like water drops that eventually fill a bucket. Six Sigma's approach, on the other hand, is to find the monster haunting a process and kill it with a single stroke, which can bring large and immediate benefits (see the later section "The pros and cons of Six Sigma: The dealbreakers").

Six Sigma believes *nothing* in a process is sacred. Often, the solution to a problem lies in an area that workers believe is flawless or that's politically untouchable (such as a part of the process implemented and fawned over by a company executive). By eliminating the infected area or altering it so that it runs smoother, Six Sigma can increase positive output substantially. When processes represent a collection of personal preferences and internal politics, Six Sigma can make big changes — all based on the data your team collects.

Here are some justifications you may hear that should serve as clues about seemingly "untouchable" processes:

- ✓ "We always do things that way."
- ✓ "The boss protects jobs so he becomes more important."
- ✓ "That was some executive's pet project."
- ✓ "Corporate headquarters requires this part of the process."
- ✓ "The last guy did it this way, so I'm going to follow suit so I don't get into trouble."

Meeting Six Sigma experts: The necessity

An important resource for starting and running a Six Sigma program is a certified Six Sigma expert. The expert provides encouragement, pointers on what to try next, and a kick in the pants for lazy Six Sigma students. In most organizations, the expert is the driving force that keeps the program moving forward.

One of the odder aspects of Six Sigma is its use of martial arts analogies to indicate the expertise levels of Six Sigma practitioners. Experts range from those familiar with the techniques to masters of the art. The typical Six Sigma expertise levels are

- ✓ **Champion:** Requires two days of training for executives. The training explains how to break down the internal political barriers that prevent improvement and how to manage the Six Sigma process.
- ✓ **Yellow Belt:** Requires two days of training. A Yellow Belt works part time as a Green or Black Belt team member.
- ✓ **Green Belt:** Requires one week of training and one completed project. A Green Belt works part time in his or her own department addressing problems.

✔ **Black Belt:** Requires four weeks of training, a passed written exam, and two completed projects. A Black Belt works full-time on process issues, trains Green and Yellow Belt team members, and mentors his or her projects.

✔ **Master Black Belt:** Requires experience as a Black Belt and completion of an enterprise-wide project. A Master trains and mentors Black Belt team members.

Most companies use outside experts to get their program well underway. At about six months, a company hires a Master Black Belt as a full-time employee and begins training several of its most promising Black Belts to be Master Black Belts. A key emphasis in Six Sigma training is to reinforce what employees learn by working on real projects that benefit their employers. Often, the savings from the project more than pays for the training.

Don't waste time looking for a "standard" organization for certifying an employee as a Six Sigma "belt." The best bet for an employee interested in Six Sigma certification is to look for a reputable organization that specializes in quality improvement. Here are a few we can recommend:

✔ American Society for Quality (ASQ): `www.asq.org/training-and-certification.html`

✔ Juran Institute: `www.juran.com/ store/results.cfm?category=4`

✔ Datazinc: `www.datazinc.com`

✔ Six Sigma Qualtec: `www.sixsigmaqualtec.com`

✔ Air Academy Associates: `www.airacad.com/SpecializedToolsTraining.aspx`

Considering the pros and cons of Six Sigma: The dealbreakers

Like many good things in life, Six Sigma's advantages may be offset by its limitations. When it comes to mysterious and persistent process problems, the technique shines. However, in most situations, Six Sigma is more than what an organization needs. A hammer is a great tool for pounding a nail, but it's a bit much for swatting a spider, if you catch our drift.

The pros of Six Sigma include the following:

✔ Elimination of stubborn problems by identifying their root causes

✔ Effective customer- and cost-focused quality technique

✔ Breakthrough process improvements (see the earlier section "Driving for breakthrough results: The goal")

✔ Typical annual savings of $250,000 per Black Belt project (see the previous section for more expert information)

Six Sigma isn't the right tool for every situation, however. The techniques involved take time to work their magic. Six Sigma programs have failed in numerous companies that have tried to apply them to all sorts of problems. You need to avoid the thinking that "If all I have is a hammer, every problem is a nail." Cons of Six Sigma include the following:

✔ It takes time to run a Six Sigma project. A solution typically requires three to six months.

✔ A program requires an investment in training employees (see the section "Meeting Six Sigma experts: The necessity" for more on training).

✔ Over time, executives may become bored and stop breaking down internal barriers for projects.

✔ A Six Sigma program works best after a company applies other process-improvement techniques to address simple issues. Most companies apply Lean processes (Chapter 11) and 5S (Chapter 13) prior to implementing Six Sigma, which clears up the easy issues and leaves the tough nuts for Six Sigma to crack.

Taking Important Steps to Implement Six Sigma

Starting a Six Sigma initiative in a company is a big step. Properly done, it generates excitement and high expectations across the company (although you shouldn't let those expectations rise *too* high). The key is to carefully plan what to do and who will participate. Make the first impression a good one!

In the following sections, we explain the importance of selecting a good project (or a good bad project, we suppose); we walk you through steps that your organization should complete before you implement Six Sigma; and we get to the heart of Six Sigma with a process called DMAIC.

Project selection: The key to success

The careful selection of projects is essential for Six Sigma to be successful. An organization must choose a project based on its potential benefit in cost savings and customer satisfaction, and the decision can be a tough one. Not every Six Sigma project *must* save money. If a problem has an impact on customer satisfaction or product or service quality, fixing it is just the right thing to do.

Often, a Six Sigma expert must root out a problem that needs to be solved (see the earlier section "Meeting Six Sigma experts: The necessity" for more on Six Sigma experts). Why do we say "root out"? We're not implying that your company has a lack of problems; the more likely scenario is that your managers are reluctant to admit that any problems exist in their departments.

We give examples of good and bad project selections in the following sections.

Good projects to fix

The following list presents some areas your quality team may want to investigate for possible Six Sigma projects. At this stage, your quality team is just building a list of potential problems. After you identify the problems you want to correct, the Six Sigma team focuses on correcting the problem, no matter where it resides in your process.

- Customer complaints
- Scrapped materials
- Reworked material
- Customer returns
- Warranty claims
- Overtime labor
- Excess inventory
- Cost to deliver product or service
- Cost of customer service
- Operating below industry norms

Bad projects to fix

Avoid selecting the following projects for Six Sigma implementation:

- **Projects with a predetermined solution.** If the solution is obvious, why spend time studying it? Try the "obvious" solution first and then apply Six Sigma if it doesn't solve the problem. For example: A shipping department's scanner guns can't read the bar codes on outgoing containers, which causes record-keeping errors. The IT manager is cutting costs by forcing employees to use old, unreliable equipment.

- **Projects that cross department boundaries without executive support.** Turf battles between managers can kill a quality improvement project. (This is often the reason that no one has tried to fix a problematic process before.) Top bosses must champion a project and break down internal barriers. A Six Sigma Champion should address this issue; one of the Champion's roles is to address internal political struggles (see the section "Meeting Six Sigma experts: The necessity").

✔ **Projects focused purely on headcount reduction.** The focus should be on improving a process, and if fewer workers are required afterward, let that be a result and not the goal of the improvement project. Some companies take pains to reassign all displaced workers in order to maintain labor goodwill toward their Six Sigma programs.

Proceed with caution: Doing upfront work before you implement Six Sigma

Before your quality team implements Six Sigma on a problematic process within your organization, you need to follow these steps:

1. **Examine the process you've selected (see the previous section) and try to eliminate it all together.**

   This advice shocks people, but upon examination, you may find that the requirement to make an improvement may no longer exist. Why improve a process that your organization should blow up?

   For example, in one data center, a study was made for a more efficient way to print reports and stage them for pickup. The final answer was to send all reports to local printers, where the person requesting them could pick them up and eliminate the print room altogether.

2. **Clean up the problematic process with Lean techniques (which we cover in the chapters of Part III).**

   Beginning with Lean simplifies the steps of Six Sigma and often resolves the problem entirely. If the problem persists, the factors are now easier to identify.

DMAIC: A five-step program, Six Sigma style

Six Sigma uses a five-phase approach for attacking a quality problem: Define, Measure, Analyze, Improve, and Control (better known as DMAIC). We explain the five phases in detail in the following sections.

Define

This stage makes clear what the problem is and how you measure it. Now's the time to set the boundaries of the study and explain how the defect impacts customer perceptions. Here are the steps you take to define:

1. **Clearly state the problem to keep your effort focused.** One method of defining a problem is describing exactly what's meant by the term "defect" (see Chapter 4 for more about defects). Here are some questions you should ask:

   - How many defects can the item or service have? If it has just one, is the whole product or service bad, or is it acceptable to customers?

   - How do you measure defects? Each type of defect likely has a different cause, and you must identify each separately.

2. **Investigate the process to understand how it should be working.** A Six Sigma expert asks questions of everyone involved with the process in order to look for the problem's obvious solution. Each worker has an opinion on the cause, which is referred to as *tribal knowledge*. Sometimes, many workers know the problem's solution but lack political clout to fix it. Before you proceed, try the recommended solution.

   If the tribal-knowledge approach fixes the problem, the entire effort is a success. Go on to the next Six Sigma project. Your goal is to solve process problems, not to awe your co-workers with Six Sigma statistics.

   If the tribal-knowledge approach fails, you must dig further into the process. A Six Sigma maxim is, "We don't know what we don't know." In other words, you don't know the right question to ask at this stage, so you can't find the right answer.

   Some tools typically used at this point are Value Stream Maps to visualize the process (see Chapter 12) and Standard Input and Output Charts (see the section "Painting a complete picture with a SIPOC") to break down a process into its major components.

3. **Identify the value the process adds from the customer's point of view.** For example, does the process add paint to an item? Put an order confirmation into the mail? How does the process transform the item (or service) that the customer is willing to pay for?

4. **Mark out the project boundaries (so you don't try to solve all the world's problems at once).** Company employees don't make visits to customer sites. In the manufacturing world, boundaries are usually the process's beginning and end within the facility. In the service world, the boundaries are usually the same. However, if your investigation points to a defect involving poor material received from a supplier, you must change the boundaries.

Measure

After you define the problem within the process you select, the Six Sigma expert on staff should validate that the process is repeatable and capable of delivering what your customers need. This validation points toward fixing the process or looking for variation in the inputs. (See Chapter 10 for more on assessing quality.)

If the expert determines that the problem is in the process, you look for variation there. Your process's tooling, design, and materials may not be capable of consistently delivering what your customers desire. When a correct product appears, it may be more of an accident than something your company can rely on.

If the expert determines that the process is capable and repeatable, however, the variation must be in the inputs. In that case, you follow these steps:

1. **Consider all the process inputs (men, machines, methods, environment, or materials) to identify variations (see the sections "Measuring variation with x's and Y's" and "Organizing process inputs with Ishikawa's Fishbone," later in this chapter, for more details).** Variation may be one of the following types:

   - **Positional:** Variation within the part in question or between machines or operators. Make several measurements on the same piece.

   - **Cyclical:** Variation from part to part in the same batch or between batches. Make measurements on different pieces.

   - **Temporal:** Changes that happen over time. Maybe the parts are worse on Mondays, you see variation between shifts, or you notice an hour-by-hour difference.

2. **Map the process and measure its overall performance.** At this point, you update the SIPOC and Value Stream Maps you create at the definition stage (see the previous section). Note the performance measurements made on the process map where they occur.

3. **Review the process to find a point to begin collecting data (see Chapter 8 for more about data collection).** The team begins zeroing in on where the problem may be. Up to now, the analysis has been on the process in general to identify these points for in-depth review.

4. **Gather information on previous defects.** Look for inspection records for this part of the process. You're constantly trying to tighten the point where the defect may occur while remaining flexible enough to chase the problem wherever the data takes your team.

5. **Verify that the way you detect defects is correct and consistent.** In some cases, the defect either exists or it doesn't (like a dent or a missed field in an order form). In other cases, the defect is that a product is too short, too long, not strong enough, and so on. You identify each of these defect types through measuring something. You must confirm that the way you detect a defect (or measure it) is valid.

   If you detect the defect by inspection (see Chapter 4), you can provide pictures of good and bad results. If you detect the defect with a measuring device (micrometer, voltmeter, and so on), you should prove that the device making the measurement is accurate. At this point, you've looked at the entire process and zeroed in on one or more places (or process steps) to focus on. You can't spread your Six Sigma efforts everywhere — it would take way too long.

Analyze

During the analyze phase, you examine your collected data and, in many cases, collect even more. Sometimes, your data leads you to believe that other process steps require data collection and analysis. And just like an old detective story, sometimes data leads to a dead end.

The final goal of this phase is to identify the cause of the defect. In general, the defect will be a variation in one of the inputs. Here, we lay out the analyze phase:

1. **Analyze the data you collect during the measuring stage (see the previous section) to identify the cause of the variation.** When one of the inputs changes, what happens to the output? Look for statistical interactions between the inputs. There are times when a problem occurs only when two random things meet at once; sort of like two feuding people that can fight only when brought together. Statistical interactions show that this occurs in a process. An example may be when an operator from deep in the Mississippi countryside takes a service call from an excited person in Boston.

2. **Pinpoint any areas of improvement.** Often, this step requires additional measurement. When you give attention to a process, it isn't unusual to identify small improvements you can make that aren't a part of the Six Sigma investigation.

Improve

During the improve phase, you form ideas about how to fix the problem in your process. This can be the most fun (or the most frustrating) part of the Six Sigma experience. Based on the data you've collected, your team proposes one or more ways to change the process to eliminate the problem. If a proposed change is cheap (such as changing the sequence of process steps), you can easily test it. If the change requires an expensive piece of equipment, the team must prove that the purchase will fix the problem (a tough but not impossible task).

Here are the steps you go through in the improvement phase:

1. **Begin improving the guilty process step(s) by identifying ways to fix it.** Based on the data you've collected, create a list of actions for correcting the problem. One or two major things and many minor things generally cause a defect. Focus on correcting the major issues, and if the minor causes are obvious and easy to fix, clean them up also.

2. **Experiment with various solutions, and propose the one that solves the problem with the least amount of cost or complexity.** This step can be fun. It involves purposely varying the input you think causes the problem to prove your theory. If you find the right cause, everyone can watch as your team makes the elusive defect appear and disappear at will by varying the guilty input.

3. **Obtain approval and install the solution.** With the true problem's identity proven, your team proposes a solution to eliminate the problem. Draft a proposal for changing the process for approval by the project's sponsor (see Chapter 5 for more on sponsors).

4. **Look for mistake-proofing opportunities (see Chapter 14 for more about mistake proofing).** When eliminating the problem, look for ways to reduce the chance that it will ever appear again.

5. **Statistically demonstrate the amount of improvement in the process after you implement the solution (see Chapter 9 for more on the role of statistics).** After you implement the fix, compare the result to the original defect level — the true test that the process is really repaired. In some cases, you can prove the result immediately. However, many companies wait anywhere from two weeks to a month before sampling the error rate to prove the change made the process better and not worse.

Control

An important part of Six Sigma is controlling the process you improve so that it stays fixed. After you take steps to improve the process, implement a control process that alerts you if the process changes back to its dysfunctional ways. A control process also ensures that workers don't go back to the "old way" of doing something.

Six Sigma teams can maintain control several ways. One way is to monitor the quality of the output to see if the defect reappears. However, the monster may awaken later when no one is watching. Another way is to review an FMEA chart you create (see the section "Putting Everything Together with Process-Review Tools" later in this chapter).

Crunching Some Six Sigma Numbers

A hallmark of the Six Sigma process is its dependence on hard data (which you can see in the DMAIC steps from the previous section). Instead of having each person on your quality team read and interpret every line of data you collect during a Six Sigma project, you can summarize it by using numbers to indicate relationships. For example, you may want to examine the relationship of how many units were started versus how many were completed the first time through a process without rework — known as the Rolled Throughput Yield (RTY) — in order to identify a variation (a problem in the process). In the following sections, we show you how to calculate RTY, explain the meaning of "Sigma" in Six Sigma, and give you a few handy ways to interpret process data.

Calculating the Rolled Throughput Yield

The most important part of any process is the result — the finished product or service that you produce or deliver. The *Rolled Throughput Yield* (RTY) is the number of finished units a process produces the first time through without any rework. RTY is an indicator of the number of units that go into a process compared to the number that come out complete at the end. The higher the RTY, the more efficient the process.

The RTY is mathematically related to the Sigma level, but explaining natural logs (mathematical logs, not big wooden sticks) isn't something for this *For Dummies* book (sorry for the curious!).

In Figure 17-1, you can see material on the left that's entering a process. After entry, workers handle the material, and most of it exits to the right as finished goods. However, a small amount of material is defective and is set aside and restarted through the process for rework or total scrap.

Unfortunately, life isn't as simple as a one-step process. Imagine a three-step process in shaping wood:

- ✔ In the first step, 100 pieces of wood enter the process, but the workers make only 95 properly for the second step. The workers didn't cut the other 5 pieces according to specification, so the pieces are discarded.

- ✔ The second step takes the output from the first and makes additional cuts. Of the 95 pieces that enter the second step, only 98 percent (93 pieces) are fit to pass on. The other two pieces are discarded.

- ✔ The third step takes the results from the second and drills some holes into the wood pieces as a finishing touch. Of the pieces that enter the third step, 99 percent (92 pieces total) are delivered as finished products.

So, you calculate the Rolled Throughput Yield by multiplying the percent of good material that leaves each process step. Here are the results for the wood example:

Step 1: $95 \div 100 = 0.95$ (95 percent)

Step 2: $93 \div 95 = 0.978$ (98 percent)

Step 3: $92 \div 93 = 0.989$ (99 percent)

RTY: 95 percent $\times$ 98 percent $\times$ 99 percent $=$ 92 percent

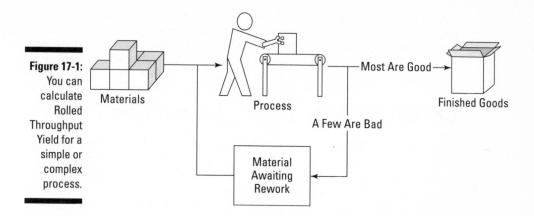

Figure 17-1: You can calculate Rolled Throughput Yield for a simple or complex process.

The total RTY is 92 percent. Out of 100 pieces of wood that enter the process, only 92 acceptable ones come out.

After calculating the RTY, you need to consider the money lost in buying the other eight pieces of material and the labor lost by working on the material lost in the third step. Now, consider the impact of a 20- or 30-step process. How much would you save by improving a process with so many steps? That's where Six Sigma comes in.

Consider the example of filling in a home loan application form with 30 blanks. If customers experience a 99-percent success rate for filling in each blank, you'd calculate the RTY by multiplying 99 percent times itself 30 times. The result is a 74-percent chance of a customer filling out a form correctly the first time. Not a very efficient process! Imagine the cost of reworking all the defective forms to clear up the bad data in the blanks.

Understanding the meaning of "Sigma"

A *sigma* is a standard deviation on a normal curve — a deviation away from the mean. In quality terms, it indicates the number of defects that emerge from a process. The higher the sigma level, the fewer the defects.

Figure 17-2 shows the sigma in a normal curve. You can think of the area under the curve as all the items produced, or the output. Down the middle is the mean, or average, value. The figure identifies results as above or below this average. The closer to the mean a result falls, the more commonly that value occurs. Some results appear farther from the mean, but those values should occur very rarely.

Figure 17-2 allows you to put Six Sigma to use in a practical example. Suppose you're making wooden yard sticks that hardware stores give away to attract customers. Looking at the scale on the bottom of Figure 17-2, each yardstick should be exactly 36 inches long, per customer specifications. You can use that value for the mean. Based on your stick-making experience, you know that some will be slightly shorter or slightly longer than the mean. The normal curve indicates that very few will be a lot longer or shorter; most will be very close to the center, or the desired value.

If your customers don't care that a yardstick is ³⁄₁₀ of an inch longer or shorter than an exact yard, the process meets customer needs. However, if you're creating a tool for measuring cloth for sale, this amount of variation can be detrimental to your customers, who may have cloth that's too short, or to the seller, who may cut the cloth too long. In this case, the variation of plus or minus 0.3 inches is unacceptable. In short, the customer determines the amount of acceptable variation.

You can see numerical breakdowns for a normal curve in Table 17-1. A two-sigma process (one sigma above and one sigma below the mean) provides about two-thirds of the results; in other words, two-thirds of a company's products or services are free of defects. At four sigma (two sigma on either side of the mean), defect-free results include over 99 percent of the output. The higher the sigma you calculate, the better.

Table 17-1	Percentage of Defect-Free Products and Services in Six Sigma	
σ	*Defects per Million Opportunities*	*Percent of Defect-Free Products and Services*
One Sigma	690,000	31%
Two Sigma	308,000	69%
Three Sigma	66,800	93%
Four Sigma	6,210	99.4%
Five Sigma	230	99.97%
Six Sigma	3.4	99.9966%

Most U.S. companies operate between three and four sigma in quality terms, and they still spend 20 percent of their costs on correcting defects in completed products or services. Some companies, like those in the airline industry, operate in areas beyond Six Sigma. They spend a considerable amount of time and money to ensure that their hugely expensive aircraft remain safe and operational. A single defect may cost hundreds of lives and millions of dollars.

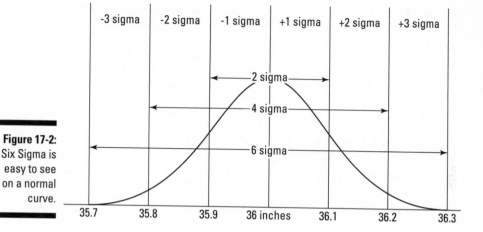

Figure 17-2:
Six Sigma is
easy to see
on a normal
curve.

Measuring variation with x's and Y's

Six Sigma focuses on variation in the output caused by variation in the input. Your input can vary due to different tools, different operators, different materials, different time of day, and so on (see the section "Measure," earlier in this chapter, for more about variation). Whatever the variation may be, after you identify it, you can measure it.

The equation for measuring variation is as follows:

$$Y = f(x)$$

In English, you say, "Y is a function of x." What values go into this equation?

- Six Sigma uses Y to symbolize the output of a process. Y could be a finished document, a machined part, or even a properly served customer. Y is the result of working on the process.

- x is anything you use to complete a task (representing just one step in a process, or whatever a worker is doing). Y, or the output, is the result of the x's that you use to create it (sort of "you are what you eat").

You can apply this concept to small tasks or to an entire process. On its surface, the idea seems basic. It isn't much different from making soup. The worker pours inputs (labor, materials, tools, instructions, and so on) into a process, shakes it up, and something comes out the other end (soup, dirty pans, heat in the air, and so on). The value of listing everything that goes in and everything that pops out is identifying what's involved so a quality team can focus on where the problem may be.

Any given Y has numerous x's. To identify and categorize all the x's, you use a Fishbone chart (which we cover later in this chapter). Some x's are more significant than others. You may want to list major factors as capital X's and minor factors as lowercase x's. For example, when making soup, the significant X's are the amount of heat applied, water, potatoes, celery, and carrots. The minor x's may be the amount of black pepper added.

Putting Everything Together with Process-Review Tools

With so much information swirling around the heads of Six Sigma team members — from process research, to RTYs, to sigma, to measurements, and the implementation of Six Sigma — it helps to gather it all into one place for analysis purposes (a place bigger than your head, of course). Three tools — SIPOC, Fishbone charts, and FMEA — are easy-to-use and effective for process analysis. You can use these tools to dissect a process to figure out what makes it tick.

A classic rule in Six Sigma is, "You don't know what you don't know." If someone doesn't know that something exists, he or she can't ask questions about it. A team should never approach a process assuming that the members know all there is to know about it. You can use the simple tools in the following sections to break down processes to methodically study them.

Painting a complete picture with a SIPOC

You can use a *Standard Input and Output Chart* (SIPOC) (pronounced sigh-pock) to organize the inputs and outputs of a process onto a single sheet of paper. A SIPOC is an excellent tool for beginning the examination of a process, which we explain in the earlier section "DMAIC: A five-step program, Six Sigma style." You can complete the chart with pictures or as text. A sample SIPOC is shown in Figure 17-3, and the following list outlines its elements. To create the chart, you just have the following five columns with space underneath for information.

✔ **Suppliers:** Anyone who contributes to making a process work. Some categories that suppliers contribute to may be materials, specific labor skills, tooling, or machines or repair services. In Figure 17-3, the suppliers are a copier company, an office supplies store, and a person making copies. Focus on the major suppliers to the process; don't get caught up in the minutia.

✔ **Inputs:** The resources necessary to make a process work, such as the operators or specific materials. In Figure 17-3, the inputs are a copier service technician (if needed), a page for copying, blank paper, and toner.

✔ **Process:** The process is like the soup pot — it's where everything comes together. In Figure 17-3, the only process is the actual copying of a document.

✔ **Outputs:** The products that result from the inputs and the workings of a process. You may list critical product characteristics on this part of the chart. In Figure 17-3, the outputs are the copies of a document and a "click" counter. (The click counter is the way the machine keeps track of how many copies it has made so that workers can replace usage-sensitive components before they fail.) Listing the critical characteristics of a correct process output anchors the analysis of customer requirements.

✔ **Customers:** The people who receive the value-added product. The customers in Figure 17-3 are the person making the copies and folks in other departments who may receive the copies.

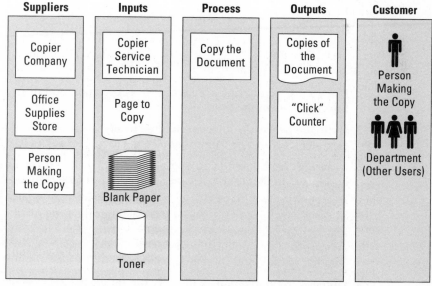

Figure 17-3: A SIPOC gives a clear overview of a process's inputs and outputs.

Organizing process inputs with Ishikawa's Fishbone

An easy way to organize the inputs of a process is by using an *Ishikawa's Fishbone chart* (also known as a Cause and Effect Diagram; see Figure 17-4). Think of the chart as a visual Y = f(x) equation for measurement (see the earlier section "Measuring variation with x's and Y's" for more about this formula). The head of the fish is the "Y" of the process, and each of the "ribs" is an "x" and represents one of the major sources of inputs. This type of diagram is an excellent tool for an in-depth identification of everything that goes into a process.

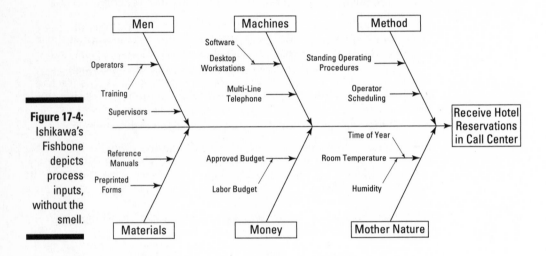

Figure 17-4:
Ishikawa's
Fishbone
depicts
process
inputs,
without the
smell.

To create a Fishbone chart, follow these steps:

1. **Draw a horizontal line across the sheet of paper, and draw a box on the right side of the line.**

2. **Write the process's objective in the "head," such as "Run the kitchen" (big picture view) or "Make soup" (specific process view).**

3. **Draw six "fishbones" at an angle toward the left — three lines on top and three on the bottom, evenly spaced apart (see Figure 17-4).**

   You'll fill this space with detail, so use the whole page. You attach a label to each of these six fishbones. Old-timers use the 6 Ms (men, machines, materials, money, method, and mother nature). Over time, people have substituted more politically correct terms like "environment" for "mother nature" and "people" for "men."

4. **Off each of the fishbones, identify the things the process needs in order to work properly.**

   For example, you see the following fishbones in Figure 17-4:

   • **Men:** Anything dealing with the labor used by the process, such as skilled workers or training.

   • **Machines:** All the tools used in a process, such as a conveyor, a mop and bucket, and so on.

- **Materials:** The "things" used in the process. You may identify an order form (paper or electronic), a piece of wood, and so on. Usually, workers use several materials in a process step.

- **Money:** This could include budget money, petty cash, capital purchases, and so on.

- **Method:** The process steps that fuel the process. Hopefully, the steps are clearly documented and available to everyone who works on the process steps. You also include safety requirements, labor scheduling, and all the actions taken to execute this task.

- **Mother Nature:** We all work in an environment that directly impacts performance. Is the work area well lit, dry, and at a comfortable temperature? Is the facility sound or falling apart?

Continue breaking down each of the entries attached to the fishbones, so long as the information is useful. If one of the fishbones becomes too crowded (called a fishbone becoming a whale bone), break it down as its own fishbone diagram.

Some flowcharting tools, such as Microsoft's Visio software, have prebuilt fishbone diagrams to speed things up.

Pinpointing potential process errors with FMEA

Another powerful analytical tool used to scour a process is *Failure Modes and Effects Analysis* (FMEA). The tool examines a step within a process for all the things that can go wrong so you can work to prevent the most pressing issues. Most FMEA tools are built with spreadsheets, following these steps:

1. **Make a list of potential problems for the step.**

2. **Come up with mitigation actions to avoid the problems.**

3. **Rank the list of problems and solutions by sorting the "score."**

   See the following section "The problem component" for more on the ranking process.

4. **Work on mitigating the highest-scoring issues and adding their solutions into the process to prevent the problems from occurring.**

A FMEA isn't confined only to existing processes. You can use it to improve the product flow of new processes before their implementation. Furthermore, a FMEA isn't a one-shot tool. Always a keep a copy of a process FMEA handy for the people who use the process. If they detect a problem, the FMEA may indicate what causes it.

A FMEA is easy to implement, though it often takes a day or more to create. Your quality team may have a lot to discuss about the process at hand. Some companies apply FMEAs to every step of every process. Others apply them only to process steps that cause them the greatest problems. However, given the amount of time necessary to create a FMEA, Six Sigma practitioners usually apply one only to a problematic process step.

You should involve everyone who works on a step in the process in a FMEA, as well as workers from the preceding and follow-up steps in the process. A team effort works best (see Figure 17-5).

As you can see from the previous list and explanatory info in this section, a FMEA has two primary components: possible problems within a process and the proposed mitigation actions for the problems. We describe both parts in further detail in the following sections.

The problem component

The following items make up the problem component of a FMEA:

- **Part/process:** The problem part or process step, such as "customer order entry" or, in the case of Figure 17-5, "office fax machine"
- **Failure mode:** What caused the problem
- **Failure effects:** The damage from the problem
- **SEV (severity of the error):** Ranked on a 1 to 10 scale, with 10 being the worst
- **Possible causes:** The team lists everything that could've caused the problem
- **OCC (occurrence):** Ranked on a 1 to 10 scale, with 10 being most often
- **Controls in place:** The things used today to mitigate the problem
- **DET (detection):** How obvious the error is when it occurs, ranked on a 1 to 10 scale, with 10 being the hardest to detect
- **Score:** The product of severity, multiplied by the occurrence, multiplied by the detection

    You sort the results in descending order to bring the most serious issues to the top for action and push the least likely and least damaging issues to the bottom. In the case of Figure 17-5, you'd move the last issue of not being able to receive faxes to the top for action.

    Traditional FMEAs refer to the "Score" field as a *Risk Priority Number* (RPN).

(Process Name Here)
(Date Here)

Drafted by: _____

Part/Process	Failure Mode	Failure Effects	S E V	Possible Causes	O C C	Controls in Place	D E T	S c o r e	Solution	Assigned to	Schedule Date	R S	R O	R D	S c o r e	Risk
												PROBLEM → **RECOMMENDATION** → **After Fix**				
Office fax machine	Cannot dial out	Cannot send PO to vendor	8	Operator training	5	Sign explaining fax procedure	1	40	Review sign text, move it closer to the machine's dialer	Tom Collins	4/1/07	8	1	1	8	2 - Low
Office fax machine	Cannot dial out	Cannot send PO to vendor	7	Fax is receiving	5	Window on machine indicates it is receiving	1	35	Receive faxes into e-mail		5/5/07	7	1	1	7	4 - Medium
Office fax machine	Cannot receive	Cannot receive customer orders	4	Fax is sending	3	Window on machine indicates it is receiving	4	48	Add another fax machine		4/1/07	4	4	1	16	4 - Medium

Figure 17-5: A FMEA looks at possible problems within a process.

The recommendation component

The following items comprise the recommendation component of a FMEA:

- ✔ **Solution:** Explain the proposed solution (in project management, this is a *mitigation action*).

- ✔ **Assigned to:** Person responsible for installing a change.

- ✔ **Schedule date:** When the proposed solution is in place.

- ✔ **RS:** After application of the solution, determine the anticipated severity of the mitigated problem, using a scale of 1 to 10, with 10 being the worst.

- ✔ **RO:** After application of the solution, determine the anticipated frequency of occurrence of the mitigated problem, using a scale of 1 to 10, with 10 being most often.

- ✔ **RD:** After application of the solution, determine how obvious future errors will be, using a scale of 1 to 10, with 10 being the hardest to detect.

- ✔ **Score:** The product of severity, times the frequency, times the detection. You can compare the results to the earlier score (see the previous section) to determine a magnitude of improvement.

- ✔ **Risk:** The risk that your solution will fail. The risk is higher if the solution is expensive.

Chapter 18

Delving into Quality Function Deployment

. . . .

In This Chapter

▶ Looking at Quality Function Deployment basics

▶ Building a House of Quality from the ground up

. . . .

The concept of quality can mean different things to different organizations. To a factory, quality is a problem-free product. To a hotel reservation center, quality is accurate and timely data. However, you can spot a different aspect to quality that's missing from both of these examples. The key to quality is the value that the customer places on the product, and value is how well a product's characteristics fulfill the customer's needs and wants.

Quality Function Deployment (QFD) is a disciplined approach to collecting the wants and needs of the customer and then translating them into product or service characteristics. You waste time and money if you create a defect-free product or service that no one wants. You must design quality (in this context, customer value) into your product or service from the beginning. In this chapter, we explain the basics of QFD and give you the full scoop on an important QFD tool: the House of Quality.

Organizing the Nuts 'n' Bolts of Quality Function Deployment

When you use Quality Function Deployment, you gather information from potential customers, evaluate it, and convert it into product specifications. You organize the information in a matrix called the House of Quality. In the following sections, we introduce this matrix and the pros and cons of QFD.

The QFD matrix

QFD uses a series of matrices to break down customer data further and further, starting with the voice of the customer. How many matrices you want to create for the project is simply a matter of where you want your company to stop. Matrices are time consuming to construct, so you want to create only as many as are necessary. In this chapter, we describe only the most foundational layer: the overall House of Quality.

The pros and cons of QFD

QFD is a powerful tool that visually ties customer wants and product characteristics to individual components and the processes that create them. However, if a company lacks the patience to go through the process, and if representatives from all departments aren't participating, then the results will be skewed and the customer will be dissatisfied.

The pros

Quality Function Deployment can improve the success of your new products and services and revise existing ones. Pluses of QFD include the following:

- ✔ You significantly reduce the risk of introducing products (or services) that customers don't want. You base products on data, not guesswork.
- ✔ You base tradeoffs between design considerations on data and agreement of a cross-functional team.
- ✔ You can determine the market position of the product to its competitors, based on value to the customer.
- ✔ QFD matrices allow you to visualize the issues at hand, and they increase cross-functional communications between the design team, production team, marketing department, and so on.
- ✔ You can eliminate problems in products long after they hit the market.

The cons

A company applying QFD for the first time must spend considerable upfront preparation. By its nature, QFD is a cross-functional, team-oriented strategy. At a minimum, you must train several team members from various departments (marketing, engineering, production, sales, and so on) before you can begin the process, which can be difficult to arrange and expensive.

Additional minuses of QFD include the following:

- ✔ QFD is time consuming because you have to identify target customers and collect data.

- ✔ The design doesn't reflect the cost of the changes.

- ✔ The relationships between various specifications and requirements are subjective and easily skewed. Values in the House of Quality are based on the opinions of the participants. One dominant person can skew priorities as higher or lower, block the labeling of some of the relationships between tradeoffs, and so on.

- ✔ A large House of Quality is incomprehensible. Even a medium-sized chart with 40 customer requirements and 40 design requirements has 1,600 possible relationships that you have to understand.

If You Build a House of Quality, Customers Will Come

Quality Function Deployment is as complex and detailed as you and your organization want to make it. Some charts expand into detailed technical-design analysis, feasibility, detailed competitor analysis, and so on. The basic QFD process, as we describe in the following sections, is as follows:

1. **Collect information from potential customers that specifies their wants and needs regarding a new product (or service) or the revision of an existing product.**

   You refer to the wants and needs of potential consumers as the *voice of the customer,* or VOC. Be sure to include a measure for how important each want or need is.

2. **Compare the customers' requirements with how well your competitors meet them.**

3. **Create design requirements that will fulfill the customers' requirements.**

4. **Rate the strength of relationships between the design requirements and the customer requirements.**

5. **Identify the tradeoffs between design requirements.**

6. **Determine technical targets to fulfill customer requirements.**

You put the information you gather on perceived customer needs, methods of measuring them, and so on into the rooms of the House of Quality (see Figure 18-1), and you should update the rooms as your product or service evolves.

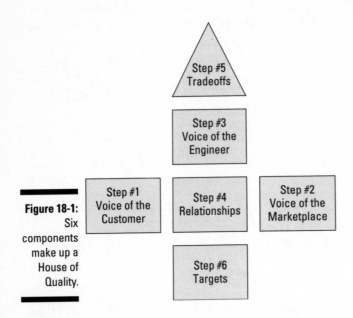

Figure 18-1:
Six
components
make up a
House of
Quality.

It may be necessary to create a separate House of Quality for each major market segment. Different groups of people, such as engineers, clerks, office workers, physicians, and so on, may use the same product very differently.

Identifying customer requirements

At times, the voice of the customer is long and loud. The customer voices opinions about your product or service through complaints, service calls, and warranty returns. You should analyze each communication for ways to improve your existing product features and delivery. However, for new products, you haven't yet heard the voice of the customer because you haven't created the product or delivered the service.

In the following sections, we explain the differences between customer needs and wants and show you how to collect data to start your House of Quality. Chapter 6 has details on gathering information from (and about) customers.

Distinguishing between demands and delighters

One of your most important jobs is to question customers about what they demand in a product or service (the needs) and what would be very nice to have (the wants). The more thoroughly you question and gather information, the better your product decisions will be. The following list dives a bit deeper into customer requirements:

- ✔ *Expected requirements* are customer requirements that you must fill. If the requirements aren't present, the product ceases to be of value to the customers, and they become dissatisfied. For example: A restaurant's waiters are expected to be polite. Rude service drives people away.

- ✔ Requirements that merely excite the customer may be harder to uncover. Their presence is exciting, but their absence doesn't keep the customer from wanting the product or service. These *delighters* wow the customers and add value in their mind. The trick is to question potential customers about what these features may be and how much they may value each feature. Often the customers don't know themselves.

Collecting information to start your House of Quality

Take action by following these steps to collect customer data:

1. **Make a list of all potential end-users (or people who will use the item).** If your product is a new company computer network service, for example, you could consider the secretary, the boss, the employees, or any customers that may need to use the network. If your product is a new broom, you could consider children, handicapped persons, janitors, or able-bodied persons with either older or no children.

2. **Develop a list of questions regarding the product or service.** Prepare questions for each type of user. Consider factors such as the following:

   - What skills do the users or clients need to use the product or service?

   - What would make it more comfortable or easy for consumers?

   - What does the customer like about the current product or service?

   - What does the customer dislike about the current product or service?

   - How does the customer typically use the product or service?

   - What would the customer change about the product or service?

The best data-collection methods involve personal contact. Interview potential customers and observe your product or service (or a competitor's) in use. Organize focus groups to discuss the product. Surveys and questionnaires help but don't give as much information.

3. **Organize the wants and needs of your customers into a list that categorizes them.** You want labels such as "critical to delivery," "critical to cost," and so on. This is the "what" section of the matrix — in other words, what the customer wants (see Figure 18-2). The left-most column lists the categories of customer wants and needs, and the second column contains brief descriptions of the wants or needs.

If the list of wants and needs is more than 20 items, reduce it or break it down into several smaller lists. Keep your charts to manageable sizes — especially if you have to present them to executives in your organization.

4. **Determine how important each described feature is to the final product.** Quantify each feature on a 1 to 5 scale, with 1 being of little importance and 5 being of high importance. Add each figure to the column titled "Importance."

Sometimes a paired comparison is useful for determining relative importance. Ask prospective customers to compare two features and pick one as more important than the other. Pair all the features against each other to determine the relative score of a particular feature's importance.

5. **Ask customers about the same wants and needs as they apply to competing products.** If you have a conceptually new product, you may have to identify several products, where each has one characteristic of the solution. Again, rate each want and need on a 1 to 5 scale. Be sure to include any competing products considered to be the "best in class." (See the following section for more on the uses of this data).

Figure 18-2:
Find out about customer wants and needs to start building a House of Quality.

Voice of Customer			Importance
Category	Need		
	Need		
	Want		
Category	Need		
	Need		
	Want		

Poorly conducted data gathering is the primary reason that QFD fails. Some companies actually believe that they know more than their customers, so they fill in the information for themselves! If a company lacks a team that routinely researches markets, then it should consider using a nonbiased, third-party organization to gather its customer data.

Listening to the voice of the marketplace

A critical goal of QFD is to create a product or service that provides significantly more value than competing models. When surveying products in the marketplace with prospective customers, focus on published problems with competing products. Identify the gap between what customers say they want and what the competitors are delivering. This gap is where you can find your immediate opportunities.

Along the top of Figure 18-3, list the various competitors you use for comparison when gathering customer information (see the previous section). For each customer want or need, identify how well each competitor meets it on a 1 to 5 scale, with 5 being the best. Compare this column with the "Importance" column. The result identifies things that your product does well (which should be protected) and areas in which the product can improve.

Figure 18-3:
Compare your competitors' performance in addressing customer wants and needs against your company's.

Voice of Customer			Importance		Voice of Market			
					Your Company	Competitor #1	Competitor #2	Competitor #3
	Category	Need						
		Need						
		Want						
	Category	Need						
		Need						
		Want						

You can use benchmarking to help choose among several design concepts that you're considering. During the process, consider recombining some ideas that seemed to have promise but didn't rank too well with customers. You may create an even better product as a result.

Converting customer requirements into design specifications

After your quality control team gathers a sufficient amount of customer data, you can begin interpreting it. But what amount is sufficient, though? At some point, no more new ideas will pop up in your research.

You start your data interpretation by rephrasing each customer observation about a product into a need for the product (in other words, a *design specification*). Here are some traits of proper needs statements:

- ✔ **Put the focus on the product.** The product should be the subject, as opposed to "I" or "the user." Each need describes something about the product.

- ✔ **Be positive.** State what the product does do, not what it doesn't do. By being positive, you can actively add a useful feature as opposed to merely avoiding an undesirable trait.

- ✔ **Be specific.** Describe the product in objectively measurable terms, such as the product weighing less than eight ounces.

- ✔ **Stay functional.** State what the product does, not how it does it. For example: "An MP3 player runs continuously for eight hours" doesn't state *how* the player runs continuously.

- ✔ **Stay simple.** Break down complex statements into individual needs. Each statement addresses only one function or characteristic. If the function has two characteristics, then each one is a separate item.

Figure 18-4 is the "how" section of the House of Quality matrix — also known as the *voice of the engineer*. You fill it out to indicate which design specifications apply to each of the customer wants and needs. You list the voice of the engineer along the top of the matrix.

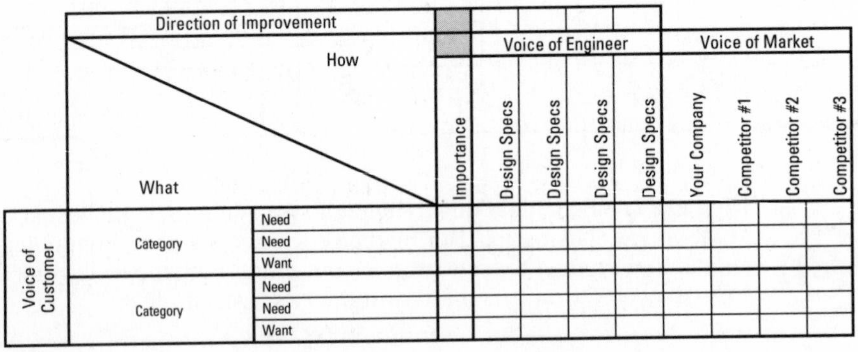

Figure 18-4:
The voice of the engineer is the "how" section of the House of Quality.

You may notice that a field called "Direction of Improvement" now appears in Figure 18-4. Feel free to ignore it for now; we explain what it means in the "Targets" section later in this chapter.

Determining relationships between requirements and specifications

You know that state-of-the-relationship talk most newly formed couples dread? Well, to move forward in your quality relationship with your customers, you need to determine the state of the relationship between customer requirements and your design specifications. We show you what to do in the following sections.

Making sure that you can measure customer requirements

Ensuring that your organization meets each customer need requires an objective way to measure the needs. The good news is that you can measure virtually all needs. If the need is for your product to be light in weight, for example, you can set a metric for the object to weigh less than a specific number of pounds.

Some metrics require additional thought. If a customer want or need is for the car you produce to be attractive, for example, talk to a panel of potential customers and determine what the consensus is for "attractive" (see the earlier section "Identifying customer requirements" for details). Perhaps the metric will be that 70 percent of the panelists agree that the car is attractive, or that fewer than 10 percent say they "wouldn't be caught dead in it." Some metrics have a binary value: Either the metric will be true or it won't. For example, either an MP3 player is sold with a carrying strap or it isn't.

Focus on what's needed to meet customer requirements, not on how to do it. Take care not to include or infer how to do something in technical specifications; this hinders the flow of ideas later.

Mapping relationships

In the House of Quality matrix, under the design requirements and to the right of the customer needs, indicate the relationship you find between customer wants or needs and design requirements. You're filling out the "what-to-how" section of the matrix (refer to Figure 18-4 to see the area we're talking about).

Not every design requirement you have will relate to a customer need, so you'll have to leave many of these blocks blank. (For example, a ground wire on an electrical device may be required to meet electrical safety codes, but the customer will rarely ask about it.) But when a specification does apply to a customer requirement, indicate the relationship as one of the following:

✔ **Weak relationship:** Indicate this relationship with a "–" symbol and score it as a "1." This means that if the specification becomes looser or tighter, it very slightly changes the performance of the customer requirement.

✔ **Moderate relationship:** Indicate this relationship with a "0" and score it as a "3." This means that if the specification becomes looser or tighter, it changes some of the performance of the customer requirement.

✔ **Strong relationship:** Indicate this relationship with a "+" symbol and score it as a "9." This means that if the specification becomes looser or tighter, it directly changes the performance of the customer requirement.

You'll use the numeric scores in the later section "Absolute importance."

Quality tradition calls for you to use a power of 3 in each relationship cell that you place a number in. The numbers you use are 1, 3, and 9, which correspond to 3^0, 3^1, and 3^2, respectively.

Laying the roof

If we want to keep the drips away, we need a roof for our House of Quality (see Figure 18-5). The *roof* is a correlation matrix that illustrates interactions between technical requirements.

When considering the potential designs of a product, you may find that some features sacrifice quality in one area to improve it in another. For example, buying a computer with a relatively large amount of memory will give the consumer more speed, but it will cost the consumer more money, too. In the business situation where you must make all products the same, it's important to consider how one feature impacts another.

Above the direction-of-improvement indicators (see the "Targets" section later in this chapter), you see a matrix at an angle. This matrix shows how one metric affects another. The easiest way to visualize the roof of the house — in other words, to look at the relationships between your design specifications — is to grade the relationships with the following symbols:

✔ "– –" for a strong negative relationship: If one characteristic is decreased, the other characteristic is significantly increased. In essence, they move in opposite directions; one goes up, the other goes down.

✔ "–" for a negative relationship: If one characteristic is decreased, the other characteristic is increased.

✔ "+" for a positive relationship: If one characteristic is decreased, the other characteristic is decreased. They move in the same direction.

✔ "++" for a strong positive relationship: If one characteristic is increased, the other characteristic is significantly increased.

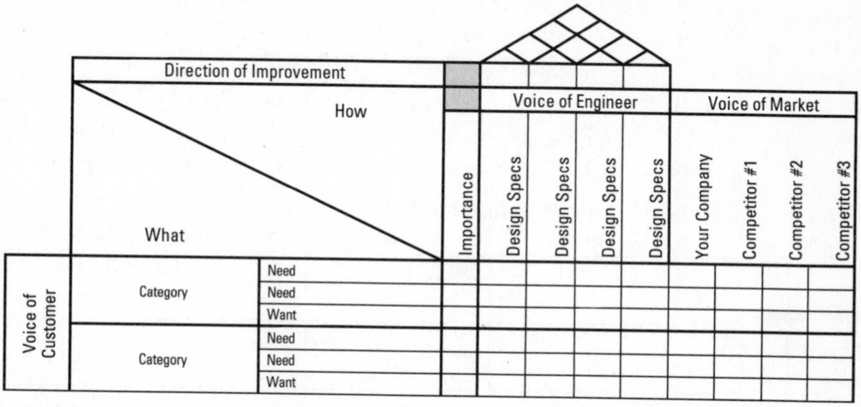

Figure 18-5:
The roof is
a finishing
touch to the
House of
Quality that
highlights
relationships
between
technical
require-
ments.

Digging a basement

It isn't always possible to provide every feature that your customers want or need in your product (or service). Your job is to determine the difficulty that comes with developing the product and the relative value of the product by considering the technical characteristics and customer wants and needs.

In Figure 18-6, we've added rows to the bottom of the House of Quality matrix for you to indicate the relative importance of each specification and a measurable target for each. We cover these rows in the following sections.

Absolute importance

Absolute importance is value you get when you multiply the "Importance" column with the relationship boxes. The relationships carry symbols (–, 0, or +) — each of which you equate to a numeric score of 1, 3 or 9, respectively (see "Mapping relationships," earlier in this chapter, for details). You multiply these values by the values in the "Importance" column and put the total into the "Absolute Importance" box.

Relative importance

You have two possibilities when filling out the "Relative Importance" row:

- You can rank the "Absolute Importance" values from highest (most crucial to your product's success) to lowest; the highest value(s) gets a 1, the next highest gets a 2, and so on.

- You can rank by calculating the percentage of each "Absolute Importance" value in context with the rest of the values. This makes it easier to see how important each value is relative to the others and relative to the project as a whole.

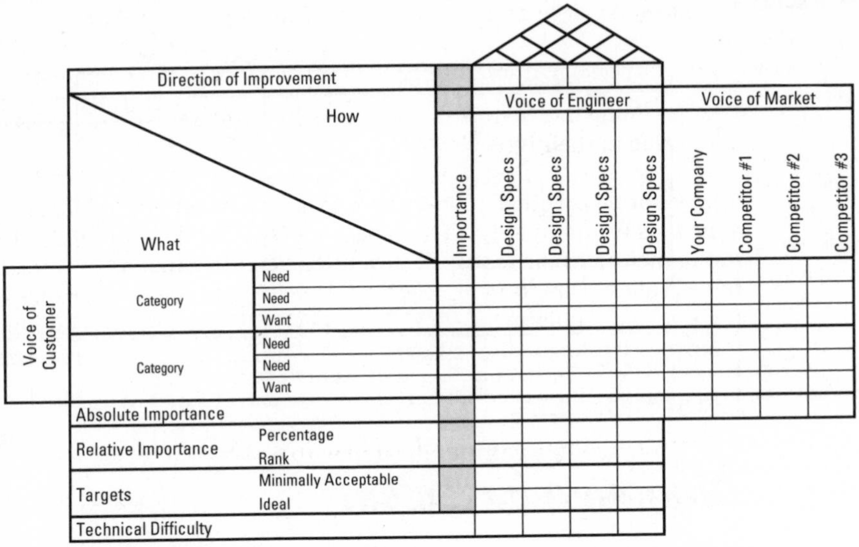

Figure 18-6:
Four rows
make up the
basement of
the House of
Quality.

For example, say you have the following five values in the "Absolute Importance" blanks: 20, 40, 80, 50, and 10. You can rate them from most important to least important, like so: 4, 3, 1, 2, 5. You could also put their importance in percentage form: 10, 20, 40, 25, and 5. (The House of Quality shown in the figures throughout this chapter has two rows, so you can use both strategies if you desire.)

The "Relative Importance" row ranks the scores to indicate which area you should address first, second, and so on.

Targets

Targets specify the required values for each metric. The House of Quality in Figure 18-6 has two rows next to Targets so that you have room to indicate both the minimally acceptable and the ideal values. You need to identify a minimally acceptable target so that your product always meets consumer expectations. However, most consumers appreciate having their expectations exceeded; this is more likely to happen when a metric approaches or even exceeds its ideal value.

You should make a chart that indicates both the optimal value and minimally acceptable value for each metric. By specifying both values, you allow for some design leeway. The leeway helps prevent a value from being lowered too much to attain excellence elsewhere, and it may help find a happy medium between two metrics that have adverse effects on each other (see the section "Laying the roof" for an example).

You normally determine these values in a couple of ways:

- A physical feature: An engineering analysis of the component
- An intangible feature: Based on what customers identified as an optimal value in their interviews

It may not be practical to indicate a target value for everything. It can be almost as useful to indicate that "more of this" or "less of this" is better. Along the top of the matrix, above the design requirements, you see a row of boxes called "Direction of Improvements." They indicate whether the value for a design requirement should increase, decrease, or stay the same with the following symbols:

- **Maximize this value:** Indicated with a "↑"
- **Minimize this value:** Indicated with a "↓"
- **Optimal value:** Indicated with a "0"

Technical difficulty

The quality team should discuss each technical design specification and assign numerical values indicating the foreseen difficulty for the organization to meet the requirements. Rate on a scale of 1 to 5, with 1 being easy to meet the requirement and 5 being very difficult (in other words, expensive). Use the scale to weed out requirements that provide little value at high cost.

The hard part of the technical process is ranking those requirements in the middle — requirements that provide moderate value at a slightly higher cost. These may require additional review in a separate House of Quality that breaks them down further, or you can hold out for a later version of the product, after you gain a better understanding of its manufacture.

Always consider the maturity of the marketplace, technical maturity, business risk, supplier capability, and so on when making your product rankings. Limit the number of high-risk items.

Chapter 19

Considering the Theory of Constraints

r. Eliyahu Goldratt, in his book *The Goal* (North River Press), proposes the Theory of Constraints (TOC). The theory views an organization as a chain of processes. Each chain has a weak link that limits how much it can produce; this limitation is known as its *constraint.*

Dr. Goldratt thinks that we're missing the point. Quality improvement techniques are okay, but they don't address the big picture. What good is it to increase the efficiency of one step of the process if it's already making more than the process's bottleneck can handle?

If a company has tried Lean processes, Total Quality Management, or Quality Function Deployment without the desired results, why not try something different? The Theory of Constraints says that the key to a quality process is the constraint — the one unplanned place that sets the pace for everything else. Manage this bottleneck, and the entire process will flow more smoothly. In this chapter, we cover the fundamentals and unique concepts of the Theory of Constraints.

Focusing on the Fundamentals of the Theory of Constraints

The Theory of Constraints isn't a typical quality control technique. The TOC approaches quality control from its own unique angle, whereas other quality improvement initiatives build on other techniques (Six Sigma is a classic example of borrowing from everyone; see Chapter 17 for more about this technique). In the following sections, we explain the basic principles behind the TOC and its advantages and disadvantages.

Highlighting the principles behind the TOC

The Theory of Constraints is a comprehensive technique for identifying and managing an organization's constraints for obtaining maximum output from a process (or throughput).

The TOC says that a traditional approach of optimizing individual processes only occasionally helps throughput. For years, companies have spent large amounts of money to improve their processes. They have eliminated waste, shrunk inventories, and so on, but these improvements haven't delivered a corresponding quantity of savings. The disconnect occurs because the companies focused on speeding up individual processes to become more efficient, often with no overall improvement in throughput.

Why optimize a process to produce a product or deliver a service faster or more efficiently if its output will just pile up further down the chain next to a constraint? The key to improving throughput is to manage the constraint that prevents maximum process throughput.

Much of a company's internal friction is between departments and processes. As measurements and improvements are applied to one process at a time — often confined to the same department — no one is looking at the "touch points" where products and responsibility move into someone else's hands. The TOC has a big-picture approach to quality that encompasses problems occurring between processes.

In the following sections, we go into more detail on two of the main principles of the TOC: focusing on throughput and avoiding the overfeeding of a process.

The TOC aims to identify and resolve internal conflicts — often between policies. You need to make sure that the result of resolved conflicts is a win-win situation for all involved parties; if you use the TOC to bludgeon processes and managers, you'll see it quickly fade away.

Concentrate on throughput upfront

Most companies measure their production or service processes individually. They look at how efficiently orders are received or how promptly bills are paid. They encourage managers who oversee their processes to optimize them through improvement tools, outside advisors, and even cost reductions, and give rewards for jobs well done. However, each isolated improvement may have a negative effect on another process. Many companies don't rate improvement by how much they improve output of the facility to the customer; they rate only on how much faster one individual process works, and they emphasize only the cost-cutting benefits of improving quality.

The TOC's global view perceives improving the speed of individual processes as a waste of time and money. If the accounts-payable process isn't constraining the speed of throughput, why spend time and money to improve it? Although cutting costs provides an immediate bottom-line impact, it can go only so far in quality improvement. After all, costs can drop only to zero.

Lean (which we cover in Part III), Six Sigma (which we cover in Chapter 17), and the Theory of Constraints all have different ideas of the nature of waste:

- ✔ Lean's emphasis on process flow stipulates that waste is anything that doesn't add value.
- ✔ Six Sigma fights waste in the form of variation in a process or its inputs.
- ✔ The TOC defines waste as a constraint on a system's throughput.

The TOC focuses first on increasing income, as its potential is unlimited. (Of course, income has an upper limit, but how many companies have fully exploited and dominated their own markets?) Cutting costs is a secondary priority. The TOC uses throughput, inventory, and operating expense as measures to guide company decisions:

- ✔ *Throughput* is the rate at which the company's processes create cash for the company through sales of its products or services.
- ✔ *Inventory* is an investment in tooling, labor, materials, and any other items needed to create goods for sale.
- ✔ *Operating expense* is the cash spent to convert inventory into throughput.

The biggest gains from the TOC technique come from increasing throughput. After that, companies should pay attention first to inventory and last to operating expense. This hierarchy conflicts with the traditional quality concerns of first cutting inventory and labor to improve profits.

Don't overfeed the process!

If you find that a constraint limits the throughput of an important process in your organization, it doesn't make sense for you to improve upstream processes to run faster. Doing so just creates piles of work-in-process material at the bottleneck. The TOC refers to this problem as *overfeeding the process*.

Implementation of the TOC (combined with Lean; see Part III) reduces the rate of upstream processes to keep the constraint supplied without piling up excess work. As you consolidate and then shrink the work-in-process materials, workers can see that the amount of inventory on hand isn't related to the facility's output.

People are funny creatures. If they have jobs like printing paychecks, counting nails, or whatever, and they can work so fast as to pile up work ahead of a constraint, they quickly learn to slow down and soak up the time. The maxim that "work expands to fill the time allotted" is true. What this means for your organization is that a constraint may not always be obvious if the behavior of other links in the operating chain disguises it. Look at the entire process from end to end to identify areas that may be walking slowly — adding non-value-added steps (see Chapter 12) — to soak up the excess time. This review also brings out any "near constraints" that you can address.

Weighing the pros and cons of the TOC

The TOC is a breakthrough approach to quality control. If your organization properly applies it, the TOC can quickly transform your organization by eliminating artificial internal barriers. Think about it: Major improvements to your bottom line without major capital investment, all because you defeated the company's worst enemy — itself! But the TOC isn't all peaches and cream. We cover both the pros and cons of the TOC in the following sections.

The pros

The TOC quality improvement technique has many advantages:

✔ Instead of improving every step of every process within the building, the TOC focuses improvement efforts (in other words, expense) on those places where it can provide the greatest benefits. This strategy provides greater return for the process-improvement dollar. For example:

- If a single manager must approve every customer order, what happens if the manager gets sick? Why let orders pile up in front of one person when order entry software can accomplish the same review?

- If the entire cleaning crew shares a single floor buffer, providing a second buffer may finish jobs quicker and permit the crew to move on to other places.

✔ The TOC is similar to Lean in that it minimizes inventory (see Part III for more about Lean). So how does this minimization save money? Inventory costs money to purchase and hold until it's finally included in a finished product. This ties up money in things that may sit around half finished for months. The company must pay for floor space to store everything and for someone to shuffle it around. And this material loses value through corrosion, theft, damage, humidity, and so on.

✔ The TOC is similar to Six Sigma (see Chapter 17) in its breakthrough improvements. While some techniques value small, everyday improvements that eventually add up to big money, the TOC believes that by breaking up a constraint, you can immediately realize a significant improvement. Consider emptying a big tub of water: You can leave it in the sun to evaporate, or you can pull the plug and drain it in no time.

✔ The TOC saves money in critical areas:

- Eliminates unnecessary internal constraints that only add wasted work to a process

- Shrinks work-in-process inventory into a few buffers focused on the constraint

- Improves customer response time through reduced work in a process

- Frees employee time to improve quality and eliminate constraints

✔ Policies and measurements are management's way to signal work priorities to employees; if you focus your policies and measurements on breaking down constraints, so will your workforce.

Make the identification and elimination of throughput constraints an important part of every company meeting. Each discussion should begin with identifying the current constraint and ensuring that previously discussed constraints remain fixed. By following this strategy, you ensure that the entire organization is focused on managing work product throughput.

✔ With the TOC, participants understand how much the junction points between processes and departments contribute to product or service delivery. You must constantly manage these interface points to ensure their normal variability doesn't disturb overall process throughput.

The cons

One hurdle that comes with using the TOC is manager and worker acceptance. The hard part is setting aside all the previously accepted performance measures and quality initiatives to look at processes in a different light. Until now in your organization, each process was in contention with the others through internal optimization of the chain, but the TOC's view is system-wide (see the earlier section "Highlighting the principles behind the TOC").

For example, imagine two departments where the first one feeds the second one. Each department manager's promotions and pay raises are based on efficient operations. So Operation A saves everything they make for an entire week and then sends it over to Operation B. In this way, Operation A pays for a single shipment. Meanwhile, Operation B (which has limited floor space) is overwhelmed with material and shuffles it here and there to keep it out of the way, or late in the week, it's starved for material with people sitting around. Operation A's manager is viewed as efficient, while Operation B's manager is seen as ineffective.

The solution is to make a single person responsible for each product from end to end and to reward everyone in the chain the same way. Align the incentives with the desired behaviors.

Other disadvantages of the TOC include the following:

✔ It may be hard for some department managers to let go of the policies and measurements that have big parts of their daily routines.

✔ The key people implementing the TOC must be trained, and a TOC expert needs to be on site to help roll out this new way of thinking (see Chapter 5 for general information on training employees).

✔ An existing reward system in your organization may be locally focused and will resist your attempts to act globally with the TOC. During the TOC rollout, expect internal political turbulence as you discard the assumptions used to build careers or to create personal empires within your organization.

TOC may not fit everywhere. "Old" companies with strongly entrenched cliques and heavily negotiated work rules may not have the will to break down their barriers. (But we would bet that such companies would reap huge benefits if they did.)

Understanding the Drum-Buffer-Rope System

An efficient process works at its maximum rate, based on its tools, materials, labor, and process work instructions. The *Drum-Buffer-Rope system* is a simple way to illustrate how a constraint controls the speed at which a process can work. Managing a process using the Drum-Buffer-Rope system focuses attention where it belongs: on the process's bottlenecking constraint.

The following sections go into detail on each part of the system; see Figure 19-1 for an outline of how the Drum-Buffer-Rope system works.

Marching to the beat of the drum

A constraint in your process sets the maximum speed that the process can achieve and maintain acceptable quality. The pace or the person who controls it is called the *drum*. Somewhat similar to Takt Time in a Lean operation (see Chapter 11 for more about Takt Time), the drum sets the beat for the upstream processes. As you improve the constraint's throughput, the drum beats faster for the upstream processes to pick up the pace.

Figure 19-1:
The Drum-
Buffer-Rope
system is
essential
to the
application
of the
Theory of
Constraints.

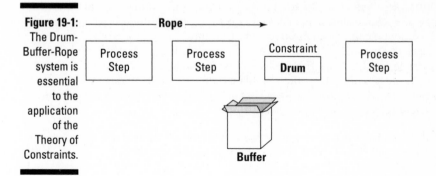

A good example of a constraint is a bathtub drain. Water can exit the bathtub only as fast as the drain can handle it — no faster. Shout, threaten, dish out incentives — no matter what — the draining process moves only as fast as the drain can take water. The drain sets the rate at which work (draining the water) is done; it's the drumbeat of the process. Water in excess of the drain's capacity backs up in the tub until it's drained. If water is added faster than the drain can let it out, eventually the tub overflows.

Processes work the same way. Work flows along until it hits the constraint. If the processes feeding the constraint can produce faster than the constraint can process it, then work backs up. This backed-up work means that the workers in the processes feeding the constraint have nothing to do until the backlog is emptied — or they continue piling up even more work-in-process inventory.

To eliminate inefficiency, the constraint must set the work rate for processes that feed it. Think of the process from end to end rather than as islands of work that provide output, whether or not it's needed.

Managing buffers for maximum results

To maximize a constraint's capabilities, you need to make sure that the upstream processes keep it supplied with whatever it needs to keep running. The constraint should never run out of material. What you do is maintain a *buffer* of incoming materials next to the constraint to keep it busy. If the inflow of new work material slackens, the constraint remains running at full rate by dipping into the buffer (or safety) stock.

For example, consider a doctor's office. The doctor requires at least five minutes with each patient. If more time is needed, the waiting room begins to fill up. If someone cancels an appointment that day, the doctor would be idle and miss the income for a patient. One of the waiting patients is used to fill the time gap. In this way, the doctor's time is maximized. To ensure that the doctor is always busy, the office builds a buffer by booking one more patient per hour than the doctor can see. This action builds a buffer to ensure the constraint (the doctor) is always fed with work.

A buffer stabilizes the constraint's performance by isolating it from upstream problems. Buffer management includes several functions:

- ✔ **Minimizing the number of buffers in the operating chain to one next to the constraint and a few more along the chain.** The rates of all subprocesses that feed into the constraint are set so that they provide only enough to feed the constraint and no more. By minimizing, you gather the safety time from the individual processes and may reveal other constraints. This minimization also reduces the amount of work-in-process material clogging the facility.

- ✔ **Setting the minimal size of the buffer.** To reduce cost, you need to keep the work in process at a minimum. A minimal amount of work also provides flexibility to quickly respond to new customer requirements or urgent requests.

- ✔ **Analyzing the causes of buffer shortages that may shut down the constraint.** Whenever the constraint dips into the buffer, it gives a signal that the upstream processes have a problem that you must address. Stabilizing upstream processes allows the buffer to shrink.

Lean techniques (see Part III) reduce materials throughout the facility to expose problems to address. The TOC seeks out the problems (constraints) and resolves them before reducing materials. Both processes reduce materials to save money and improve flexibility — it's just a matter of timing.

Feeding a constraint with the rope

A TOC *rope* is the length of the operating chain that feeds the constraint. It stretches from the receiving dock all the way to the constraint. The operating processes that your material passes through on its way to your customers are known as the constraint's *subordinate processes.*

For example, consider supplying a restaurant kitchen. The "rope" refers to the actions and materials required to keep the kitchen supplied with fresh vegetables. The first step was to purchase the vegetables. Then they were unloaded and inspected. Next they were washed. Finally, they were cleaned and set aside for that day's use.

Altogether, this series of steps is considered the "rope" for supplying the constraint: the speed of the chef. The rope must ensure that there is enough material to keep the chef busy but not too much, because the vegetables will become old and tasteless.

This setup is contrary to the notion that every step of the process must always be fully busy or time is wasted. Instead of employees involved in the steps working full time, which only piles up material feeding into the chef, they should complete only what the chef can use, and then apply their time to other efforts.

Tackling Constraints in Your Process

Like all change, the Theory of Constraints is best tackled with a team of workers. Conscript one person from each process along the entire chain to provide explanations about why things are done a certain way and define the impact of proposed changes. Then follow these steps:

1. **Clearly identify the organization's goals.** Your goals are your anchors for all TOC activities. Typical goals are to be the low-cost provider of a service, to provide the highest-quality goods, to always have products on the shelf and ready to sell, and so on. These goals add up to making a profit so that your company can grow or at least keep operating.

    Not all organizations have a primary goal of increased profits. A hospital's primary goal may be perfect patient care; a university may value providing a top education; and a charity's main concern may be providing prompt, effective service. However, on examination, all these organizations need efficient, low-cost operations to achieve their goals.

2. **Identify how to measure the goals.** The way that you measure a process signals to the workers what's important to your company. If a goal is to make a profit, you must decide whether to measure in revenue or profit. If the goal is customer satisfaction, you may measure return visits, positive survey responses, reduced complaints, and so on. A process lacking meaningful measurements creates its own, which reflect someone else's priorities.

So, you have your company goals and a way to measure them. Just what's keeping your company from advancing to its goals? Somewhere in the bowels of your production or service processes lies a constraint. The TOC seeks out the constraint and eliminates it by using a five-step process; we cover the steps in the following sections.

Identifying a process constraint

A *system constraint* is a weak link in your production chain that makes every other phase wait. It acts as the throttle on how fast material can flow through your processes. Constraints can be located in one of three places:

- ✔ **Internal:** You can't make more to sell due to shortages in capacity, labor skills, and the like. Inside your organization is the place to begin tackling constraints.

- ✔ **Market:** You can make and provide more to sell, but the customers don't want more. This is true of many companies. Address market constraints after cleaning up the company's internal constraints.

- ✔ **Supplier:** You can make and sell more but cannot obtain materials perceived to be critical to your processes. This constraint isn't common. Address it by redesigning the product or service to use more common materials and by eliminating work-in-process inventories.

  Maintain excellent relationships with the suppliers (see Chapter 3 for details on accomplishing this task), and concentrate on new versions that provide the most money for the least amount of constrained material.

Constraints can come in many forms:

- ✔ Control-hungry managers who must review and approve all documents that come across their desks, even if the documents must wait until they return from vacation

- ✔ An expensive machine that every product must pass through

- ✔ Legal requirements, such as the maximum-emission limit for air-quality control

- ✔ Labor rules that restrict what workers can do on a job

Each of these constraints could limit the speed of a process. However, you can overcome each of these constraints if the company focuses on minimizing or eliminating them. So, how exactly do you find and identify a constraint?

- ✔ Internal constraints are often found near the end of a process where they aren't as obvious. A visible indicator is work in process piled up in front of a process but not after it.

- ✔ Market constraints can be identified by the ability to inform potential customers about the product and to deliver it to them. Some companies have overcome this constraint by building Internet Web sites and shipping anywhere in the world.

✔ Supplier constraints can be identified through consistently late or canceled shipments. If suppliers have few competitors, they may not be able to expand their output further. For example, consider a fiberglass molding operation that makes very large truck hoods. If no one else can make the hoods, the operation can deliver as it wishes.

Some companies use Rapid Improvement (or Kaizen) events to target constraints for improved throughput. See Chapter 14 for details about these events.

Cleaning up the constraint

The first step in cleaning up a constraint is to take control of the constraining process task. Establish a schedule in order to set an expectation for the amount of throughput required by a process, and take care not to overload it. This schedule becomes the published drumbeat for the upstream processes to support (see the section "Marching to the beat of the drum," earlier in this chapter, for more details). The schedule tells everyone how fast they must produce to keep the constraint fully "fed." After they meet this requirement, they should be assigned to do something else.

By combining the TOC with the 5S Technique (see Chapter 13 for details), you can clean up a constraint you've identified to ensure that it operates at its maximum potential. The cleanup process includes the following tasks:

✔ **Minimize setup time.** For example, how long does it take to gather all the tools, materials, and information to begin working on a task? For a restaurant, this task may mean prepackaging ingredients for popular dishes in "kits" rather than searching for each item.

✔ **Attack downtime, remembering that care of the constraint is your first priority.** A restaurant keeps its cooking equipment in peak working condition by cleaning and adjusting it during off hours.

✔ **Inspect material before it gets to the constraint to ensure only good material goes in.** Bad ingredients delay cooking because someone must scurry around and find replacement items. Inspect everything early to ensure that the constraint (the chef) isn't delayed due to bad material.

✔ **Closely manage the constraint for maximum throughput.** Ensure that the chef isn't distracted by other tasks such as taking out the trash, chopping celery, and so on. Focus the constraint on the things that only the chef can do.

✔ **Implement predictive maintenance on the constraint's equipment, where you replace parts before they wear out.** Parts (like cooking equipment) are replaced according to a schedule rather than waiting for them to fail.

After the process's clutter is cleaned up, verify that it's still a constraint. Often, applying attention to a work area speeds up the flow of material through it. If the improvement can now handle everything required of it, there is time to spare, and the constraint has moved.

Subordinating processes to keep materials moving

The cleaned-up constrained process now sets the pace for processes upstream and downstream of its location, acting as the drumbeat for your operation. The TOC calls this action *subordinating* the feeding processes. This third step is where most of the behavior change occurs in the constraint.

Subordinating other processes to the drum — the pace set by the constrained process — frees time for other things:

- ✔ You must make sure processes upstream perform at full speed until the buffer fills up and then shuts down. Use the extra time for maintenance and for inspecting goods in the buffer to ensure that only perfect parts enter the constraint. (See "Managing buffers for maximum results," earlier in this chapter, for more about buffers.) The intent is to avoid having workers make more material than is needed by the constraint, and to avoid having them stretching out the work to fill the extra time. Capture this time and use it elsewhere.

- ✔ You must make sure that processes downstream from the constraint work carefully so their actions don't damage any material already past the constraint; these pieces are too precious to waste. For instance: After a chef passes a completed plate of food to the pickup point, ensure that nothing there will spoil it, like a waiter knocking it over.

- ✔ Where possible, subordinate processes take on steps previously done by the constraint, saving the amount of work the constraint performs (and time taken up by the constraint). Consider moving low-value work (things that can be done outside of the constraint) back to the supplying processes. For example, require a dishwasher to ensure that the chef always has a pile of clean plates ready to use instead of requiring the chef to ask for more.

Elevating the constraint

Time to spend some money! The fourth step calls for you to *elevate* the constraint — in other words, to improve its capacity. You can elevate the constraint in many ways:

- ✔ Buy additional machinery or expansions to the existing machinery.

- ✔ Hire or train additional employees for improved utilization or extra work shifts.

- ✔ Implement a quick changeover process for swapping the constraint. If the constrained process performs different tasks, it's easier to change.

- ✔ Improve tooling for faster changeover and longer tool life.

So here we are. The constraint was identified and cleaned up so that it can focus on its primary purpose, every process that fed it was scheduled to meet the constraint's requirements without overfeeding it, and at the end, the constraint was expanded so it could process all that was needed. You fixed the constraint! So now what?

This is the true story of a constraint in the real world

An everyday constraint people encounter is the number of checkout lines at the local grocery store. On a Friday night or Saturday morning, the lines are long. At times, shoppers walk out of the store without buying anything because they don't want to wait in slow-moving lines that constantly call for "price checks." In the case of the grocery store, its sluggish checkout lines constrain the store's payoff for stocking the shelves, providing an attractive venue, and incurring advertising expense.

How have some grocery stores tackled this constraint?

- ✔ Some stores give up floor space that they could be using for merchandise to add checkout lines that they staff during peak

shopping periods. This tactic helps, but walking around to find a short line can take as long as waiting in a long, slow-moving line.

- ✔ Some stores have express checkout lanes that limit the number of items allowed per person.

- ✔ Some stores install self-service checkout lanes for people with only a few items so they can move quickly. This also saves on labor during peak periods.

- ✔ Some stores spin off home-delivery companies that take orders over the Internet and eliminate the checkout line all together. (If possible, you should strive to eliminate a constraint completely!)

Improving throughput all over again

Applying the Theory of Constraints to your quality program is a continuous process. Sometimes breaking down internal barriers to maximum throughput is difficult, but you should never let inertia become your next system constraint! Solving one problem only reveals the next one. Somewhere, you have another constraint lurking, waiting for its chance to take hold of your processes.

Do several of your subordinated processes have similar capabilities? If their throughput is about the same as the constraint you just addressed and eliminated, the subordinated processes may be the next targets. Although the constraint you identify should be your prime effort, sometimes improving "near constraints" moves them down the list.

Part V
The Part of Tens

The 5th Wave   By Rich Tennant

"We've got a machine over there that monitors our quality control. If it's not working, just give it a couple of kicks."

In this part . . .

*I*f time is short but you still want a few nuggets of wisdom to take with you, look into the lists of ten in this part for quick-action ideas.

To build high quality into a new process or product, consider the ten steps that focus on customer requirements and process-cost issues. And check out the ten online resources we give you whenever you need further guidance with your quality process.

Chapter 20

Ten Steps for Incorporating Quality into a New Product and/or Process

*P*rocesses exist in order to create. A process may produce a service or a physical item, but you can refer to both as "products." A high-quality process is one that creates what the customer wants. The customer could be an employee in the next workstation or a consumer driving an SUV.

High-quality products don't hit the shelves by accident. They begin with well-designed processes; the right materials and tools; and trained, motivated workers. Introducing a new product can be exciting, and stuffing the right ingredients into a new process is essential to squeezing good results out of it.

Delivering high-quality new products is essential because first impressions become lasting impressions. Most companies focus on delivering well-made products first and then on delivering them as cheaply as possible, without sacrificing quality. With careful design, your organization can achieve both objectives at once. In this chapter, we describe ten important steps you can take to ensure that you inject quality into a new product from the get-go.

Identify a Problem You Can Solve with a New Product or Service

Products and services exist to fulfill a customer need or to solve a problem. Therefore, the first step in product development is to identify a problem you can solve. You can make the identification through many channels:

- Customer surveys
- Analysis of service complaints
- Examination of emerging technology
- A look at shifts in trends

When identifying a problem to solve with a new product or service, consider customer requirements. These requirements break down into three types of attributes: Must Haves, Satisfiers, and Performance attributes (see Chapter 6 for details).

The key is to craft a product or service and a production process with features that meet the customer requirements while aligning with your company's strengths and strategic direction.

Define the Critical Characteristics of Each Customer Requirement

You must further identify each customer requirement you deem important by its characteristics. For instance, if the customer requirement is for an "interesting" Web page, what does that mean? You should further describe the customer requirement in three primary critical-to-customer categories (see Chapter 6 for details): quality, price, and delivery.

Document and protect the critical features you identify, even when changes occur down the line in a process. For instance, to increase production speeds, a company must make tradeoffs. When in doubt, always choose the option that protects a critical-to-customer characteristic. Document each decision you make in case the same option is proposed later.

An excellent tool for identifying and tracking customer requirements is a Quality Function Deployment model (see Chapter 18). It allows you to match customer requirements to process actions, and it can prioritize your list of critical-to-customer characteristics.

Translate Customer Requirements into Measurements

A customer's desire for a "durable" item can mean many things, and your organization needs to find out what your customers are thinking. Make a product too durable and money is wasted on excess materials; make it too fragile and you lose customers. You need to assign a measurement (or series of measurements) to each customer characteristic so all workers know how much of something your customers desire. In other words, you translate critical-to-quality requirements into critical-to-process actions.

During production, your workers can sample customer characteristics and measurements. Quality may slip a tiny bit at a time, but always in the direction of making things easier for a worker or toward the use of cheaper materials. By monitoring measurable results, you can detect and stop trends and detect unapproved changes to a process.

Establish a Capable Prototype Process

Set up a prototype version of the process your organization will use to create the product, and verify that the tools, materials, and workers involved are capable of creating the product. Sometimes, machinery must be upgraded to hold tight tolerances. The materials selected may be too fragile and generate high scrap rates. The font on a data-entry screen may be too small to read, or the database query may take far too long. The more similar to the final product the prototype is, the more accurate the prototype results will be.

 A useful tool for designing and improving processes is a Failure Modes and Effects Analysis (FMEA). This tool (which we cover in Chapter 17) examines everything that can go wrong with a process so that you can build steps into the process to avoid many of the potential problems.

Make Your Process Lean

After you design and test your potential process (see the previous section), draw a Value Stream Map to illustrate the flow of work through the steps (see Chapter 12 for details on this map). Look for possible areas of waste built into the process. Ensure that the product travels the minimum distance, and requires the fewest steps, to go from raw material to finished item. This step reduces work-in-process goods and waste from excessive handling.

Leaning a process gives you a great opportunity to engage the workers who will create the product. Gaining their insight can improve the process while increasing their ownership of the results. After you make the process as Lean as it can get, update the FMEA (see the previous section) to identify any new problems that have popped up. Part III has more about Lean processes.

Mistake Proof Your Process

A mistake-proof process eases the difficulty of assembly by fitting together only one way. The form can range from two parts whose shapes fit only one way to a data-entry form that uses a drop-down list of states to ensure that only valid data can be entered. You can even provide kits to assemblers that identify the correct number of each type of part; if any parts remain in a kit after assembly, the work product is missing a part.

Another mistake proofing approach is to detect a problem before it leaves the workstation. For example, a worker can fit the finished item into a fixture to ensure that it's the right size. You could also include a scale to weigh the work product to ensure that everything is inside of it.

Examine the process using your previously created FMEA (see the section "Establish a Capable Prototype Process") to identify areas for mistake proofing.

Prepare the Kanban

Kanban (see Chapter 15) is a plan for material flow, such as materials taken from the receiving dock to the assembly line. Kanban planning ties the use of an item to its resupply without piling up material in the intermediate steps. Here are some steps for undertaking the Kanban process:

1. **Determine how you'll order materials and deliver them to fabrication or assembly points.**

2. **Identify the appropriate quantity per container for each item.**

3. **Integrate the parts into the existing replenishment process.**

   Be sure the process reaches all the way back to where the component is ordered from the supplier.

4. **Lay out the workstation so that you present components to your workers in a logical order.**

   Heavy items may require additional material-handling units.

Test the Process

Enough with all the preparatory work; it's time to run the process. You should measure the critical-to-quality points to ensure that they're repeatable, given any of the machinery, workers, or materials that become part of the process. After you have the process running at full speed, begin tracking results with run charts and Statistical Process Control (see Chapter 10 for details). The test will demonstrate the process's capability, which you can compare to its designed capability.

A few process teams are so perfect that they can get every detail right the very first time — and then there is reality. At this point, the process works, but can you make it more efficient? Gather your process-creation team to review the FMEA charts for possible changes and spots to improve (see the section "Establish a Capable Prototype Process"). Sometimes, the FMEA indicates a symptom and a cause of a problem for which you can't add a preventative action to the process. If the symptom and cause occur, the FMEA quickly points back to the origin.

Incorporate Improvements into the Process Design

When a process is fully functional, opportunities for improving it will appear. Some improvement opportunities involve the following components:

- ✓ **Performance:** Make the process complete its tasks more efficiently by eliminating built-in delays, rebalancing work among various steps, or using different tools.
- ✓ **Delivery:** Make modifications to provide a product or service to the customer more quickly. Examples include quick responses to orders for special colors or providing tracking information for a shipped package.
- ✓ **Cost:** You can suggest the use of different materials or suppliers.

The process designers must always look for ways to improve each process step. You can hold meetings of everyone involved with the process to critique the process and make suggestions for improvement. Many suggestions will be for small changes, but collectively they can make a big difference.

Keep the original process design documents (FMEA, Value Stream Map, and so on) up to date with any changes to the process. As time passes and memories fade, these documents provide a snapshot of the process creation team's ideas at a given time.

Create a Customer-Feedback Mechanism

Feedback is nature's way of telling you how your process is working. Before making a process fully operational to produce items or services for the customer, create a feedback mechanism to gather information for quick action. Feedback can include

- Service desk calls
- Product returns
- Inspection rejections
- Customer complaints of any type
- Customer satisfaction surveys

And so on. Be sure the feedback immediately goes to your process team for prompt consideration. (See Chapter 6 for more information on gathering feedback from customers.)

To reduce the number of problems at the initial rollout of new processes, many companies "test market" their products in one area for a short time to gather customer opinions. The companies use the opinions to update the products before rolling them out to their target markets.

Chapter 21

Ten (Or So) Web Sites with Quality Control Tips and Techniques

*T*he Internet is a wonderful tool. In just a few moments, you can find information on a wide range of subjects and locate links to others. Some general sites, such as Wikipedia (www.wikipedia.com), can provide a quick overview of most quality control subjects. In this chapter, we give you a handful of Web sites that are chock-full of useful quality knowledge.

You can often find additional information on the Web sites of companies that are trying to sell their services or products. Companies often use white papers, copies of presentations, and general tutorials to introduce their services. When researching topics for your organization, look for these as valuable "second points of view" on the same issues.

International Organization for Standardization

The official Web site for the International Organization for Standardization, www.iso.org, is the authoritative source of ISO information. It contains information on various ISO standards and news about ISO as well as basics about the ISO process. Like all self-respecting businesses, it also offers many documents you can purchase for download. See Chapter 2 for ISO details.

American Society for Quality

The American Society for Quality provides information, training, and certification in a wide range of quality techniques. The Web site has some excellent information on the basics of quality management and a list of training opportunities. However, to view most of the material on the site, you must become a member. Check out www.ASQ.org for info, and see Chapter 2 for more information about ASQ.

Lean Aerospace Initiative

The Massachusetts Institute of Technology has a Web site containing information about Lean techniques, including some success stories that illustrate ways you can apply Lean techniques in your organization. You can download interesting documents that explain Lean concepts, and links to other universities offer Lean training (maybe a training session is near you). Head to lean.mit.edu. Chapter 11 has general info about Lean techniques.

Curious Cat Management Improvement Library

The Web site for Curious Cat Management Improvement Connections contains a series of articles illustrating Lean thinking and Lean manufacturing. It features a directory of Web sites containing additional information. The site, at www.curiouscat.net/library/leanthinking.cfm, provides a broad range of perspectives of Lean and how various industries have applied it. It also has links to other Web sites that discuss Lean thinking.

The Northwest Lean Networks

The most informative site for Value Stream Mapping that we can find is a PDF file that steps through the Value Stream process: www.nwlean.net/toolsCD/VSM/4%20steps%20to%20VSM.pdf. Head to Chapter 12 for more about Value Stream Mapping.

Kaizen Institute

Kaizen is an "imported" quality concept that enjoys support from a number of organizations. One of the many Kaizen Web sites is www.kaizen-institute. com. See Chapter 14 for more about Kaizen (also called Rapid Improvement Events [RIEs]).

Replenishment Technology Group Inc.

You can find many companies that sell Kanban consulting and its "tools." One interesting commercial site is www.kanban.us. We cover Kanban in detail in Chapter 15.

Total Quality Management

One interesting Web site with many articles about applying Total Quality Management (TQM) and links to other sites is www.managementhelp.org/ quality/tqm/tqm.htm.

Two other significant sites for TQM are run by organizations founded by two of TQM's major contributors:

- ✔ The Juran Institute's site, www.juran.com
- ✔ The W. Edwards Deming Institute's site, www.deming.org

Chapter 16 has the full scoop on TQM.

i Six Sigma

You can think of Six Sigma as a toolbox of quality initiatives glued together by statistics. Therefore, a Web site that provides detailed Six Sigma support also provides information on a wide range of quality tools. A good Web site for information on Six Sigma and on a wide range of other quality tools is www.isixsigma.com. Chapter 17 has details on Six Sigma.

QFD Institute

The QFD Institute is the official Quality Function Deployment Web site. The site contains useful information on Quality Function Deployment as well as training. Head to www.qfdi.org, and see Chapter 18 for more about QFD.

AGI

AGI (the Avraham Y. Goldratt Institute) is the authoritative source for information on the Theory of Constraints. After all, Mr. Goldratt wrote the book on the TOC! The AGI Web site contains information about the Theory of Constraints and how a wide range of enterprises has successfully applied it. Check out www.goldratt.com, and head to Chapter 19 for an overview of the Theory of Constraints.

Index

• P •

BUSINESS, CAREERS & PERSONAL FINANCE

0-7645-9847-3

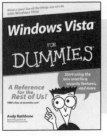

0-7645-2431-3

Also available:
- Business Plans Kit For Dummies
  0-7645-9794-9
- Economics For Dummies
  0-7645-5726-2
- Grant Writing For Dummies
  0-7645-8416-2
- Home Buying For Dummies
  0-7645-5331-3
- Managing For Dummies
  0-7645-1771-6
- Marketing For Dummies
  0-7645-5600-2

- Personal Finance For Dummies
  0-7645-2590-5*
- Resumes For Dummies
  0-7645-5471-9
- Selling For Dummies
  0-7645-5363-1
- Six Sigma For Dummies
  0-7645-6798-5
- Small Business Kit For Dummies
  0-7645-5984-2
- Starting an eBay Business For Dummies
  0-7645-6924-4
- Your Dream Career For Dummies
  0-7645-9795-7

HOME & BUSINESS COMPUTER BASICS

0-470-05432-8

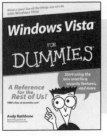

0-471-75421-8

Also available:
- Cleaning Windows Vista For Dummies
  0-471-78293-9
- Excel 2007 For Dummies
  0-470-03737-7
- Mac OS X Tiger For Dummies
  0-7645-7675-5
- MacBook For Dummies
  0-470-04859-X
- Macs For Dummies
  0-470-04849-2
- Office 2007 For Dummies
  0-470-00923-3

- Outlook 2007 For Dummies
  0-470-03830-6
- PCs For Dummies
  0-7645-8958-X
- Salesforce.com For Dummies
  0-470-04893-X
- Upgrading & Fixing Laptops For Dummies
  0-7645-8959-8
- Word 2007 For Dummies
  0-470-03658-3
- Quicken 2007 For Dummies
  0-470-04600-7

FOOD, HOME, GARDEN, HOBBIES, MUSIC & PETS

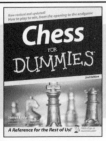

0-7645-8404-9

0-7645-9904-6

Also available:
- Candy Making For Dummies
  0-7645-9734-5
- Card Games For Dummies
  0-7645-9910-0
- Crocheting For Dummies
  0-7645-4151-X
- Dog Training For Dummies
  0-7645-8418-9
- Healthy Carb Cookbook For Dummies
  0-7645-8476-6
- Home Maintenance For Dummies
  0-7645-5215-5

- Horses For Dummies
  0-7645-9797-3
- Jewelry Making & Beading For Dummies
  0-7645-2571-9
- Orchids For Dummies
  0-7645-6759-4
- Puppies For Dummies
  0-7645-5255-4
- Rock Guitar For Dummies
  0-7645-5356-9
- Sewing For Dummies
  0-7645-6847-7
- Singing For Dummies
  0-7645-2475-5

INTERNET & DIGITAL MEDIA

0-470-04529-9

0-470-04894-8

Also available:
- Blogging For Dummies
  0-471-77084-1
- Digital Photography For Dummies
  0-7645-9802-3
- Digital Photography All-in-One Desk Reference For Dummies
  0-470-03743-1
- Digital SLR Cameras and Photography For Dummies
  0-7645-9803-1
- eBay Business All-in-One Desk Reference For Dummies
  0-7645-8438-3
- HDTV For Dummies
  0-470-09673-X

- Home Entertainment PCs For Dummies
  0-470-05523-5
- MySpace For Dummies
  0-470-09529-6
- Search Engine Optimization For Dummies
  0-471-97998-8
- Skype For Dummies
  0-470-04891-3
- The Internet For Dummies
  0-7645-8996-2
- Wiring Your Digital Home For Dummies
  0-471-91830-X

Separate Canadian edition also available
Separate U.K. edition also available

Available wherever books are sold. For more information or to order direct: U.S. customers visit www.dummies.com or call 1-877-762-2974.
U.K. customers visit www.wileyeurope.com or call 0800 243407. Canadian customers visit www.wiley.ca or call 1-800-567-4797.

SPORTS, FITNESS, PARENTING, RELIGION & SPIRITUALITY

0-471-76871-5

0-7645-7841-3

Also available:

- Catholicism For Dummies
  0-7645-5391-7
- Exercise Balls For Dummies
  0-7645-5623-1
- Fitness For Dummies
  0-7645-7851-0
- Football For Dummies
  0-7645-3936-1
- Judaism For Dummies
  0-7645-5299-6
- Potty Training For Dummies
  0-7645-5417-4
- Buddhism For Dummies
  0-7645-5359-3

- Pregnancy For Dummies
  0-7645-4483-7 †
- Ten Minute Tone-Ups For Dummies
  0-7645-7207-5
- NASCAR For Dummies
  0-7645-7681-X
- Religion For Dummies
  0-7645-5264-3
- Soccer For Dummies
  0-7645-5229-5
- Women in the Bible For Dummies
  0-7645-8475-8

TRAVEL

0-7645-7749-2

0-7645-6945-7

Also available:

- Alaska For Dummies
  0-7645-7746-8
- Cruise Vacations For Dummies
  0-7645-6941-4
- England For Dummies
  0-7645-4276-1
- Europe For Dummies
  0-7645-7529-5
- Germany For Dummies
  0-7645-7823-5
- Hawaii For Dummies
  0-7645-7402-7

- Italy For Dummies
  0-7645-7386-1
- Las Vegas For Dummies
  0-7645-7382-9
- London For Dummies
  0-7645-4277-X
- Paris For Dummies
  0-7645-7630-5
- RV Vacations For Dummies
  0-7645-4442-X
- Walt Disney World & Orlando
  For Dummies
  0-7645-9660-8

GRAPHICS, DESIGN & WEB DEVELOPMENT

0-7645-8815-X

0-7645-9571-7

Also available:

- 3D Game Animation For Dummies
  0-7645-8789-7
- AutoCAD 2006 For Dummies
  0-7645-8925-3
- Building a Web Site For Dummies
  0-7645-7144-3
- Creating Web Pages For Dummies
  0-470-08030-2
- Creating Web Pages All-in-One Desk
  Reference For Dummies
  0-7645-4345-8
- Dreamweaver 8 For Dummies
  0-7645-9649-7

- InDesign CS2 For Dummies
  0-7645-9572-5
- Macromedia Flash 8 For Dummies
  0-7645-9691-8
- Photoshop CS2 and Digital
  Photography For Dummies
  0-7645-9580-6
- Photoshop Elements 4 For Dummies
  0-471-77483-9
- Syndicating Web Sites with RSS Feeds
  For Dummies
  0-7645-8848-6
- Yahoo! SiteBuilder For Dummies
  0-7645-9800-7

NETWORKING, SECURITY, PROGRAMMING & DATABASES

0-7645-7728-X

0-471-74940-0

Also available:

- Access 2007 For Dummies
  0-470-04612-0
- ASP.NET 2 For Dummies
  0-7645-7907-X
- C# 2005 For Dummies
  0-7645-9704-3
- Hacking For Dummies
  0-470-05235-X
- Hacking Wireless Networks
  For Dummies
  0-7645-9730-2
- Java For Dummies
  0-470-08716-1

- Microsoft SQL Server 2005 For Dummies
  0-7645-7755-7
- Networking All-in-One Desk Reference
  For Dummies
  0-7645-9939-9
- Preventing Identity Theft For Dummies
  0-7645-7336-5
- Telecom For Dummies
  0-471-77085-X
- Visual Studio 2005 All-in-One Desk
  Reference For Dummies
  0-7645-9775-2
- XML For Dummies
  0-7645-8845-1